German
phrase book

Berlitz Publishing Company, Inc.

Princeton   Mexico City   Dublin   Eschborn   Singapore

Contents

Pronunciation

This section is designed to make you familiar with the sounds of German using our simplified phonetic transcription.

You'll find the pronunciation of the German letters and sounds explained below, together with their "imitated" equivalents. This system is used throughout the phrase book: simply read the pronunciation as if it were English, noting any special rules below.

The German language

German is the national language of Germany and Austria and is one of the four official languages of Switzerland. In addition, it is also spoken by groups of Germans in other countries. These are the countries where you can expect to hear German spoken (figures are approximate):

Germany Deutschland

German is spoken properly, i.e. without a noticeable accent is called **Hochdeutsch**. Native speakers often have accents or speak dialects that vary from region to region.

Austria Österreich

German is the national language for over 7.8 million people.

Switzerland Schweiz

German is spoken by 70% of the population, mainly in the north and east. Other languages: **French** (20% of the population) in the west; **Italian** in the south; and the much rarer **Romansh.**

German is also one of the languages spoken in eastern France (**Alsace-Lorraine**), northern Italy (**Alto Adige**), eastern Belgium, Luxembourg and Liechtenstein. There are also about 1.5 million German-speakers in the U.S., 500,000 in Canada and sizeable groups in South America, Namibia and Kazakhstan.

The German alphabet is the same as English, with the addition of the letter **ß**. It also uses the **Umlaut** (diaeresis) on the vowels **ä, ü, ö** (see below for pronunciation).

English has its origins in German and so some German words, such as **Hand, Butter** and **Name**, mean exactly the same as in English. You'll probably be able to guess the meaning of many other words that have slight spelling variations such as **Silber** (silver), **Fisch** (fish) and **blau** (blue).

Consonants

Letter	Approximate pronunciation	Symbol	Example	
f,h,k,l,m, n,p,t,x	as in English			
b	1) at the end of a word or between a vowel and a consonant. like **p** in u**p**	p	**ab**	ap
	2) elsewhere as in English	b	**bis**	biss
c	1) before **e, i, ö** and **ä**, like **ts** in hi**ts**	ts	**Celsius**	tselziuss
	2) elsewhere like **c** in **c**at	k	**Café**	kafay
ch	1) after back vowels (e.g. **ah, o, oo**) like **ch** in Scottish lo**ch**, otherwise more like **h** in **h**uge	kh	**doch**	dokh
	2) sometimes, especially before **s**, like **k** in **k**it	k	**Wachs**	vaks
d	1) at the end of a word or between a vowel and a consonant, like **t** in ea**t**	t	**Rad**	raat
	2) elsewhere like **d** in **d**o	d	**durstig**	doorstikh
g	1) always hard as in **g**o, but at the end of a word more often like **ck** in ta**ck**	g	**gehen**	gayen
		k	**weg**	vek
j	like **y** in **y**es	y	**ja**	yaa
qu	like **k** followed by **v** as in **v**at	kv	**Quark**	kvark
r	generally rolled in the back of the mouth	r	**warum**	varum
w	usually like **v** in **v**oice	v	**Wagon**	vagon
s	1) before or between vowels like **z** in **z**oo	z	**sie**	zee
	2) before **p** and **t** at the beginning of a syllable like **sh** in **sh**ut	sh	**spät**	shpait
	3) elsewhere, like **s** in **s**it	s/ss	**es ist**	ess ist
ß	always like **s** in **s**it	s/ss	**heiß**	hiess
sch	like **sh** in **sh**ut	sh	**schnell**	shnel
tsch	like **ch** in **ch**ip	ch	**deutsch**	doych

	tz	like **ts** in hi**ts**	ts	**Platz**	*plats*
	v	1) like **f** in **f**or	f	**vier**	*feer*
		2) in most words of foreign origin, like **v** in **v**ice	v	**Vase**	*vaazer*
w		like **v** in **v**ice	v	**wie**	*vee*
z		like **ts** in hi**ts**	ts	**zeigen**	*tsiegen*

Vowels

a	1) short like **u** in c**u**t	a	**lassen**	*lassen*
	2) long like **a** in c**a**r	aa	**Abend**	*aabent*
ä	1) short like **e** in l**e**t	e/eh	**Lärm**	*lehrm*
	2) long like **ai** in h**ai**r	ai	**spät**	*shpait*
e	1) short like **e** in l**e**t	e	**sprechen**	*shprekhen*
	2) long like **a** in l**a**te, but pronounced without moving tongue or lips	ay/eh	**geben**	*gayben*
	3) at the end of a word, generally like **er** in oth**er**	er	**bitte**	*bitter*
i	1) short like **i** in h**i**t	i	**billig**	*billikh*
	2) long like **ee** in m**ee**t	ee	**ihm**	*eem*
ie	like **ee** in b**ee**	ee	**hier**	*heer*
o	1) short like **o** in g**o**t	o	**voll**	*fol*
	2) long like **o** in n**o**te, but pronounced without moving tongue or lips	oa	**ohne**	*oaner*
ö	like **ur** in f**ur** (long or short)	ur	**können**	*kurnen*
u	1) short like **oo** in f**oo**t	u	**Nuss**	*nuss*
	2) long like **oo** in m**oo**n	oo	**gut**	*goot*
ü	like **ew** in n**ew**; round your lips	ew	**über**	*ewber*
y	like German **ü**	ew	**typisch**	*tewpish*

Diphthongs

ai, ay, ei, ey	like **ie** in t**ie**	ie	**einen**	*ienen*
au	like **ow** in n**ow**	ow	**auf**	*owf*
äu, eu	like **oy** in b**oy**	oy	**neu**	*noy*

Stress

Generally, as in English, the first syllable is stressed in German, except when short prefixes are added to the beginning of the word. Then the second syllable is stressed (e.g. **bewegen** – to move, **gesehen** – seen). As most English speakers will naturally put the stress on the correct syllable, we have not included stress on individual words.

Pronunciation of the German alphabet

In this phrase book, we have used a friendly system to achieve a close proximation of the pronunciation, although this inevitably means some simplification of the more subtle aspects of German pronunciation.

A	*aa*		**O**	*oa*
Ä	*ai*		**Ö**	*ur*
B	*bay*		**P**	*pay*
C	*tsay*		**Q**	*koo*
D	*day*		**R**	*ehr*
E	*ay*		**S**	*ess*
F	*ef*		**T**	*tay*
G	*gay*		**U**	*oo*
H	*haa*		**Ü**	*ew*
I	*ee*		**V**	*fow*
J	*yot*		**W**	*vay*
K	*kaa*		**X**	*eeks*
L	*el*		**Y**	*ewpsillon*
M	*em*		**Z**	*tset*
N	*en*			

In addition to these letters, there is the **ß** sign, a combination of **s** and **z**. It is pronounced exactly like **ss**.

9

Basic Expressions

ESSENTIAL

Yes.	**Ja.** *yaa*
No.	**Nein.** *nien*
Okay.	**In Ordnung.** *in oardnung*
Please.	**Bitte.** *bitter*
Thank you.	**Danke.** *danker*
Thank you very much.	**Vielen Dank.** *feelen dank*

Greetings / Apologies
Begrüßung/Entschuldigung

Hello./Hi!	**Hallo!** *haloa*
Good morning.	**Guten Morgen.** *gooten morgen*
Good afternoon.	**Guten Tag.** *gooten taag*
Good evening.	**Guten Abend.** *gooten aabent*
Good night.	**Gute Nacht.** *gooter nakht*
Good-bye.	**Auf Wiedersehen.** *owf veederzayen*
Excuse me! (getting attention)	**Entschuldigen Sie bitte!** *entshuldigen zee bitter*
Excuse me. (may I get past?)	**Gestatten Sie?** *geshtatten zee*
Excuse me!/Sorry!	**Entschuldigung!/Verzeihung!** *entshuldigung/fehrtsieung*
It was an accident.	**Es war ein Versehen.** *ess vaar ien fehrzayen*
Don't mention it.	**Gern geschehen.** *gehrn geshayen*

INTRODUCTIONS ➤ 118

Communication difficulties
Verständigungsschwierigkeiten

Do you speak English?	**Sprechen Sie Englisch?** shprekhen zee ennglish
Does anyone here speak English?	**Spricht hier jemand Englisch?** *shprikht heer yaymant ennglish*
I hardly speak any German.	**Ich spreche kaum Deutsch.** *ikh shprekher kowm doych*
Could you speak more slowly?	**Könnten Sie etwas langsamer sprechen?** *kurnten zee etvass langzaamer shprekhen*
Could you repeat that?	**Könnten Sie das wiederholen?** *kurnten zee dass veederhoalen*
Excuse me?	**Wie bitte?** *vee bitter*
Sorry, I didn't catch that.	**Ich habe das leider nicht verstanden.** *ikh haaber dass lieder nikht fehrshtanden*
What was that?	**Was haben Sie gesagt?** *vass haaben zee gezaagt*
Could you spell it?	**Könnten Sie das buchstabieren?** *kurnten zee dass bookhshtabeeren*
Please write it down.	**Bitte schreiben Sie es auf.** *bitter shrieben zee ess owf*
Can you translate this for me?	**Können Sie mir das übersetzen?** *kurnen zee meer dass ewberzetsen*
What does this/that mean?	**Was bedeutet das?** *vass bedoytet dass*
How do you pronounce that?	**Wie spricht man das aus?** *vee shprikht man dass ows*
Please point to the phrase in the book.	**Bitte zeigen Sie mir den Ausdruck im Buch.** *bitter tsiegen zee meer dayn owsdruck im bookh*
I understand.	**Ich verstehe.** *ikh fehrshtayer*
I don't understand.	**Ich verstehe nicht.** *ikh fehrshtayer nikht*
Do you understand?	**Verstehen Sie?** *fehrshtayen zee*

> – *Das macht einhundertfünfunddreißig Mark.*
> – Ich verstehe nicht.
> – *Das macht einhundertfünfunddreißig Mark*
> – Bitte schreiben Sie es auf …
> Ach so. "135 DM" … Bitte schön.

Questions Fragen

Questions can be formed in German:
1. by inverting the subject and the verb:
   Sprechen Sie Englisch?   Do you speak English?
2. by using a question word (➤12-17) + the inverted order:
   Wie möchten Sie zahlen?   How would you like to pay?

Where? Wo?

Where is it?	**Wo ist es?** *voa ist ess*
above the bank	**über der Bank** *ewber dehr bank*
across the road	**auf der anderen Straßenseite** *owf dehr anderen shtraassensieter*
at the meeting place	**am Treffpunkt** *am trefpunkt*
here/there	**hier/dort** *heer/dort*
in the car	**im Auto** *im owto*
in the town	**in der Stadt** *in dehr shtat*
in Germany	**in Deutschland** *in doychlant*
near the bank	**in der Nähe der Bank** *in dehr naier dehr bank*
on the left/right	**links/rechts** *links/rekhts*
in front of the café	**vor dem Café** *foar daym kafay*
under the bridge	**unter der Brücke** *unter dehr brewker*

Where to? Wohin?

Where are you going?	**Wohin gehen Sie?** *voahin gayen zee*
across the road	**über die Straße** *ewber dee shtraasser*
around the town	**durch die Stadt** *doorkh dee shtat*
(to) here/(to) there	**hierher/dorthin** *heerhayr/dorthin*
into the museum	**in das Museum** *in dass muzayum*
into the town	**in die Stadt** *in dee shtat*
to the hotel	**zum Hotel** *tsum hottel*
under the bridge	**unter die Brücke** *unter dee brewker*
up to the traffic lights	**bis zur Ampel** *biss tsoor ampel*
inside/outside	**drinnen/draußen** *drinnen/drowssen*
toward Berlin	**in Richtung Berlin** *in rikhtung behrleen*

12

When ...? Wann ...?

When does the train arrive?	**Wann kommt der Zug an?** *van komt dehr tsoog an*
10 minutes ago	**vor zehn Minuten** *foar tsayn minooten*
after lunch	**nach dem Mittagessen** *naakh daym mittaagessen*
always	**immer** *immer*
around midnight	**gegen Mitternacht** *gaygen mittehrnakht*
at 7 o'clock	**um sieben Uhr** *um zeeben oor*
before Friday	**vor Freitag** *foar frietaag*
by tomorrow	**bis morgen** *biss morgen*
daily	**täglich** *taiglikh*
during the summer	**während des Sommers** *vairent des zommers*
early	**früh** *frew*
every week	**jede Woche** *yayder vokher*
for 2 hours	**zwei Stunden** *tsvie shtunden*
from 9 a.m. to 6 p.m.	**von neun bis achtzehn Uhr** *von noyn biss akhtsayn oor*
immediately	**sofort** *zofoart*
in 20 minutes	**in zwanzig Minuten** *in tsvantsikh minooten*
never	**nie** *nee*
not yet	**noch nicht** *nokh nikht*
now	**jetzt** *yetst*
often	**oft** *oft*
on March 8	**am achten März** *am akhten mehrts*
on weekdays	**an Werktagen** *an vehrktaagen*
once a week	**einmal in der Woche** *ienmaal in dehr vokher*
sometimes	**manchmal** *mankhmaal*
soon	**bald** *balt*
then	**dann** *dan*
within 2 days	**innerhalb von zwei Tagen** *innehalp fon tsvie taagen*

TIME ➤ 220; DATE ➤ 218

13

What sort of …? Was für ein …?

It's … **Es ist …** *ess ist*

beautiful/ugly	**schön/hässlich**	*shurn/hehsslikh*
better/worse	**besser/schlechter**	*besser/shlekhter*
big/small	**groß/klein**	*groass/klien*
cheap/expensive	**billig/teuer**	*billikh/toyer*
clean/dirty	**sauber/schmutzig**	*zowber/shmutsikh*
dark/light	**dunkel/hell**	*dunkel/hel*
delicious/revolting	**köstlich/scheußlich**	*kurstlikh/shoysslikh*
early/late	**früh/spät**	*frew/shpait*
easy/difficult	**einfach/schwer**	*ienfakh/shvayr*
empty/full	**leer/voll**	*layr/fol*
good/bad	**gut/schlecht**	*goot/shlekht*
heavy/light	**schwer/leicht**	*shvayr/liekht*
hot/warm/cold	**heiß/warm/kalt**	*hiess/varm/kalt*
modern/old-fashioned	**modern/altmodisch**	*modayrn/altmoadish*
narrow/wide	**eng/weit**	*eng/viet*
next/last	**nächste/letzte**	*naikhster/letster*
old/new	**alt/neu**	*alt/noy*
open/closed	**geöffnet/geschlossen**	*geurfnet/geshlossen*
pleasant/nice/unpleasant	**freundlich/nett/unfreundlich**	*froyndlikh/net/unfroyndlikh*
quick/slow	**schnell/langsam**	*shnell/langzaam*
quiet/noisy	**leise/laut**	*liezer/lowt*
right/wrong	**richtig/falsch**	*rikhtikh/falsh*
tall/short	**groß/klein**	*groass/klien*
thick/thin	**dick/dünn**	*dik/dewn*
vacant/occupied	**frei/besetzt**	*frie/bezetst*
young/old	**jung/alt**	*yung/alt*

All nouns in German are either masculine, feminine or neuter, and the adjectival endings change accordingly. See page 169 for more explanation.

How much/many? Wie viel/Wie viele?

How much is that?	**Was kostet das?**	*vass kostet dass*
How many are there?	**Wie viele gibt es?**	*vee feeler gipt ess*
1, 2, 3	**eins, zwei, drei**	*ienss, tsvie, drie*
4, 5	**vier, fünf**	*feer, fewnf*
none	**keine**	*kiener*
about 100 Marks	**etwa hundert Mark**	*etvaa hundert mark*
a little	**ein wenig**	*ien vaynikh*
a lot of traffic	**viel Verkehr**	*veel fehrkayr*
enough	**genug**	*genook*
few	**wenige**	*vaynigger*
a few of them	**einige von ihnen**	*ienigger fon eenen*
many people	**viele Leute**	*feeler loyter*
more than that	**mehr als das**	*mayr als dass*
less than that	**weniger als das**	*vaynigger als dass*
much more	**viel mehr**	*feel mayr*
nothing else	**sonst nichts**	*zonst nikhts*
some bread	**etwas Brot**	*etvass broat*
too much	**zu viel**	*tsoo feel*

Why? Warum?

Why is that?	**Warum (ist das so)?**	*varum (ist dass zoa)*
Why not?	**Warum nicht?**	*varum nikht*
because of the weather	**wegen des Wetters**	*vaygen dess vetterss*
because I'm in a hurry	**weil ich es eilig habe**	*viel ikh ess ielikh haaber*
I don't know why.	**Ich weiß nicht, warum.**	*ikh viess nikht varum*

Who?/Which?
Wer/Welcher/Welche/Welches?

Which one do you want?	**Welches möchten Sie?** *velkhess murkhten zee*
one like that	**so eins** *zoa ienss*
that one/this one	**jenes/dieses** *yayness/deezess*
not that one	**nicht das da** *nikht dass daa*
none	**keiner/keine/keines** *kiener/kiener/kieness*
someone	**jemand** *yaymant*
something	**etwas** *etvass*

Whose? Wem?

Whose is that?	**Wem gehört das?** *vaym gehurt dass*
It belongs to ...	**Es gehört ...** *ess gehurt*
her/him	**ihr/ihm** *eer/eem*
me, you, them	**mir, Ihnen [dir], ihnen** *meer, eenen [deer], eenen*
no one	**niemandem** *neemandem*
This is ... bag.	**Dies ist ... Tasche.** *deez ist ... tasher*
my	**meine** *miener*
our	**unsere** *unzerer*
your	**Ihre [deine]** *eerer [diener]*
his/her	**seine/ihre** *ziener/eerer*
their	**ihre** *eerer*

How? Wie?

How would you like to pay?	**Wie möchten Sie zahlen?** *vee murkhten zee tsaalen*
by credit card	**mit Kreditkarte** *mit kredeetkarter*
How are you getting here?	**Wie kommen Sie hierher?** *vee kommen zee heerhayr*
by car	**mit dem Auto** *mit daym owto*
with a friend	**mit einem Freund/einer Freundin** *mit ienem froynt/iener froyndin*
by chance	**durch Zufall** *doorkh tsoofal*
entirely	**ganz** *gants*
equally	**gleich** *gliekh*
extremely	**äußerst** *oysserst*
on foot	**zu Fuß** *tsoo fooss*
quickly	**schnell** *shnel*
slowly	**langsam** *langzaam*
too fast	**zu schnell** *tsoo shnel*
totally	**völlig** *furllikh*
very	**sehr** *zayr*
without a passport	**ohne Reisepass** *oaner riezepass*

Is it …?/Is there …? Ist es …? Gibt es …?

Is it …?	**Ist es …?** *ist ess*
Is it free?	**Ist es frei?** *ist ess frie*
It isn't ready.	**Es ist nicht fertig.** *ess ist nikht fehrtikh*
Is/Are there …?	**Gibt es …?** *gipt ess*
Are there buses into town?	**Gibt es Busse in die Stadt?** *gipt ess busser in dee shtat*
There isn't any hot water.	**Es gibt kein warmes Wasser.** *ess gipt kien varmess vasser*
Here/There it is.	**Hier/Da ist es.** *heer/daa ist ess*
Here/There they are.	**Hier/Da sind sie.** *heer/daa zint zee*

17

Can/May …? Kann …?

Can I have …?	**Kann ich … haben?** *kan ikh … haaben*
Can we have…?	**Können wir … haben?** *kurnen veer … haaben*
Can you show me …?	**Können Sie mir … zeigen?** *kurnen zee meer … tsiegen*
Can you tell me …?	**Können Sie mir sagen …?** *kurnen zee meer zaagen*
Can you help me?	**Können Sie mir helfen?** *kurnen zee meer helfen*
Can you direct me to …?	**Können Sie mir den Weg nach … zeigen?** *kurnern zee meer dayn vayk naakh … tsiegen*
Sorry, I can't.	**Leider nicht.** *lieder nikht*

What would you like? Was wünschen Sie?

I'd like …	**Ich hätte gern …** *ikh hehtter gehrn*
Could I have …?	**Könnte ich … haben?** *kurnter ikh … haaben*
We'd like …	**Wir hätten gern …** *veer hehtten gehrn*
Give me …	**Geben Sie mir …** *gayben zee meer*
I'm looking for …	**Ich suche …** *ikh zookher*
I would like to …	**Ich möchte gern …** *ikh murkhter gehrn*
go to …	**nach … gehen** *naakh … gayen*
find …	**… finden** *… finden*
see …	**… sehen** *… zayen*
speak to …	**mit … sprechen** *mit … shprekhen*

– Entschuldigung.
 – *Ja?*
– Können Sie mir helfen?
 – *Ja, natürlich.*
– Ich möchte gern mit Frau Müller sprechen.
 – *Einen Moment, bitte.*

Other useful words
Andere nützliche Wörter

fortunately	**glücklicherweise**	*glewglikherviezer*
hopefully	**hoffentlich**	*hoffentlik*
of course	**natürlich**	*natewrlikh*
perhaps	**vielleicht**	*veelliekht*
unfortunately	**leider**	*lieder*
also	**auch**	*owkh*
and	**und**	*unt*
but	**aber**	*aaber*
or	**oder**	*oader*

Exclamations Ausrufe

At last!	**Endlich!**	*endlikh*
Damn!	**Verdammt!**	*fehrdamt*
Good God!	**O Gott!**	*oa got*
I don't mind.	**Es ist mir egal.**	*ess ist meer aygaal*
No way!	**Auf keinen Fall!**	*owf kienen fal*
Nonsense.	**Unsinn.**	*unzin*
Quite right too!	**Richtig so!**	*rikhtikh zoa*
Really?	**Wirklich?**	*veerklikh*
Rubbish!	**Quatsch!**	*kvach*
That's enough.	**Das reicht.**	*dass riekht*
That's true.	**Das stimmt.**	*dass shtimt*
You're joking!	**Das soll wohl ein Witz sein!**	
	dass zoll voal ien vits zien	
How are things?	**Wie geht's?**	*vee gayts*
great/brilliant	**ausgezeichnet**	*owsgetsiekhnet*
great	**großartig**	*groassaartikh*
fine	**gut**	*goot*
not bad	**nicht schlecht**	*nikht shlekht*
so so	**einigermaßen**	*ienigermaassen*
not good	**nicht gut**	*nikht goot*
terrible	**schrecklich**	*shreklikh*
awful	**furchtbar**	*foorkhtbaar*

Accommodations

All types of accommodations, from hotels to campsites, can be found through the tourist information center **(Fremdenverkehrsbüro).**
Hotel guides **(Hotelführer)** are on sale at book stores.
It's best to book in advance and to confirm your stay, especially during high season or special events. If you haven't booked, you're more likely to find accommodations available outside of towns and city centers.

Hotel *hottel*
Hotel; simple or fancy, your room will be spotless, usually with luxurious duck or goose-down quilts.

Hotel garni *hottel garni*
A hotel with comfortable accommodations that serves only breakfast. Usually beverages and snacks will be available.

Schlosshotel *shlosshottel*
Castle or palace converted into a hotel; often located in the countryside.

Rasthof/Motel *rasthoaf/mottel*
Roadside lodge, motel; most are located just off an expressway/motorway or principal route.

Gasthaus/Gasthof *gasthowss/gasthoaf*
Inn, providing lodging, food and drink.

Pension/Fremdenheim *penzioan/fremdenhiem*
Boardinghouse; offers full or half board. Meals served to house guests only.

Zimmer frei *tsimmer frie*
Where you see this sign, you'll find the equivalent of bed and breakfast.

Jugendherberge *yoogent hehrbehrger*
Youth hostel; in Austria, Germany and Switzerland, they are of a very high standard. A variation is the Youth Guest House, which usually has a later closing time.

Ferienwohnung *fayree-envoanung*
Furnished apartment found in holiday resorts; you'll probably have to reserve it in advance. Otherwise, contact the local tourist office.

Reservations/booking Reservierung

In advance Im Voraus

Can you recommend a hotel in …?	**Können Sie ein Hotel in … empfehlen?** *kurnen zee ien hottel in … empfaylen*
Is it near the center of town?	**Liegt es in der Nähe des Stadtzentrums?** *leegt ess in dehr naier dess shtattsentrumz*
How much is it per night?	**Was kostet es pro Nacht?** *vass kostet ess proa nakht*
Is there anything cheaper?	**Gibt es nichts Billigeres?** *gipt ess nikhts billigeress*
Could you reserve/book me a room there, please?	**Können Sie mir dort bitte ein Zimmer reservieren?** *kurnen zee meer dort bitter ien tsimmer rezehrveeren*
How do I get there?	**Wie komme ich dorthin?** *vee kommer ikh dorthin*

At the hotel Im Hotel

Do you have any vacancies?	**Haben Sie noch Zimmer frei?** *haaben zee nokh tsimmer frie*
I'm sorry, we're full.	**Wir sind leider voll belegt.** *veer zint lieder fol belaygt*
Is there another hotel nearby?	**Gibt es ein anderes Hotel in der Nähe?** *gipt ess ien anderess hottel in dehr naier*
I'd like a single/double room.	**Ich hätte gern ein Einzelzimmer/Doppelzimmer.** *ikh hehtter gehrn ien ientseltsimmer/doppeltsimmer*
A room with …	**Ein Zimmer mit …** *ien tsimmer mit*
twin beds	**zwei Einzelbetten** *tsvie ientselbeten*
a double bed	**einem Doppelbett** *ienem doppelbet*
a bath/shower	**Bad/Dusche** *baat/dusher*

– Haben Sie noch Zimmer frei?
– Wir sind leider voll belegt.
– Oh. Gibt es ein anderes Hotel in der Nähe?
– Ja. Versuchen Sie es im "Ambassador"
auf der anderen Straßenseite.

Reception Empfang

I have a reservation.
Ich habe reservieren lassen.
ikh haaber rezehrveeren lassen.

My name is ...
Mein Name ist ... *mien naamer ist*

We've reserved a double and a single room.
Wir haben ein Doppelzimmer und ein Einzelzimmer reservieren lassen.
veer haaben ien doppeltsimmer unt ien ientseltsimmer rezehrveeren lassen

I confirmed my reservation by mail.
Ich habe meine Reservierung schriftlich bestätigt.
ikh haaber miener rezehrveeerung shriftlikh beshtaitigt

Could we have adjoining rooms?
Könnten wir nebeneinander liegende Zimmer haben? *kurnten veer naybenienander leegender tsimmer haaben*

Amenities and facilities Ausstattung und Service

Is there ... in the room?
Gibt es ... im Zimmer? *gipt ess ... im tsimmer*

air conditioning
eine Klimaanlage *iener kleema-anlaager*

TV
einen Fernseher *ienen fehrnzayer*

telephone
ein Telefon *ien taylayfoan*

Does the hotel have ...?
Hat das Hotel ...? *hat dass hottel*

fax facilities
einen Telefaxdienst *ienen taylayfaksdeenst*

laundry service
einen Wäschedienst *ienen vehshedeenst*

satellite/cable TV
Satellitenfernsehen/Kabelfernsehen
zatelleetenfehrnzayen/kaabelfehrnzayen

sauna
eine Sauna *iener zowna*

swimming pool
ein Schwimmbad *ien shvimbaat*

Could you put ... in the room?
Könnten Sie ... ins Zimmer stellen? *kurnten zee ... ins tsimmer shtellen*

an extra bed
ein zusätzliches Bett *ien tsoozehtslikhess bet*

a crib/child's cot
ein Kinderbett *ien kinderbet*

Do you have facilities for ...?
Haben Sie Einrichtungen für ...? *haaben zee ienrikhtungen fewr*

the disabled
Behinderte *behinderter*

children
Kinder *kinder*

How long? Wie lange?

We'll be staying …	**Wir bleiben …**	*veer blieben*
overnight only	**nur eine Nacht**	*noor iener nakht*
a few days	**ein paar Tage**	*ien paar taager*
a week (at least)	**(mindestens) eine Woche**	*(mindestens) iener vokher*
I'd like to stay an extra night.	**Ich möchte noch eine Nacht bleiben.**	*ikh murkhter nokh iener nakht blieben*

– Guten Tag. Mein Name ist John Newton.
– *Guten Tag, Herr Newton.*
– Ich habe zwei Nächte reservieren lassen.
– *Ach ja. Bitte unterschreiben Sie hier.*

Kann ich bitte Ihren Pass sehen?	May I see your passport, please?
Bitte füllen Sie dieses Formular aus.	Please fill in this form.
Bitte unterschreiben Sie hier.	Please sign here.
Was ist Ihr Kraftfahrzeugkennzeichen?	What is your car registration number?

ZIMMER FREI	Room vacant
FRÜHSTÜCK INBEGRIFFEN	Breakfast included
MAHLZEITEN ERHÄLTLICH	Meals available
NAME/VORNAME	Name/first name
WOHNORT/STRASSE/NR.	Home address/street/number
NATIONALITÄT/BERUF	Nationality/Profession
GEBURTSDATUM/GEBURTSORT	Date/Place of birth
AUF DER DURCHREISE	In transit
VON/NACH	Coming from/going to
PASSNUMMER	Passport number
KRAFTFAHRZEUGKENNZEICHEN	Car registration number
ORT/DATUM	Place/date
UNTERSCHRIFT	Signature

Prices Preise

How much is it ...?	**Was kostet es ...?** *vass kostet ess*
per night/week	**pro Nacht/Woche** *proa nakht/vokhe*
for bed and breakfast	**für Übernachtung mit Frühstück** *fewr ewbernakhtung mit frewshtewk*
excluding meals	**ohne Mahlzeiten** *oaner maaltsieten*
for full board	**mit Vollpension** *mit folpenzioan*
for half board	**mit Halbpension** *mit halppenzioan*
Does the price include ...?	**Ist ... im Preis inbegriffen?** *ist ... im pries inbegriffen*
breakfast	**das Frühstück** *dass frewshtewk*
service	**die Bedienung** *dee bedeenung*
VAT	**die Mehrwertsteuer** *dee mayrvayrtshtoyer*
Do I have to pay a deposit?	**Muss ich eine Anzahlung leisten?** *muss ikh iener antsaloonk liesstern*
Is there a discount for children?	**Gibt es eine Ermäßigung für Kinder?** *gipt ess iener ehrmaissigung fewr kinder*

Decision Entscheidung

May I see the room?	**Kann ich das Zimmer sehen?** *kan ikh dass tsimmer zayen*
That's fine. I'll take it.	**Gut, ich nehme es.** *goot ikh naymer ess*
It's too ...	**Es ist zu ...** *ess ist tsoo*
cold/hot	**kalt/warm** *kalt/varm*
dark/small	**dunkel/klein** *dunkel/klien*
noisy	**laut** *lowt*
Do you have anything ...?	**Haben Sie nichts ...?** *haaben zee nikhts*
bigger/cheaper	**Größeres/Billigeres** *grursseress/billigeress*
quieter/warmer	**Ruhigeres/Wärmeres** *rooigeress/vehrmeress*
No, I won't take it.	**Nein, ich nehme es nicht.** *nien ikh naymer ess nikht*

Complaints Beschwerden

The … doesn't work.	**… funktioniert nicht.** *… funktsionneert nikht*
air conditioning	**die Klimaanlage** *dee kleema-anlaager*
fan	**der Ventilator** *dehr ventillaator*
heating	**die Heizung** *dee hietsung*
light	**das Licht** *dass likht*
television	**der Fernseher** *dehr fehrnzayer*
I can't turn the heat (heating) on/off.	**Ich kann die Heizung nicht anmachen/ausmachen.** *ikh kan dee hietsung nikht anmakhen/owsmakhen*
There is no hot water.	**Es gibt kein heißes Wasser.** *ess gipt kien hiessess vasser*
There is no toilet paper.	**Es ist kein Toilettenpapier da.** *ess ist kien twalettenpapeer daa*
The faucet is dripping.	**Der Wasserhahn tropft.** *dehr vasserhaan tropft*
The sink/toilet is blocked.	**Das Waschbecken/Die Toilette ist verstopft.** *dass vashbeken/dee twaletter ist fehrshtopft*
The window/door is jammed.	**Das Fenster/Die Tür klemmt.** *dass fenster/dee tewr klemmt*
My room has not been made up.	**Mein Zimmer ist nicht gemacht.** *mien tsimmer ist nikht gemakht*
The … is broken.	**… ist kaputt.** *… ist kaput*
blind	**das Rollo** *dass rolloa*
lamp	**die Lampe** *dee lamper*
lock	**das Schloss** *dass shloss*
There are insects in our room.	**In unserem Zimmer sind Insekten.** *in unzerem tsimmer zint inzekten*

Action Maßnahmen

Could you have that seen to?	**Können Sie sich darum kümmern?** *kurnen zee zikh darum kewmmern*
I'd like to move to another room.	**Ich möchte in ein anderes Zimmer umziehen.** *ikh murkhter in ien anderess tsimmer umtsee-ern*
I'd like to speak to the manager.	**Ich möchte mit dem Geschäftsführer sprechen.** *ikh murkhter mit daym geshehftsfewrer shprekhen*

Requirements Generelle Fragen

The 220-volt, 50-cycle AC is now universal in Germany, Austria and Switzerland. If you bring your own electrical appliances, buy a Continental adapter plug (round pins, not square) before leaving home. You may also need a transformer appropriate to the wattage of the appliance.

About the hotel Zum Hotel

Where's the …?	**Wo ist …?** *voa ist*
bar	**die Bar** *dee baar*
bathroom	**das Bad** *dass baat*
parking lot / car park	**der Parkplatz** *dehr paarkplats*
dining room	**der Speisesaal** *dehr shpiezezaal*
elevator / lift	**der Aufzug** *dehr owftsoog*
shower	**die Dusche** *dee dusher*
swimming pool	**das Schwimmbad** *dass shvimbaat*
TV room	**der Fernsehraum** *dehr fehrnzayrowm*
bathroom / toilet	**die Toilette** *dee twaletter*
tour operator's bulletin board	**das Anschlagbrett des Reiseveranstalters** *dass anshlaagbret dess riezefehranshtalterss*
Does the hotel have a garage?	**Gibt es eine Hotelgarage?** *gipt ess iener hottelgaraazher*
What time is the front door locked?	**Wann wird der Vordereingang abgeschlossen?** *van veert dehr forderiengang apgeshlossen*
What time is breakfast served?	**Wann wird das Frühstück serviert?** *van veert dass frewstewk zehrveert*
Is there room service?	**Gibt es einen Zimmerservice?** *gipt ess ienen tsimmerzehrvees*

AMTSANSCHLUSS: WÄHLEN SIE …	dial … for an outside line
BITTE IM ZIMMER NICHT ESSEN	no food in the room
BITTE NICHT STÖREN	do not disturb
EMPFANG: WÄHLEN SIE …	dial … for reception
FEUERTÜR	fire door
NOTAUSGANG	emergency exit
NUR FÜR RASIERAPPARATE	electric razors only

Personal needs Persönliche Fragen

The key to room ..., please.	**Den Schlüssel für Zimmer ..., bitte.** *dayn shlewssel fewr tsimmer ... bitter*
I've lost my key.	**Ich habe meinen Schlüssel verloren.** *ikh haaber mienen shlewssel fehrloaren*
I've locked myself out of my room.	**Ich habe mich aus meinem Zimmer ausgesperrt.** *ikh haaber mikh ows mienem tsimmer owsgeshperrt*
Could you wake me at ...?	**Können Sie mich um ... wecken?** *kurnen zee mikh um ... veken*
I'd like breakfast in my room.	**Ich möchte auf meinem Zimmer frühstücken.** *ikh murkhter owf mienem tsimmer frewshtewken*
Can I leave this in the safe?	**Kann ich dies in den Safe legen?** *kan ikh deez in dayn "safe" laygen*
Could I have my things from the safe?	**Kann ich meine Sachen aus dem Safe haben?** *kan ikh miener zakhen ows daym "safe" haaben*
Where can I find ...?	**Wo kann ich ... finden?** *voa kan ikh ... finden*
maid	**das Zimmermädchen** *dass tsimmermaitkhen*
porter	**den Portier** *dayn portyayr*
May I have ...?	**Kann ich ... haben?** *kan ikh ... haaben*
a bath towel	**ein Badetuch** *ien baadetookh*
an (extra) blanket	**eine (zusätzliche) Decke** *iener (tsoozehtslikher) deker*
(more) hangers	**(noch) einige Kleiderbügel** *(nokh) ieniger kliederbewgel*
a pillow	**ein Kopfkissen** *ien kopfkissen*
soap	**Seife** *ziefer*

Post and telephone Post und Telefon

Avoid high costs and surcharges when telephoning from hotel rooms in Germany, Austria and Switzerland by buying a **Telefonkarte** (phonecard) and making calls from a public phone.

Is there any mail for me?	**Ist Post für mich da?** *ist posst fewr mikh daa*
Are there any messages for me?	**Hat jemand eine Nachricht für mich hinterlassen?** *hat yaymant iener naakhrikht fewr mikh hinterlassen*

BREAKFAST ➤ 43; CHANGING MONEY ➤ 138

Lodging Unterkunft

We've reserved … in the name of …	**Wir haben … auf den Namen … reservieren lass:** *veer haaben … owf dayn naamen … rezehrveeren lassen*
an apartment	**eine Ferienwohnung** *iener fayree-envoanung*
a cottage	**ein Ferienhaus** *ien fayrienhowss*
Where do we pick up the keys?	**Wo bekommen wir die Schlüssel?** *voa bekommen veer dee shlewssel*
Where is the…?	**Wo ist …?** *voa ist*
electricity meter	**der Stromzähler** *dehr shtroamtsailer*
fuse box	**der Sicherungskasten** *dehr zikherungskasten*
stopcock	**der Absperrhahn** *dehr apshpehrhaan*
water heater	**das Heißwassergerät** *dass hiessvassergerait*
Are there any spare fuses?	**Sind Ersatzsicherungen da?** *zint ehrzatszikherungen daa*
Are there any spare gas bottles?	**Gibt es Gasflaschen als Reserve?** *gipt ess gaassflashen als rayzehrver*
Are there any spare sheets?	**Sind noch zusätzliche Bettlaken da?** *zint nokh tsoozehtslikher betlaaken daa*
Which day does the cleaner come?	**An welchem Tag kommt die Putzfrau?** *an velkhem taag komt dee putsfrow*

Problems? Probleme?

Where can I contact you?	**Wo kann ich Sie erreichen?** *voa kan ikh zee ehrriekhen*
How does the … work?	**Wie funktioniert …?** *vee funktsionneert*
cooker / water heater	**der Herd/das Heißwassergerät?** *dehr hehrt/dass hiessvassergerait*
The … has broken down.	**… ist kaputtgegangen.** *… ist kaputgegangen*
We have accidentally broken/lost …	**Wir haben versehentlich … zerbrochen/verlore** *veer haaben fehrzayentlikh … tsehrbrokhen/ fehrloaren*
That was already damaged when we arrived.	**Das war schon bei unserer Ankunft beschädigt.** *dass vaar shoan bie unzerer ankunft beshaidigt*

28   *HOUSEHOLD ARTICLES, CLEANING ITEMS ➤ 148*

Useful terms Nützliche Wörter

boiler	**der Boiler** *dehr boyler*
cooker	**der Herd** *dehr hehrt*
cutlery	**das Besteck** *dass beshtek*
freezer	**der Gefrierschrank** *dehr gefreershrank*
refrigerator	**der Kühlschrank** *dehr kewlshrank*
kettle	**der Kessel** *dehr kessel*
pot	**der Kochtopf** *dehr kokhtopf*
toaster	**der Toaster** *dehr toaster*
toilet paper	**das Toilettenpapier** *dass twalettenpapeer*
washing machine	**die Waschmaschine** *dee vashmasheener*

Rooms Zimmer

balcony	**der Balkon** *dehr balkoan*
bathroom	**das Badezimmer** *dass baadetsimmer*
bedroom	**das Schlafzimmer** *dass shlaaftsimmer*
dining room	**das Esszimmer** *dass esstsimmer*
kitchen	**die Küche** *dee kewkher*
living room	**das Wohnzimmer** *dass voantsimmer*
toilet	**die Toilette** *dee toaletter*

Youth hostel Jugendherberge

Youth hostels in Germany, Austria and Switzerland are of a very high
standard. For a Youth Hostel pass and more information contact:
(Germany) **Deutsches Jugendherbergswerk** ☎ 05231/74010;
(Austria) **Österreicher Jugendherbergsverband** ☎ 0222/533 53 53;
(Switzerland) **Schweizer Jugendherbergen** ☎ 01/360 14 14

Do you have any beds left for tonight?	**Haben Sie heute Nacht noch Plätze frei?** *haaben zee hoyter nakht nokh plehtser frie*
Do you rent bedding?	**Verleihen Sie Bettzeug?** *fehrlie-en zee bettsoyg*
What time are the doors locked?	**Wann werden die Türen abgeschlossen?** *van vehrden dee tewren apgeshlossen*
I have an International Student Card.	**Ich habe einen internationalen Studentenausweis.** *ikh haaber ienen internatsioanaalen shtuddentenowsvies*

Camping Camping

Camping is very popular in German-speaking countries and sites tend to be of a high standard. For a list of sites, facilities and rates contact:

(Germany) **Deutscher Camping-Club** ☏ (089) 33 40 21;
(Austria) **Österreicher Camping-Club** Johannesgasse 20, 1010 Vienna;
(Switzerland) **Schweizerischer Camping- und Caravanning-Verband** ☏ (041) 2 34 822.

Booking in Anmeldung

Is there a camp site near here?	**Gibt es hier in der Nähe einen Campingplatz?** *gipt ess heer in dehr naier ienen kempingplats*
Do you have space for a tent/trailer?	**Haben Sie Platz für ein Zelt/einen Wohnwagen?** *haaben zee plats fewr ien tselt/ienen voanvaagen*
What is the charge ...?	**Wie hoch sind die Gebühren ...?** *vee hoakh zint dee gebewren*
per day/week	**pro Tag/Woche** *proa taag/vokher*
for a tent/car	**für ein Zelt/ein Auto** *fewr ien tselt/ien owto*
for a trailer	**für einen Wohnwagen** *fewr ienen voanvaagen*
Can we camp anywhere on the campground?	**Können wir überall auf dem Platz zelten?** *kurnen veer ewberal owf daym plats tselten*
Can we park the car next to the tent?	**Können wir das Auto neben dem Zelt parken?** *kurnen veer dass owto nayben daym tselt parken*

Facilities Einrichtungen

Are there cooking facilities on site?	**Gibt es auf dem Platz Kochgelegenheiten?** *gipt ess owf daym plats kokhgelaygenhieten*
Are there any electric outlets?	**Gibt es hier Stromanschlüsse?** *gipt ess heer shtroamanshlewsser*
Where is/are the ...?	**Wo ist/sind** *voa ist/zint*
drinking water	**das Trinkwasser** *dass trinkvasser*
trash cans	**die Mülleimer** *dee mewlliemer*
showers	**die Duschen** *dee dushen*
Where are the laundry facilities?	**Wo kann man Wäsche waschen?** *voa kan man vehsher vashen*

ZELTEN VERBOTEN	no camping
TRINKWASSER	drinking water

Complaints Beschwerden

It's too sunny/shady/ crowded here.	**Hier ist es zu sonnig/schattig/ überfüllt.** *heer ist tsoo zonnikh/ shattikh/ewberfewlt*
The ground's too hard/ uneven.	**Der Boden ist zu hart/uneben.** *dehr boaden ist tsoo hart/unayben*
Do you have a more level spot?	**Haben Sie eine ebenere Stelle?** *haaben zee iener aybenerer shteler*

Camping equipment Campingausrüstung

backpack	**der Rucksack** *dehr rukzak*
butane gas	**das Butangas** *dass butaangaass*
camping stove	**der Camping kocher** *dehr kempingkokher*
charcoal	**die Holzkohle** *dee holtskoaler*
coolbox	**die Kühlbox** *dee kewlboks*
cot	**die Campingliege** *dee kempingleeger*
firelighter	**der Feueranzünder** *dehr foyerantsewnder*
flashlight	**die Taschenlampe** *dee tashenlamper*
folding chair/table	**der Klappstuhl/Klapptisch** *dehr klapshtool/klaptish*
hammer	**der Hammer** *dehr hamer*
ice pack	**der Kälteakku** *dehr kehlteakoo*
kerosene	**das Kerosin** *dass kehroseen*
knapsack	**der Rucksack** *dehr rukzak*
mallet	**der Holzhammer** *dehr holtshamer*
matches	**die Streichhölzer** *dee shtriekhhurltser*
(air) mattress	**die (Luft)matratze** *dee (luft)matratser*
paraffin	**das Paraffin** *dass parafeen*
pocket knife	**das Taschenmesser** *dass tashenmesser*
pump	**die Pumpe** *dee pumper*
pot	**der Kochtopf** *dehr kokhtopf*
sleeping bag	**der Schlafsack** *dehr shlaafzak*
tent	**das Zelt** *dass tselt*
tent floor	**der Zeltboden** *dehr tseltboaden*
tent pegs	**die Heringe** *dee hayringer*
tent pole	**die Zeltstange** *dee tseltshtanger*
water jug	**der Wasserkanister** *dehr vasserkanister*

Checking out Abreise

What time do we need to vacate the room?	**Bis wann müssen wir das Zimmer räumen?** *biss van mewssen veer dass tsimmer roymen*
Could we leave our baggage/luggage here until ... o'clock?	**Können wir unser Gepäck bis ... Uhr hier lassen?** *kurnen veer unzer gepehk biss ... oor heerlassen*
I'm leaving now.	**Ich reise jetzt ab.** *ikh rieze yetst ap*
Could you order me a taxi, please?	**Könnten Sie mir bitte ein Taxi bestellen?** *kurnten zee meer bitter ien taksi beshtelen*
It's been a very enjoyable stay.	**Es war ein sehr angenehmer Aufenthalt.** *ess vaar ien zayr angenaymer owfenthalt*

Paying Bezahlen

May I have my bill, please.	**Kann ich bitte die Rechnung haben?** *kan ikh bitter dee rekhnung haaben*
How much is my telephone bill?	**Wie hoch ist meine Telefonrechnung?** *vee hoakh ist miener taylayfoanrekhnung*
I think there's a mistake in this bill.	**Ich glaube, Sie haben sich verrechnet.** *ikh glowber zee haaben zikh fehrrekhnet*
I've made ... telephone calls.	**Ich habe ... Anrufe gemacht.** *ikh haaber ... anroofer gemakht*
I've taken ... from the minibar.	**Ich habe ... aus der Minibar entnommen.** *ikh haaber ... ows dehr minibaar entnommen*
Could I have my passport/deposit back?	**Kann ich meinen Pass/meine Kaution zurückhaben?** *kan ikh mienen pas/miener kowtsioan tsoorewk haaben*
Could I have a receipt, please?	**Kann ich bitte eine Quittung haben?** *kan ikh bitter iener kvittung haaben*

Tipping: a service charge is generally included in hotel and restaurant bills. However, if the service has been particularly good, you may want to leave an extra tip. The following chart is a guide:

	Germany	Austria	Switzerland
Porter	1–2 DM	10 S	1–2 F
Hotel maid, per week	5–10 DM	50 S	10 F
Waiter	round up (optional)	5% (optional)	optional

TIME ➤ 220

Eating Out

Restaurants   Restaurants

Beisel *biezel*

The Austrian equivalent to a **Gasthaus**.

Bierhalle *beerhaller*

Beer hall; besides beer served from huge barrels, you'll also be able to order hot dishes, salads and pretzels. The best-known beer halls are in Munich, which has a giant beer festival (**Oktoberfest**) in late September.

Bierstube *beershtoober*

The nearest equivalent to an English pub or an American bar though the atmosphere may be very different; usually only serves a few "dishes of the day."

Café *kafay*

Coffee shop offering pastries, snacks and drinks. A **Tanzcafé** will have a small dance floor.

Gasthaus/Gasthof *gasthowss/gasthoaf*

Inn, usually in the country. It offers home cooking and a folksy atmosphere.

Gaststätte *gaststetter*

Another word for restaurant.

Konditorei *kondeetoarie*

Pastry shop, often with a café for coffee and pastries.

Milchbar *milkhbaar*

Bar serving mainly plain and flavored milk drinks with pastries. Also called a **Milchstübl** in some regions.

Raststätte/Rasthof *rastshtetter/rasthoaf*
Roadside restaurant; Usually found on highways/
motorways with lodging and service-station facilities.
Ratskeller *raatskeller*
Restaurant in the cellar of the town hall (often an historic
building).

Restaurant *restorang*
Restaurants are usually up-scale/market establishments with a menu to
match, ranging from local specialties to international cuisine.

Schnellimbiss *shnelimbiss*
Snack bar; the English term is also seen. The principal fare is beer and
sausages. A sausage stand (**Würstchenstand**) is often quite similar.

Weinstube *vienshtoober*
Cozy restaurant found in wine-producing areas, where you can sample
new wine with simple hot dishes and snacks.

Meal times Essenszeiten

das Frühstück *dass frewshtewk*
Breakfast: from 7–10 a.m. More substantial than the typical Continental
breakfast: you'll be offered a selection of cold meats, cheeses, pâtés, jams
and marmalades, accompanied by a huge variety of different breads,
together with tea, coffee or hot chocolate. Boiled eggs are also popular.

das Mittagessen *dass mittaagessen*
Lunch: from 11.30 a.m. – 2 p.m. The majority of Germans like to eat their
main meal in the middle of the day and most restaurants will offer their
set menus (**Menü** or **Gedeck**) at midday as well as in the evening. If you
want something smaller, look under **Kleine Gerichte** or try the ever-
increasing number of snack bars and fast-food outlets.

das Abendessen/Abendbrot *dass aabentessen/aabentbroat*
Dinner/Supper: standard evening meals in German homes consist of a
variety of bread or rolls with cold meats, cheeses, pickles and maybe
salad. You'll be able to get a full menu in restaurants which tend to serve
between 6:30 and 8:30 p.m; larger restaurants may serve until 10 or 11 p.m.

Most restaurants will offer several fixed-price menus (**Tagesgedeck**) at
different price points. These usually change every day and provide typical
German dishes at a reasonable price. Or you can choose from the à la carte
menu (**Speisekarte**). Service is always included.

It's quite common to drink beer with most German meals, but if you want
to try some of the local wine ask for **eine Flasche** (bottle), **eine halbe
Flasche** (half-bottle) or **eine Karaffe** (carafe).

A table for	**Ein Tisch für** *ien tish fewr*
1/2/3/4	**eine/zwei/drei/vier** *ien/tsvie/drie/feer*
Thank you.	**Danke.** *danker*
The bill, please.	**Die Rechnung, bitte.** *dee rekhnung bitter*

Finding a place to eat Eine Gaststätte finden

Can you recommend a good restaurant?	**Können Sie ein gutes Restaurant empfehlen?** *kurnen zee ien gootess restorrang empfaylen*
Is there a(n) ... restaurant near here?	**Gibt es hier in der Nähe ein ... Restaurant?** *gipt ess heer in dehr naier ien ... restorrang*
traditional local	**traditionelles gutbürgerliches** *traditsionnelless gootbewrgerlikhess*
Chinese	**chinesisches** *khinayzishess*
Greek	**griechisches** *greekhishess*
Italian	**italienisches** *italyaynishess*
inexpensive	**preiswertes** *priesvayrtess*
Turkish	**türkisches** *tewrkishess*
vegetarian	**vegetarisches** *vegetaarishess*
Where can I find a(n) ...?	**Wo finde ich ...?** *voa finder ikh*
sausage stand	**einen Würstchenstand** *iehnen vewrstkhenshtant*
café	**ein Café** *ien kafay*
café/restaurant with a beer garden	**ein Café/Restaurant mit Biergarten** *ien kafay/restorrang mit beergarten*
fast-food restaurant	**einen Schnellimbiss** *ienen shnelimbiss*
ice-cream parlor/parlour	**eine Eisdiele** *iener iesdeeler*
pizzeria	**eine Pizzeria** *iener peetseree-ah*
snack bar	**eine Imbissstube** *iener imbiss-shtoober*
steak house	**ein Steakhaus** *ien shtaykhowss*

DIRECTIONS ➤ *94*

Reservations Bestellen

I'd like to reserve a table for 2.	**Ich möchte einen Tisch für zwei Personen bestellen.** *ikh murkhter ienen tish fewr tsvie pehrzoanen beshtelen*
For this evening/ tomorrow at …	**Für heute Abend/Morgen um …** *fewr hoyter aabent/morgen um*
We'll come at 8:00.	**Wir kommen um zwanzig Uhr.** *veer kommen um tsvantsikh oor*
A table for 2, please.	**Einen Tisch für zwei Personen, bitte.** *ienen tish fewr tsvie pehrzoanen bitter*
We have a reservation.	**Wir haben einen Tisch bestellt.** *veer haaben ienern tish beshtelt*

Ihr Name, bitte?	What's the name, please?
Es tut mir leid. Wir haben sehr viel zu tun.	I'm sorry. We're very busy.
Es tut mir leid. Wir sind völlig ausgebucht.	I'm sorry. We're completely booked.
In … Minuten wird ein Tisch frei.	We'll have a table in … minutes.
Sie müssen in … Minuten wiederkommen.	You'll have to come back in … minutes.

Where to sit Wo man sitzt

Could we sit …?	**Können wir … sitzen?** *kurnen veer … zitsen*
over there	**dort drüben** *dort drewben*
outside	**im Freien** *im frie-en*
in a non-smoking area	**in einer Nichtraucherecke** *in iener nikhtrowkhereker*
by the window	**am Fenster** *am fenster*

> – Ich möchte einen Tisch für heute abend bestellen.
> – *Für wie viele Personen?*
> – Für vier Personen.
> – *Wann kommen Sie?*
> – Wir kommen um 20 Uhr.
> – *Und Ihr Name, bitte?*
> – Evans.
> – *Gut. Bis heute abend.*

Ordering Bestellen

Excuse me, please!	**Entschuldigen Sie, bitte!** *entshuldiggen zee bitter*
May I see the wine list, please?	**Die Weinkarte, bitte.** *dee vienkarter bitter*
Do you have a set menu?	**Haben Sie ein Menü?** *haaben zee ien maynew*
Can you recommend some typical local dishes?	**Können Sie einige typische hiesige Gerichte empfehlen?** *kurnen zee ienigger tewpisher heeziger gerikhter empfaylen*
Could you tell me what … is?	**Können Sie mir sagen, was … ist?** *kurnen zee meer zaagen vass … ist*
What is in it?	**Was ist darin?** *vass ist daarin*
What kind of … do you have?	**Welche Art von … haben Sie?** *velkher aart fon … haaben zee*
I'd like …	**Ich hätte gern …** *ikh hetter gehrn*
I'll have …	**Ich nehme …** *ikh naymer*
a bottle/glass/ carafe of …	**eine Flasche/ein Glas/eine Karaffe …** *iener flasher/ien glaass/iener karaffer*

Haben Sie gewählt?	Are you ready to order?
Was nehmen Sie?	What would you like?
Möchten Sie zuerst Getränke bestellen?	Would you like to order drinks first?
Ich empfehle Ihnen …	I recommend …
… haben wir nicht.	We haven't got …
Das dauert … Minuten.	That will take … minutes.
Guten Appetit.	Enjoy your meal.

– *Haben Sie gewählt?*
– Können Sie etwas typisch Deutsches empfehlen?
– *Ja. Ich empfehle Ihnen den Sauerbraten.*
– Gut, den nehme ich, und als Beilage Kartoffeln, bitte.
– *Selbstverständlich. Und was möchten Sie trinken?*
– Eine Karaffe Rotwein, bitte.

DRINKS ➤ 49; MENU READER ➤ 53

Side dishes Beilagen

Could I have ... without ...?	**Kann ich ... ohne ... haben?** *kan ikh ... oaner ... haaben*
With a side order of ...	**Mit ... als Beilage.** *mit ... als bielaager*
Could I have salad instead of vegetables, please	**Kann ich bitte Salat statt Gemüse haben?** *kan ikh bitter zalaat shtat gemewzer haaben*
Does the meal come with vegetables/potatoes?	**Ist Gemüse/Sind Kartoffeln bei dem Essen dabei?** *ist gemewzer/zint kartoffeln bie daym essen dahbie*
Do you have any sauces?	**Haben Sie Soßen?** *haaben zee zoassen*
Would you like ... with that?	**Möchten Sie ... dazu haben?** *murkhten zee ... dahtsoo haaben*
vegetables	**Gemüse** *gemewzer*
salad	**Salat** *zalaat*
potatoes	**Kartoffeln** *kartoffeln*
French fries	**Pommes frites** *pom frit*
sauce	**Soße** *zoasser*
ice	**Eis** *iess*
May I have some ...?	**Könnte ich etwas ... haben?** *kurnter ikh etvass ... haaben*
bread	**Brot** *broat*
butter	**Butter** *butter*
lemon	**Zitrone** *zitroaner*
mustard	**Senf** *zenf*
pepper	**Pfeffer** *pfefer*
salt	**Salz** *zalts*
seasoning	**Würze** *vewrtser*
sugar	**Zucker** *tsukker*
artificial sweetener	**Süßstoff** *sewsshtof*

MENU READER ➤ 52

General questions Allgemeine Fragen

Could I/we have ..., please? | **Kann ich/Können wir bitte ... haben?** *kan ikh/kurnen veer bitter ... haaben*

ashtray | **einen Aschenbecher** *ienen ashenbekher*

cup/glass | **eine Tasse/ein Glas** *iener tasser/ien glas*

fork/knife | **eine Gabel/ein Messer** *iener gaabel/ien messer*

napkin | **eine Serviette** *iener zehrvietter*

plate/spoon | **einen Teller/Löffel** *ienen teller/lurfel*

I'd like some more ..., please. | **Ich hätte gern noch etwas ...** *ikh hetter gehrn nokh etvaas*

Nothing more, thanks. | **Nichts mehr, danke.** *nikhts mayr danker*

Where is the bathroom? | **Wo sind die Toiletten?** *voa zint dee twaletten*

Special requirements Sonderwünsche

I mustn't eat food containing ... | **Ich darf nichts essen, was ... enthält.** *ikh darf nikhts essen vass ... ent-hehlt*

salt/sugar | **Salz/Zucker** *zalts/tsukker*

Do you have meals/drinks for diabetics? | **Haben Sie Gerichte/Getränke für Diabetiker?** *haaben zee gerikhter/getrehnker fewr dee-abaytiker*

Do you have vegetarian meals? | **Haben Sie vegetarische Gerichte?** *haaben zee vegetaarisher gerikhter*

For the children ... Für Kinder ...

Do you do children's portions? | **Haben Sie Kinderportionen?** *haaben zee kinderpoartsioanen*

Could we have a child's seat, please? | **Können wir bitte einen Kinderstuhl haben?** *kurnen veer bitter ienen kindershtool haaben*

Where can I warm the baby's bottle? | **Wo kann ich das Fläschchen wärmen?** *voa kan ikh dass flehshkhen vehrmen*

Where can I feed/change the baby? | **Wo kann ich das Baby füttern/wickeln?** *voa kan ikh dass baby fewttern/vikeln*

CHILDREN ➤ 113

Fast food Schnellgerichte

Something to drink Etwas zu trinken

I'd like …	**Ich hätte gern …** *ikh hetter gehrn*
(hot) chocolate	**(heiße) Schokolade** *(hiesser) shokolaader*
coffee	**Kaffee** *kafay*
black/with milk	**schwarz/mit Milch** *shvarts/mit milkh*
tea	**Tee** *tay*
I'd like a … of red/white wine.	**Ich hätte gern … Rotwein/Weißwein.** *ikh hetter gehrn … roatvien/viessvien*
bottle	**eine Flasche** *iener flasher*
glass	**ein Glas** *ien glas*
A small/large beer, please.	**Ein kleines/großes Bier, bitte.** *ien klienes/groasses beer bitter*

Bitte schön?	Can I help you?
… haben wir nicht mehr.	We've run out of…
Sonst noch etwas?	Anything else?

And to eat … Und zu essen …

A piece of …, please.	**Ein Stück …, bitte.** *ien shtewk … bitter*
I'd like two of those.	**Ich hätte gern zwei davon.** *ikh hetter gehrn tsvie dahfon*
burger	**Hamburger** *hamboorger*
cake	**Kuchen** *kookhen*
French fries	**Pommes frites** *pom frit*
sandwich	**belegtes Brot** *belaygtess broat*
sausage	**Wurst** *voorst*

Eis *iess*

ice cream; some common flavors are **Erdbeereis** (strawberry), **Schokoladeneis** (chocolate), **Vanilleeis** (vanilla).

A … portion, please.	**Eine … Portion, bitte.** *iener … poartsioan bitter*
small	**kleine** *kliener*
medium/regular	**mittlere/normale** *mitlerer/normaaler*
large	**große** *groasser*
It's to take out.	**Es ist zum Mitnehmen.** *ess ist tsum mitnaymen*
That's all, thanks.	**Danke, das ist alles.** *danker dass ist aless*

- *Was hätten Sie gern?*
- Zwei Kaffee, bitte.
- *Schwarz oder mit Milch?*
- Mit Milch, bitte.
- *Etwas zu essen?*
- Ja, zwei Stücke Kuchen, bitte.
- *Sonst noch etwas?*
- Danke, das ist alles.

Complaints Beschwerden

I have no knife/fork/spoon.	**Ich habe kein Messer/keine Gabel/keinen Löffel.** *ikh haaber kien messer/kiener gaabel/kienen lurfel*
There must be some mistake.	**Es muss ein Irrtum vorliegen.** *ess muss ien irtoom foarleegen*
That's not what I ordered.	**Das habe ich nicht bestellt.** *dass haaber ikh nikht beshtelt*
I asked for …	**Ich wollte …** *ikh volter*
I can't eat this.	**Das kann ich nicht essen.** *dass kan ikh nikht essen*
The meat is …	**Das Fleisch ist …** *dass fliesh ist*
overdone	**zu stark gebraten** *tsoo shtark gebraaten*
underdone	**zu roh** *tsoo roa*
too tough	**zu zäh** *tsoo tsai*
This is too …	**Das ist zu …** *dass ist tsoo*
bitter/sour	**bitter/sauer** *bitter/zower*
The food is cold.	**Das Essen ist kalt.** *dass essen ist kalt*
This isn't fresh.	**Das ist nicht frisch.** *dass ist nikht frish*
How much longer will our food be?	**Wie lange dauert unser Essen noch?** *vee langer dowert unzer essen nokh*
We can't wait any longer. We're leaving.	**Wir können nicht länger warten. Wir gehen.** *veer kurnen nikht lehnger varten. veer gayen*
Have you forgotten our drinks?	**Haben Sie unsere Getränke vergessen?** *haaben zee unzerer getrehnker fehrgessen*
This isn't clean.	**Das ist nicht sauber.** *dass ist nikht zowber*
I'd like to speak to the head waiter/manager.	**Ich möchte mit dem Oberkellner/Geschäftsführer sprechen.** *ikh murkhter mit daym oaberkelner/geshehftsfewrer shprekhen*

Paying Bezahlen

Tipping: Service is generally included in the bill, but if you are happy with the service, a personal tip for the waiter is appropriate and appreciated – in Germany it's usual to round up the bill.

I'd like to pay.	**Ich möchte bezahlen.**	*ikh murkhter betsaalen*
Could I have the bill, please?	**Bezahlen, bitte.**	*tbesaalen bitter*
We'd like to pay separately.	**Wir möchten getrennt bezahlen.**	*veer murkhten getrent betsaalen*
It's all together, please.	**Alles zusammen, bitte.**	*aless tsoozammen bitter*
I think there's a mistake in this bill.	**Ich glaube, Sie haben sich verrechnet.**	*ikh glowber zee haaben zikh fehrrekhnet*
What is this amount for?	**Wofür ist dieser Betrag?**	*voafewr ist deezer betraag*
I didn't have that. I had …	**Das hatte ich nicht. Ich hatte …**	*dass hatter ikh nikht. ikh hatter*
Is service included?	**Ist die Bedienung inbegriffen?**	*ist dee bedeenung inbegriffen*
Can I pay with this credit card?	**Kann ich mit dieser Kreditkarte bezahlen?**	*kan ikh mit deezer kredeetkarter betsaalen*
I've forgotten my wallet.	**Ich habe meine Brieftasche vergessen.**	*ikh haaber miener breeftasher fehrgessen*
I haven't got enough money.	**Ich habe nicht genug Geld.**	*ikh haaber nikht genook gelt*
Could I have a receipt, please?	**Kann ich bitte eine Quittung haben?**	*kan ikh bitter iener kvittung haaben*
Can I have an itemized bill, please?	**Kann ich eine spezifizierte Rechnung haben?**	*kan ikh iener shpetsifitseerter rekhnung haaben*
That was a very good meal.	**Das Essen war sehr gut.**	*dass essen vaar zayr goot*

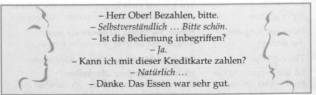

– Herr Ober! Bezahlen, bitte.
– *Selbstverständlich … Bitte schön.*
– Ist die Bedienung inbegriffen?
– *Ja.*
– Kann ich mit dieser Kreditkarte zahlen?
– *Natürlich …*
– Danke. Das Essen war sehr gut.

PAYING (SHOPPING) ➤ 136; PAYING (HOTEL) ➤ 32

Course by course
Die verschiedenen Gänge

Breakfast Frühstück

No trip to Germany would be complete without sampling some of the wonderful breads: **Weißbrot** (white), **Vollkornbrot** (whole grain), **französisches Weißbrot/Baguette** (French), **Zwiebelbrot** (onion), **Rosinenbrot** (raisin), **Roggenbrot** (rye), **Sesambrötchen** (sesame seed rolls), **Mohnbrötchen** (poppy seed rolls).

I'd like …	**Ich hätte gern …** *ikh hetter gehrn*
bread	**Brot** *broat*
butter	**Butter** *butter*
cereal	**Müsli/Cornflakes** *mewsli/"cornflakes"*
cheese	**Käse** *kaizer*
cold meats	**Aufschnitt** *owfshnit*
eggs	**Eier** *ie-er*
boiled egg	**ein gekochtes Ei** *ien gekokhtes ie*
fried eggs	**Spiegeleier** *shpeegelie-er*
scrambled eggs	**Rühreier** *rewrie-er*
honey	**Honig** *hoanikh*
jam	**Marmelade** *marmelaader*
marmalade	**Orangenmarmelade** *oranzhgen-marmelaader*
milk	**Milch** *milkh*
orange juice	**Orangensaft** *orangshenzaft*
toast	**Toast** *toast*

Appetizers Vorspeisen

Aufschnittplatte   *owfshnitplatter*
assorted cold cuts served with gherkins and bread
Bauernomelette   *bowern omletter*
diced bacon and onion omelet
Bündnerfleisch   *bewndnerfliesh*
cured, dried beef served in thin slices (Swiss)
Fleischpastete   *flieshpastayter*
meat loaf
Matjesfilet nach Hausfrauenart   *matyehsfillay nakh howsfrowenart*
fillets of herring with apples and onions
Russische Eier   *russisher ieer*
hard-boiled eggs with mayonnaise
Stolzer Heinrich   *stoalzer hienrikh*
fried pork sausage in beer sauce (Bavarian)

NON-ALCOHOLIC DRINKS ➤ *51*

Soups Suppen

Soups appear on menus in two main forms: **Suppe** (soup) and **Brühe** (broth). Look out for these specialties.

Backerbsensuppe	*bakehrpsenzupper*	type of split-pea soup
Bauernsuppe	*bowernzupper*	cabbage and frankfurter soup
Champignonsuppe	*shampinyongzupper*	mushroom soup
Erbsensuppe	*ehrpzenzupper*	pea soup
Flädlesuppe	*flaydlezupper*	broth with pancake strips
Gemüsesuppe	*gemewsezupper*	vegetable soup
Gulaschsuppe	*goolashzupper*	spiced soup of stewed beef
Hühnerbrühe	*hoonerbrewer*	chicken broth
Leberknödelsuppe	*layberknurdelzupper*	liver-dumpling soup
Nudelsuppe	*noodelzupper*	noodle soup
Ochsenschwanzsuppe	*okhsenshvantszupper*	oxtail soup
Serbische	*sehrbisher*	spiced bean soup
Bohnensuppe	*boanenzupper*	
Tomatensuppe	*tomaatenzupper*	tomato soup

Fish and seafood Fisch und Meeresfrüchte

You'll recognize **Hering, Karpfen** and **Makrele;** other popular fish and seafood are listed below or appear in the Menu Reader.

Dorsch	*dorsh*	cod
Forelle	*foreller*	trout
Garnelen	*garnaylen*	prawns/shrimps
Kabeljau	*kaabelyow*	cod
Lachs	*laks*	salmon
Languste	*langooster*	crayfish
Muscheln	*musheln*	clams/mussels
Salm	*zalm*	salmon
Scholle	*sholler*	plaice
Tintenfisch	*tintenfish*	squid, octopus

Meat Fleisch

Ich hätte gern ...	*ikh hetter gehrn*	I'd like some ...
Rindfleisch	*rintfliesh*	beef
Hähnchen	*hainkhern*	chicken
Ente	*enter*	duck
Schinken	*shinken*	ham
Lammfleisch	*lammfliesh*	lamb
Schweinefleisch	*shvienefliesh*	pork
Kaninchen	*kaneenkhern*	rabbit
Würste	*vewrster*	sausages
Truthahn	*troothaan*	turkey
Kalbfleisch	*kalpfliesh*	veal
Reh	*ray*	venison

Meat cuts Fleischstücke

To find out what type of cut you'll be getting for your meal, look to
the end of the word: the meat comes first (e.g. **Schweine-**), followed by
the cut (**-kotelett**)

-braten	*braaten*	joint, roast
-brust	*brust*	breast
-hachse/haxe	*hakser*	shank
-herz	*herts*	heart
-kotelett	*kotlett*	cutlet, chop
-klößchen	*klurskhen*	meatballs
-leber	*layber*	liver
-plätzli	*plehtslee*	cutlet
-rücken	*rewken*	back
-spießchen	*shpeeskhen*	skewered meat
-zunge	*tsunger*	tongue

Meat dishes Fleischgerichte

Eisbein	*iesbien*	pickled pig's knuckle
Faschiertes	*fasheertes*	minced meat
Fleischkäse	*flieshkaizer*	meat loaf
Gehacktes	*gehaktes*	minced meat
Kalbshaxen	*kalpshaksen*	roast shank of veal
Leberkäse	*layberkaizer*	type of meat loaf
Wiener Schnitzel	*veener shnitsel*	breaded veal cutlet

45

Bauernschmaus *bowenshmowss*
sauerkraut garnished with boiled bacon, smoked pork,
sausages, dumplings, potatoes (Austrian)

Berner Platte *behrner platter*
sauerkraut or green beans liberally garnished with pork chops,
boiled bacon and beef, sausages, tongue and ham (Swiss)

Holsteiner Schnitzel *holstiener shnitsel*
breaded veal cutlet topped with fried egg, garnished with vegetables
and usually accompanied by bread and butter, anchovies, mussels and
smoked salmon

Kohlroulade *koalroolaader*
cabbage leaves stuffed with minced meat

Maultaschen *mowltashen*
Swabian-style ravioli filled with meat, vegetables and seasoning

Pfefferpotthast *pfefferpot-hast*
spicy meat and onion casserole

Rouladen *roolaaden*
slices of beef or veal filled, rolled and braised (in brown gravy)

Sauerbraten *zowerbraaten*
beef roast, marinated with herbs and braised in a rich sauce

Schlachtplatte *shlakhtplatter*
platter of various sausages and cold meats

Sausages Würste

Bierwurst	*beervoorst*	pork and beef, smoked
Blutwurst	*blootvoorst*	blood sausage
Bockwurst	*bokvoorst*	large frankfurter
Bratwurst	*braatvoorst*	pork, fried or grilled
Fleischwurst	*flieshvoorst*	mildly seasoned, popular with children
Jagdwurst	*yaagtvoorst*	smoked pork, similar to salami
Leberwurst	*laybervoorst*	liver sausage
Katenrauchwurst	*kaatenrowkhvoorst*	country-style, smoked
Regensburger	*raygensburger*	highly spiced, smoked
Rotwurst	*roatvoorst*	blood sausage/black pudding
Weißwurst	*viesvoorst*	veal and bacon with parsley and onion
Zervelat(wurst)	*tservelaat(voorst)*	pork, beef and bacon, seasoned and smoked
Zwiebelwurst	*tsveebelvoorst*	liver and onion

Side dishes Beilagen

Kartoffeln *kartoffeln*
potatoes, which may appear as: **Bratkartoffeln/Röstkartoffeln**
(fried), **Geröstete/Rösti** (hash-brown), **Kartoffelbrei/-püree**
(mashed), **Kartoffelsalat** (potato salad), **Salzkartoffeln** (boiled).

Klöße/Knödel *klursser/knurdel*
dumplings – another specialty that comes highly recommended; they are
often served with soups, stews and meat dishes. Some varieties are
Grießklöße (semolina), **Kartoffelklöße** (potato), **Leberknödel** (liver), **Mehlklöße**
(flour), **Nockerl** (small), **Semmelknödel** (Bavarian bread dumplings). Note that
dumplings are called **Klöße** in northern Germany, but **Knödel** in the south.

Teigwaren *tiegwaaren*
pasta; some varieties include **Nudeln** (noodles), **Spätzle** and **Knöpfli**
(types of gnocchi).

You'll recognize these vegetables: **Brokkoli, Karotten, Sauerkraut, Sellerie,
Tomaten.**

Blumenkohl	*bloomenkoal*	cauliflower
Bohnen	*boanen*	beans
Cornichons	*kornishons*	small pickles
Erbsen	*ehrpsen*	peas
Gurke	*goorker*	cucumber
Karfiol	*karfioal*	cauliflower
Kopfsalat	*kopfzalaat*	head of lettuce
Mohrrüben	*moarrewben*	carrots
Zwiebeln	*tsveebeln*	onions
gemischter Salat	*gemishter zalaat*	mixed salad
grüner Salat	*grewner zalaat*	green salad
Rettichsalat	*rettichzalaat*	white radish salad
Rotkrautsalat	*roatkrowtzalaat*	red cabbage salad
Tomatensalat	*tomaatenzalaat*	tomato salad

Kohl/Kraut *koal/krowt*
cabbage; a popular vegetable with many variations: **Grünkohl** (kale),
Krautsalat (coleslaw), **Rotkohl/-kraut** (red cabbage), **Sauerkraut** (pickled,
shredded cabbage), **Weißkohl/-kraut** (white cabbage).

Pilze *piltser*
mushrooms. Common varieties used in German cuisine include
Champignons (white), **Pferrlinge** (wild), and **Pfifferlinge** (chanterelle).

Cheese Käse

Most of the cheeses produced in Germany, Austria and Switzerland are mild, though there are some strong cheeses – usually classified in three grades: **würzig**, **pikant** and **scharf**.

hard cheeses	(mild)	**Allgäuer Bergkäse** (like Swiss cheese), **Appenzeller**, **Räucherkäse** (smoked), **Schichtkäse**, **Tilsiter**
	(sharp)	**Handkäse**, **Harzer Käse**, **Schabzieger**
soft cheeses	(mild)	**Allgäuer Rahmkäse**, **Altenburger** (goat's milk cheese), **Edelpilz** (blue cheese), **Frischkäse** (curd cheese), **Kümmelkäse** (with caraway seeds), **Sahnekäse** (cream cheese)
Swiss cheeses	(mild)	**Emmentaler**, **Greyerzer**

Fruit Obst

Apfelsine	*apfelzeener*	orange
Birne	*beerner*	pear
rote/schwarze Johannisbeeren	*roater/shvartser yohanisbayren*	red/black currants
Kirschen	*keershen*	cherries
Pflaumen	*pflowmen*	plums
Zitrone/Limone	*tsitroaner/limoaner*	lemon/lime
Zwetschgen	*tsvetshgen*	plums

Dessert Nachtisch

And you'll recognize: **Apfel, Banane, Mandarine, Melone, Aprikosen, Datteln, Kokosnuss, Orange, Rhabarber**.

Apfelkuchen	*apfelkookhen*	apple tart
Dampfnudeln	*dampfnoodeln*	sweet dumplings
gemischtes Eis	*gemishtes iess*	mixed ice cream portion
Germknödel	*gehrmknurdel*	sweet dumpling
Obstsalat	*oabstzalaat*	fruit salad
Pfannkuchen	*pfankookhen*	pancakes
Rote Grütze	*roater grewtser*	red berry compote
Streuselkuchen	*stroyselkookhen*	coffee cake with crumble topping
Zwetschgenkuchen	*zvetshgenkookhen*	plum tart

Drinks Getränke

Beer Bier

Beer is by far the most popular drink in Germany and Austria – and it's not all lager! For easy ordering, ask for **Bier vom Fass** (draft beer). To be more specific, ask for **ein Helles** (light beer) or **ein Dunkles** (dark beer). And look out for:

Alkoholfreies Bier: alcohol-free

Altbier: with high hops content; similar to British ale

Berliner Weiße mit Schuss: pale beer with a shot of raspberry syrup

Bockbier, Doppelbock, Märzen, Starkbier: with high alcoholic and malt content

Export: pale and strong, higher in alcoholic content and less bitter than a Pilsener

Hefeweizen/Hefeweißbier: pale, brewed from wheat

Kölsch: golden and light, brewed in Cologne; similar to the beer of Canada and the U.S.

Kulmbacher Eisbock: with the highest alcohol content of all German beer

Malzbier: dark and sweet, low in alcohol

Pilsener (Pils): pale and strong with an aroma of hops

Radlermaß/Alsterwasser: lager shandy (beer with lemonade)

Weißbier: light, brewed from wheat grain

Wine Wein

The Association of German Wine Estates (VDP) acts as a quality control and ensures that wines carrying the VDP label are of superior quality. The wine seal **(Weinsiegel)** on the neck of the wine bottle is color-coded for easy recognition: yellow seal for dry **(trocken)**, green for medium-dry **(halbtrocken)** and red for sweet **(lieblich)**.

Kabinett: light, dry wine

Spätlese: riper, more full-bodied, often sweeter

Auslese: slightly dry wine, richer than Spätlese

Beerenauslese: slightly sweet wine, honeyed and rich

Trockenbeerenauslese: sweet, dessert wine, comparable to the best Sauternes

Eiswein: intensely sweet, fairly scarce and expensive

Tafelwein: table wine; lowest quality

Qualitätswein bestimmter Anbaugebiete: medium-quality wine

Qualitätswein mit Prädikat: highest quality wine

ORDERING DRINKS ➤ 40

Wine regions   Weinregionen

Ahr (region south of Bonn)
The region's pale red wines are the best in Germany; produced around the towns of Ahrweiler, Neuenahr and Walporzheim.

Rheingau (area producing the most highly reputed wines)

Rheinhessen (region on the left bank of the Rhine, south of Mainz)

Niersteiner, Domtal, Oppenheimer
Wine of lesser quality is sold under the name of Liebfraumilch. Towns producing wines of exceptional quality include Alsheim, Bingen, Bodenheim, Dienheim, Guntersblum, Ingelheim, Nackenheim, Nierstein, Oppenheim and Worms.

Rheinpfalz (further south of Rheinhessen; mainly produces white wines)
Dürkheimer, Deidesheimer, Forster, Ruppertsberger, Wachenheimer.

Mittelrhein (wine-growing area between Rüdesheim and Koblenz)
Vineyards in Bingen, Bacharach, Boppard and Oberwesel.

Mosel (Moselle Valley; green bottles, instead of the brown glass of the Rhine wines)
The best quality Moselle wines are produced in the vineyards of Bernkastel, Brauneberger, Graach, Piesport, Wehlen, Zeltingen. Names to look out for: Bernkasteler, Graacher, Piesporter, Zeltinger.

Baden (mostly whites, a few light reds; south-west Germany)
Markgräfler, Mauerwein, Seewein, Rulander, Gutedel, Kaiserstuhl, Sauser (sweet).

Württemberg (good wine-growing region of red wines)
Look for Trollinger (red), Schillerwein (rosé) and Stettener Brotwasser.
The best wine of the region is produced at Cannstatt, Feuerbach and Untertürckheim.

Franken (Franconia: region around Würzburg producing dry, strong, white wines)
Wine-growing areas: Iphofen, Eschendorf, Andersacker, Rödelsee, Würzburg. Names to look out for: Bocksbeutel, Steinwein.

Nahe (full-bodied white wines)
Look for Schloss Böckelheim or areas such as Bad Kreuznach, Bretzenheim, Münster, Niederhausen, Nordheim, Roxheim and Winzerheim for some excellent wines.

Austria (some good white wines, unremarkable reds)
Look out for: Gumpoldskirchner (south of Vienna); Dürnsteiner, Loibner, Kremser (Wachau area); table wines such as Nussberger, Grinzinger, Badener (Vienna region).

Switzerland (red and white table wines)
German-speaking cantons produce mainly light red wines: Hallauer, Maienfelder, Stammheimer.

Other drinks Andere Getränke

You'll recognize **Cognac, Rum, Wodka, Whisky.** Other drinks you may want to order in German-speaking countries include **Apfelwein** (fermented cider), **Bowle** (punch), **Glühwein** (mulled wine), **Portwein** (port), **Weinbrand** (brandy). More common are the many liqueurs and brandies, typical of Germany, Austria and Switzerland. Try some of the following:

Schnaps *shnaps*

the generic term for spirits or brandies, often distilled from fruit. Varieties include **Apfelschnaps** (apple); **Birnenschnaps** (pear); **Bommerlunder** (caraway-flavored brandy); **(Doppel)korn** (aqua vitae); **Dornkaat/Steinhäger** (similar to gin); **Heidelbeergeist** (blueberry brandy); **Kirschwasser** (cherry brandy); **Obstler** (fruit brandy); **Pflümli(wasser)/Zwetschgenwasser** (plum brandy); **Träsch** (pear and apple brandy); **Weizenkorn** (aqua vitae).

Likör *likur*

liqueur; look out for varieties such as **Aprikosenlikör** (apricot), **Eierlikör** (eggnog), **Himbeerlikör** (raspberry), **Kirschlikör** (cherry), **Kümmel** (caraway-flavored).

You'll have no trouble finding your favorite soft drinks or sodas such as *Coca-Cola®, Fanta®, Pepsi®*. Also popular is **Kaffee und Kuchen** (coffee and cakes) in the afternoon, and in Austria there are many varieties of coffee to choose from.

I'd like …	**Ich hätte gern …** *ikh hetter gehrn*
(hot) chocolate	**eine (heiße) Schokolade** *iener (hiesser) shokkolaader*
(glass of) milk	**(ein Glas) Milch** *(ien glas) milkh*
mineral water	**Mineralwasser** *minneraalvasser*
carbonated	**mit Kohlensäure** *mit koalenzoyrer*
non-carbonated	**ohne Kohlensäure** *oaner koalenzoyrer*
fruit juice	**Fruchtsaft** *frukhtzaft*
coffee	**Kaffee** *kafay*
tea	**Tee** *tay*

Menu Reader

A

Aal eel
Aalsuppe eel soup
Abendbrot supper
Abendessen dinner
alkoholfrei non-alcoholic
alkoholfreies Bier low alcohol beer
alkoholfreies Getränk non-alcoholic drinks
alle Preise inklusive Bedienung und Mehrwertsteuer (MwSt.) service charge and VAT (sales tax) included
Allgäuer Käsesuppe cheese soup from the Allgäu
Alsterwasser beer w/lemonade
Altbier similar to British ale
Ananas pineapple
Anis aniseed
Aperitif aperitif
Apfel apple
Apfelcreme apple cream dessert
Apfelkuchen apple tart
Apfelküchlein apple fritters
Apfelsaft apple juice
Apfelschnaps apple brandy
Apfelsine orange
Apfelsinensaft orange juice
Apfelstrudel apple strudel
Apfelwein cider
Appetithäppchen canapés
Aprikosen apricots
Aprikosenlikör apricot liqueur
... Art ...-style
Auberginen eggplant
-auflauf soufflé
Aufschnitt(platte) cold cuts ➤43
auf Vorbestellung advance orders only
Auslese wine classification ➤49
Austern oysters

B

Bachsaibling brook trout
Back- baked
Backerbsensuppe type of pea soup ➤44
Backpflaumen prunes
Baguette French bread
Banane banana
Barsch freshwater perch
Basilikum basil
Basler Mehlsuppe flour soup with grated cheese (Swiss)
Bauernomelette diced bacon and onion omelet
Bauernschmaus sauerkraut with meats, dumplings and potatoes ➤46
Bauernsuppe cabbage and frankfurter soup
(deutsches) Beefsteak hamburger
Beerenauslese wine classification ➤49
Beilagen accompaniments
belegtes Brot open-face sandwich
Berliner jelly doughnut

Berliner Weiße pale beer ➤49
Berner Platte sauerkraut or green beans with meats ➤46
Bete beet
Bethmännchen marzipan balls
Beuschel veal with lemon sauce
Bienenstich honey-almond cake
Bier beer ➤49
Bierwurst smoked pork and beef sausage
Birne pear
Birnen, Bohnen & Speck pears, green beans and bacon
Birnenschnaps pear brandy
Bismarckhering pickled herring with onions
blau boiled in bouillon
Blaubeer-Kaltschale chilled blueberry soup
Blaubeeren blueberries
Blaukraut red cabbage
Blindhuhn Westphalian vegetable stew
Blumenkohl cauliflower
blutig rare/underdone
Blutwurst blood sausage
Bockbier strong beer ➤49
Bockwurst large frankfurter
Bohnen beans
Bohnensuppe bean soup with bacon
Bommerlunder caraway-flavored brandy
Borretsch borage
Bouillon clear soup
Bowle punch

Brachse/Brasse bream
Brat- roast
-braten joint, roast
Bratkartoffeln fried potatoes
Bratwurst fried pork sausage
Brechbohnen string beans
Brokkoli broccoli
Brombeeren blackberries
Brot bread
Brötchen rolls
-brust breast
Bückling kipper
Buletten meat patties
Bündnerfleisch cured beef ➤43
Butterkuchen butter crumble cake
Butterreis buttered rice

C **Cayenne-Pfeffer** cayenne pepper
Champignons white mushrooms
Champignonsuppe mushroom soup
Chicorée chicory
Christstollen Christmas fruitcake
Cornichons small pickles
-creme pudding
Cremeschnitte napoleon/millefeuille
Curryreis curried rice

D **Dampfnudeln** sweet dumplings

53

dasselbe mit ... the same served with ...

Datteln dates

Dill dill

Doornkaat German gin, juniperberry brandy

Doppelbock strong beer ➤49

(Doppel)Korn grain-distilled liquor, similar to whisky

Doppelrahm-Frischkäse cream cheese

Dorsch cod

dunkles Bier dark beer

(gut) durchgebraten well-done

E **Edelpilz** blue cheese, similar to Stilton

Egli perch

Eier eggs

Eierlikör eggnog

Eierspeisen egg dishes

Eintopfgerichte stews

Eis/-eis ice cream

Eisbein pickled pig's knuckle

Eistee iced tea

Eiswein wine classification ➤49

Endivien curly endive

Endiviensalat curly endive salad

Endpreise einschließlich Service und Mehrwertsteuer service and VAT included

Ente duck

Erbsen peas

Erbsensuppe pea soup

Erdbeeren strawberries

Erdnüsse peanuts

Essig vinegar

Essiggurken pickles/gherkins

Estragon tarragon

Export strong, pale beer ➤49

Expresso espresso coffee

F **falscher Hase** meat loaf

Fasan pheasant

Faschiertes minced meat

Feigen figs

Felchen kind of trout

Fenchel fennel

Filetsteak beef steak

Fisch fish ➤44

Fischbeuschelsuppe fish roe and vegetable soup

Fischfrikadellen fish croquettes

Fischgerichte fish dishes

Fischsuppe fish soup

Fisolen French (green) beans

Flädlesuppe broth with pancake strips

Fleisch (gerichte) meat (dishes) ➤45–46

Fleischkäse type of meat loaf

Fleischklößchen meatballs

Fleischpastete type of meat loaf

Fleischsalat diced meat salad with mayonnaise

Fleischwurst mildly seasoned sausage ➤46

Fondue bread dipped into melted cheese

Forelle trout

Frankfurterwürstchen frankfurter

französisches Weißbrot
French baguette

Fridattensuppe broth with
pancake strips

Frikadellen meat patties

**Frisch geräucherte Gänsebrust
auf Toast** freshly smoked breast
of goose on toast

Frischkäse cream cheese

frittiert deep-fried

Früchtetee fruit tea

Fruchtjogurt fruit yogurt

Fruchtsaft fruit juice

Frühstück breakfast ➤43

für unsere kleinen Gäste
children's meals

für zwei Personen for two

G **Gans** goose

Gänseleberpastete goose
liver pâté

Garnelen prawns/shrimps

Gebäck pastries

gebacken baked
**(im schwimmenden Fett)
gebacken** deep-fried
(in der Pfanne) gebraten fried
(im Ofen) gebraten roasted

gebrühter Weißkrautsalat
parboiled white cabbage
coleslaw

gedämpft steamed

Geflügel poultry

gefüllt stuffed

gegrillt grilled/broiled

gehackt
diced

Gehacktes minced
meat

gekocht boiled

gekochtes Ei boiled egg

Gelbwurst mildly seasoned
sausage, popular with
children

Gelee jelly/jam

gemischter Salat mixed salad

gemischtes Gemüse mixed vegetables

Gemüse vegetables ➤47

Gemüse nach Wahl choice of
vegetables

geräuchert smoked

Germknödel sweet dumpling

Geröstete hashed-brown
potatoes

geschmort braised

Geschnetzeltes chopped veal in
wine sauce

(in Butter) geschwenkt sautéed
(in butter)

Geselchtes salted and smoked
meat, usually pork

gespickter Hirsch larded
venison

Getränke drinks ➤49–51

Gewürz spice

Glace/-glace ice cream

Glühwein mulled wine

Glutenfreies Brot gluten-free
bread

Götterspeise fruit jelly (Jell-O)

Grießbrei cream of
wheat

Grießklöße semolina dumplings

Grießnockerlsuppe semolina-dumpling soup

grüne Bohnen French (green) beans

grüner Salat green salad

Grünkohl kale

Gugelhupf pound cake

Gulasch gulash; chunks of beef stewed in a rich paprika gravy

Gulaschsuppe spiced soup of stewed beef

Gurken cucumber

H **-hachse** shank

Hackbraten meat loaf

Hackepeter spiced pork tartare

Haferbrei oatmeal

Hähnchen chicken

halbfester Käse medium-hard cheese

halbtrocken medium-dry

Hammelfleisch mutton

hart hard

Hase hare

Haselnüsse hazelnuts

Hauptgerichte main courses

Häuptlsalat lettuce salad

hausgemacht homemade

-haxe shank

Hecht pike

Hefeklöße yeast dumplings

Hefekranz ring-shaped cake of yeast dough, with almonds and sometimes candied fruit

Hefeweizen pale beer ➤49

Heidelbeeren blueberries

Heidelbeergeist blueberry brandy

Heidschnucken mutton from the Lüneberg Heath

Heilbutt halibut

heiß hot

heißer Apfelwein hot apple cider

helles Bier light beer

-hendl chicken

Hering(salat) herring (salad)

-herz heart

Himbeeren raspberries

Himbeerlikör raspberry brandy

hohe Rippe roast ribs of beef

Holsteiner Schnitzel breaded veal cutlet topped with fried egg ➤46

Honig honey

Honigkuchen honey biscuits

Hoppel-Poppel scrambled eggs with diced sausages or bacon

Huhn chicken

Hühnerbrühe chicken broth

Hummer lobster

Hummerkrabben large prawns

Hüttenkäse cottage cheese

I **Imbiss** snacks

... im Preis inbegriffen ... included in the price

Ingwer ginger

J **Jagdwurst** smoked pork sausage, similar to salami

Jakobsmuscheln scallops

Jogurt yogurt

Johannisbeersaft currant juice

K **Kabeljau** cod

Kabinett wine classification ►49

Kaffee coffee ►51

Kaffeesahne creamer

Kaisergranate kind of shrimp

Kaiserschmarren shredded pancake with raisins served with syrup

Kakao hot chocolate

Kalbfleisch veal

Kalbshaxen roast shank of veal

Kalbsleber veal liver

kalt cold

Kaltschale chilled fruit soup

Kaninchen rabbit

Kapaun capon

Kapern capers

Karamel caramel

Kardamon cardamon

Karfiol cauliflower

Karotten carrots

Karpfen carp

Kartoffelauflauf potato casserole

Kartoffelbälle potato balls

Kartoffelbrei mashed potatoes

Kartoffelchips chips

Kartoffelklöße potato dumplings

Kartoffelkroketten potato croquettes

Kartoffelmus mashed potatoes

Kartoffeln potatoes

Kartoffelpuffer potato fritters

Kartoffelsalat (mit Speck) potato salad (with bacon)

Kartoffelstock mashed potatoes

Kartoffelsuppe potato soup

Käse cheese ►48

Käsebrett/Käse nach Ihrer Wahl cheese selection

Käseschnitte open, melted cheese sandwich

Käsestangen cheese sticks

Käsewähe hot cheese tart

Kasseler Rippenspeer smoked pork chops

Katenrauchwurst country-style, smoked sausage

Kekse cookies

Kerbel chervil

-keule haunch

Kirschcreme cherry cream dessert

Kirschen cherries

Kirschlikör cherry liqueur

Kirschwasser cherry brandy

kleine Mahlzeiten light meals/snacks

Klöße dumplings

Knoblauch garlic

Knödel dumplings

Knödelsuppe dumpling soup

Knöpfli kind of gnocchi

koffeinfreier Kaffee decaffeinated coffee

Kognak brandy

Kohl cabbage ►47

Kohlrabi kohlrabi

Kohlroulade cabbage leaves stuffed with minced meat

Kokosnuss coconut

Kompott/-kompott stewed fruit, commpote

Königinpastete diced meat and mushrooms in puff-pastry

Königinsuppe soup with beef, sour cream and almonds

Königsberger Klopse meatballs in white caper sauce

Kopfsalat lettuce

-kotelett chop

Krabben shrimps

Kraftbrühe beef consommé

Kräuter herbs

Kräutersalz herb-flavored salt

Kräutertee herb tea

(roher) Krautsalat coleslaw

Krautstiel white beet

Krautwickel braised cabbage rolls

Krebs river crayfish

Kren horseradish

Krenfleisch pork served with shredded vegetables and horseradish

Kresse cress

Kuchen/-kuchen cake

Kulmbacher Eisbock very strong beer ➤49

Kümmel caraway; caraway-flavored liquor

Kürbis pumpkin

Kuteln tripe

L **Labskaus** thick stew of minced and marinated

meat with mashed potatoes

Lachs salmon

Lammfleisch lamb

Languste spiny lobster

Lauch leeks

Laugenbrötchen pretzel rolls

Leber liver

Leberkäse type of meat loaf

Leberknödel liver dumplings

Leberknödelsuppe liver-dumpling soup

Leberwurst liver sausage

Lebkuchen gingerbread

Leckerli ginger biscuits

leicht light

Leipziger Allerlei peas, carrots and asparagus

Lenden- fillet of beef (tenderloin)

Lendenstück loin

lieblich sweet

Likör liqueur ➤51

Limette lime

Limonade lemonade

Limone lemon

Linsen lentils

Linsensuppe lentil soup

Lorbeer bay leaf

M **Maibowle** white wine punch, flavored with sweet woodruff

Mais sweet corn

Maispoularde corn-fed chicken

Majoran marjoram

Makrele mackerel

Makronen macaroons

Malzbier low-alcohol beer ➤49
Mandarine tangerine
Mandeln almonds
Marillen apricots
mariniert marinated
Marmelade jam
Märzen strong beer ➤49
Masthühnchen chicken
Matjesfilet nach Hausfrauenart herring fillets ➤43
Matjeshering salted young herring
Maultaschen type of ravioli
Meeresfrüchte seafood
Meerrettich horseradish
Mehlklöße flour dumplings
Mehlnockerln small dumplings
Melone melon
Mettwurst spicy smoked pork sausage
Milch milk
Milchkaffee coffee with milk
Milchmixgetränk milk shake
Mineralwasser mineral water
mit Ei with egg
mit Eis on the rocks/with ice
mit Kohlensäure carbonated
mit Milch with milk
mit Sahne with cream
mit Zitrone with lemon
mit Zucker with sugar
Mittagessen lunch
mittel medium
Mohnbrötchen poppy seed rolls
Mohrrüben carrots

Mokka mocha; coffee-flavored
Muscheln clams/mussels
Muskatblüte mace
Muskatnuss nutmeg

N **nach ... Art** ... style
nach Wahl with choice of
Nachspeisen/Nachtisch desserts ➤48
Nelke clove
Nieren kidneys
Nockerl small dumpling
Nudeln noodles ➤47
Nudelsuppe noodle soup
nur auf Bestellung made to order
Nürnberger Bratwurst fried, veal and pork
Nürnberger Rostbratwurst Nuremberg-style pork sausage
Nuss- nut-flavored
Nüsse nuts

O **Obst** fruit ➤48
Obstler fruit brandy
Obstsalat fruit salad
Ochsenschwanzsuppe oxtail soup
ohne Kohlensäure non-carbonated
Öl oil
Omelett(e) omelet
Orangeade orangeade
Orangen oranges
Orangenmarmelade orange marmelade

Orangensaft orange juice

P Palatschinken
when listed under desserts, pancakes with a jam or cream cheese filling, otherwise they are a savory dish

Pampelmuse grapefruit

paniert breaded

Paradeiser tomatoes

Pellkartoffeln potatoes boiled in their jackets

Petersilie parsley

Petersilienkartoffeln parsley potatoes

Pfeffer pepper

Pfefferkörner pepper corns

Pfefferminze peppermint

Pfefferpotthast spicy meat and onion casserole

Pfifferlinge chanterelle mushrooms

Pfirsich peach

Pflaumen plums

Pflümli(wasser) plum brandy

Pharisäer coffee with rum and whipped cream

Pichelsteiner Eintopf meat and vegetable stew

pikant pungent/biting

Pickelsteiner Franconia casserole with horseradish, garlic, salsify

Pilsener pils ➤49

Pilze mushrooms ➤47

Piment all-spice

-plätzli cutlet

Pökelfleisch salted meat

Pommes frites French fries

Porree leek

Portwein port

Poulet chicken

Preiselbeeren cranberries

Presskopf pork headcheese

Printen honey biscuits

Prinzessbohnen thick string beans

pur straight (neat)

-püree creamed

Q Quark dairy product
similar to plain yogurt

Quitte quince

R Raclette melted cheese
with potatoes and pickles

Radieschen radishes

Radlermaß beer w/ lemonade

Räucheraal smoked eel

Räucherhering smoked herring

Rebhuhn partridge

Regensburger highly spiced, smoked sausage

Reh(pastete) venison paté

Reibekuchen fried potato pancake

reif ripe

Reis rice

Reisgerichte rice dishes

Rettichsalat white radish salad

Rhabarber rhubarb
Ribisel currants
Rindfleisch beef
Rindswurst grilled beef sausage
Rippensteak rib steak
Rochen ray
Roggenbrot rye bread
Rohschinken cured ham
Rollmops pickled herring
Rosenkohl brussels sprouts
Rosinen raisins
Rosinenbrot raisin bread
Rosmarin rosemary
Rösti hashed-brown potatoes
Röstkartoffeln fried potatoes
rot red
Rotbarsch red sea-bass
Rote Grütze red berry compote
rote Beete beet
rote Johannisbeeren red currants
Rotkohl red cabbage
Rotkrautsalat red cabbage salad
Rotwurst blood sausage
Rouladen slices of rolled and braised beef or veal
Rüben beet
-rücken back
Rüdesheimer Kaffee coffee with brandy and whipped cream
Rüebli carrots
Rühreier scrambled eggs
Rum rum
Russische Eier hard-boiled eggs with mayonnaise

S Safran saffron
saisonbedingt seasonal
Salate salads ➤47
Salbei sage
Salm salmon
Salz salt
Salzgurke pickled cucumber
Salzkartoffeln boiled potatoes
Sardinen sardines
Sauerbraten marinated, braised beef ➤46
Sauerkirsch-Kaltschale chilled sour cherry soup
Sauerkraut sauerkraut
Sauerkraut und Rippchen sauerkraut and ribs
Schalotten shallots
scharf piquant/hot/sharp
Schellfisch haddock
Schillerlocke pastry cornet with vanilla cream filling
Schillerwein type of rosé
Schinken ham
Schinkenröllchen mit Spargel rolled ham with asparagus filling
Schlachtplatte platter of various sausages and cold meats
Schlesisches Himmelreich smoked pork loin cooked with mixed dried fruits
Schmelzkäse spreadable cheese
Schnaps strong spirit or brandy ➤51
Schnecken snails

Schnepfe wood cock

Schnittlauch chives

Schnitzel cutlet

(heiße) Schokolade hot chocolate

Schokoladen- chocolate ...

Scholle plaice

Schupfnudeln rolled potato noodles

schwarze Johannisbeeren black currants

schwarzer Kaffee black coffee

Schwarzwälder Kirschtorte Black Forest cake

Schwarzwurzeln salsify

Schweinefleisch pork

Schweinekamm pork shoulder

Schweinekotelett pork chop

Schweinshaxe knuckle of pork

Seebarsch sea bass

Seebutt brill

Seehecht hake

Seezunge sole

sehr trocken extra dry

Sekt sparkling wine

selbstgemacht homemade

Sellerie celery

Selleriesalat celeriac root salad

Semmelknödel Bavarian bread dumplings

Semmelsuppe dumpling soup

Senf mustard

Seniorenmenü senior citizens' meals

Serbische Bohnensuppe spiced

bean soup ➤44

Sesambrötchen sesame seed rolls

Soleier eggs pickled in brine

Spanferkel suckling pig

Spargel(spitzen) asparagus (tips)

Spätlese wine classification ➤49

Spätzle kind of noodle

Speck bacon

Speckknödel bread dumplings with bacon

Spekulatius almond cookies

Spezialität des Hauses specialty of the house

Spezialitäten der Region local specialties

Spiegeleier fried eggs

Spiegeleier mit Schinken/Speck ham/bacon and eggs

-spießchen skewered ...

Spinat spinach

Sprotten sprats

Stachelbeeren gooseberries

Starkbier strong beer ➤49

Steckrüben turnips

Steinbutt turbot

Steinhäger juniperberry brandy, similar to gin

Steinpilze wild yellow mushrooms

Steinpilze Försterinnenart mushrooms forestiere

Stolzer Heinrich sausage in beer ➤43

Stör sturgeon

Strammer Max bread with ham, fried eggs and maybe onions

Streichkäse spreadable cheese

Streuselkuchen coffee cake with crumble topping

Stückchen pastries

Sülze headcheese

Sülzkotelett pork chops in aspic

Suppen soups

süß sweet

Süßspeisen desserts

Süßstoff artificial sweetener

T **Tafelspitz mit Meerrettich** boiled beef with horseradish cream sauce

Tagesgedeck set menu of the day

Tagesgericht dish of the day

Taube pigeon, squab

Tee tea

Teewurst soft, spreadable sausage

Teigwaren pasta ➤47

Teilchen pastries

Teltower Rübchen baby turnips

Thymian thyme

Tintenfisch squid/octopus

Toast toast

Tomaten tomatoes

Tomatenketchup ketchup

Tomatensaft tomato juice

Tomatensalat tomato salad

Tomatensuppe tomato soup

Topfbraten pot roast

Topfenstrudel flaky pastry filled with vanilla-flavored cream cheese, rolled and baked

Torte/-torte layer cake

Töttchen Westphalian sweet and sour veal stew

Träsch pear and apple brandy

Trauben grapes

Traubensaft grape juice

trocken dry

Trockenbeerenauslese wine classification ➤49

Truthahn turkey

U **überbacken** oven-browned

unser Küchenchef empfiehlt
… the chef recommends …

V **Vanille** vanilla

VDP (Verband Deutscher Prädikats- & Qualitäts Weingüter) officially recognized wine ➤49

Vollkornbrot whole grain bread

vollmundig full-bodied

vom Rost grilled/broiled

Vorspeisen appetizers/starters ➤43

W **Wacholder** juniper

Wachsbohnen yellow wax beans

Wachtel quail

Waldmeister sweet woodruff

Walnüsse walnuts

wärme Getränke hot beverages
Wasser water
Wassermelone watermelon
weich soft
Wein wine ➤49
Weinbrand brandy
Weincreme wine cream dessert
Weintrauben grapes
weiß white
Weißbier pale, light beer ➤49
Weißbrot white bread
weiße Bohnen white beans
Weißherbst type of rosé
Weißkohl/-kraut white cabbage
Weißwurst veal and bacon sausage with parsley and onion
Weizenkorn wheat-distilled liquor, similar to whisky
Wermut vermouth
Whisky whisky
Wiener Schnitzel breaded veal cutlet
Wienerli Vienna-style frankfurter
Wild game
Wildschwein wild boar
Windbeutel cream puff
Wirsing savoy cabbage
Wodka vodka
Würste sausages ➤46
Wurstplatte assorted cold cuts
Würze seasoning
würzig aromatic

Z **Zander** (giant) pike-perch
Zervelat(wurst) pork, beef and bacon sausage ➤46
Zimt cinnamon
Zitrone lemon
zu allen Gerichten servieren wir ... all meals are served with...
Zucchetti zucchini
Zucker sugar
Zuckererbsen young green peas
Zunge/-zunge tongue
Zungenwurst blood sausage with pieces of tongue and diced fat
Zuschlag extra charge/ supplement
Zwetschgen plums
Zwetschgenkuchen plum tart
Zwetschgenwasser plum brandy
Zwiebelbrot onion bread
Zwiebeln onions
Zwiebelsuppe onion soup
Zwiebelwurst liver and onion sausage
Zwischengerichte for the small appetite

Travel

ESSENTIAL

A ticket to …	**Eine Fahrkarte nach …** *iener faarkarter naakh*
How much is …?	**Wie viel kostet …?** *Vee feel kostet*
When?	**Wann?** *van*
When will … arrive?	**Wann kommt … an?** *van komt … an*
When will … leave?	**Wann fährt … ab?** *van fairt … ap*

Germany, Austria and Switzerland all have well-developed public transport systems, so you should be able to enjoy trouble-free traveling.

Safety Sicherheit

Would you accompany me to the bus stop?	**Würden Sie mich zur Bushaltestelle begleiten?** *vewrden zee mikh tsoor busshalteshteler beglieten*
I don't want to … on my own.	**Ich möchte nicht allein …** *ikh murkhter nikht allien*
stay here	**hier bleiben** *heer blieben*
walk home	**zu Fuß nach Hause gehen** *tsoo fooss naakh howzer gayen*
I don't feel safe here.	**Ich fühle mich hier nicht sicher.** *ikh fewler mikh heer nikht zikher*

Arrival Ankunft

Document Requirements

UK   valid passport; visitors passport; or British Excursion document (valid 60 hours)

U.S./Can   valid passport

Duty Free Into:	Cigarettes	Cigars	Tobacco	Spirits	Wine
Germany	200	50	250g	1*l* or	2*l*
Switz./Austria 1)	200 or	50 or	250g	1*l* and	2*l*
2)	400 or	100 or	500g	1*l* and	2*l*
Canada	200 and	50 and	400g	1*l* or	1*l*
UK	200 or	50 or	250g	1*l* and	2*l*
U.S.	200 and	100 and	discretionary	1*l* or	1*l*

1) EU residents; 2) non-EU residents

Import restrictions between EU countries have been relaxed on items for personal use or consumption that are bought duty-paid within the EU.

Suggested maximum: 90*l* wine or 60*l* sparkling wine, 20*l* fortified wine, 10*l* spirits and 110*l* beer.

Passport control Passkontrolle

We have a joint passport.	**Wir haben einen gemeinsamen Pass.** *veer haaben ienen gemiensaamen pass*
The children are on this passport.	**Die Kinder sind auf diesem Pass eingetragen.** *dee kinder zint owf deezem pass iengertraagen*
What's the purpose of your visit?	**Was ist der Zweck Ihres Aufenthalts?** *vass ist dehr zvayk eeress owfenthalts*
I'm here on vacation.	**Ich bin im Urlaub hier.** *ikh bin im oorlowp heer*
I'm here on business.	**Ich bin geschäftlich hier.** *ikh bin geshehftlikh heer*
I'm just passing through.	**Ich bin nur auf der Durchreise.** *ikh bin nur owf dehr durkhriezer*
I'm going to …	**Ich reise nach …** *ikh riezer nakh*
I'm …	**Ich reise …** *ikh riezer*
on my own	**allein** *allien*
with my family	**mit meiner Familie** *mit miener fameelier*
with a group	**mit einer Gruppe** *mit iener grupper*

Customs Zoll

I have only the normal allowances.

Ich habe nur die normalen erlaubten Mengen.
ikh haaber nur dee normaalen ehrlowbten mengen

It's a gift.

Es ist ein Geschenk.
ess ist ien geshenk

It's for my personal use.

Es ist für meinen persönlichen Gebrauch.
ess ist fewr mienen payrzurnlikhen gebrowkh

Haben Sie etwas zu verzollen?	Do you have anything to declare?
Das müssen Sie verzollen.	You must pay duty on this.
Wo haben Sie das gekauft?	Where did you buy this?
Bitte öffnen Sie diese Tasche.	Please open this bag.
Haben Sie noch mehr Gepäck?	Do you have any more luggage?

PASSKONTROLLE	passport control
GRENZÜBERGANG	border crossing
POLIZEI	police
ZOLL	customs
ANMELDEFREIE WAREN	nothing to declare
ANMELDEPFLICHTIGE WAREN	goods to declare
ZOLLFREIE WAREN	duty-free goods

Duty-free shopping Zollfreier Einkauf

What currency is this in?

In welcher Währung ist das?
in velkher vairung ist dass

Can I pay in …

Kann ich mit … bezahlen?
kan ikh mit … betsaalen

dollars

Dollars *dollarz*

marks

D-Mark *day-mark*

pounds

Pfund *pfunt*

Plane Flugzeug

The National airlines, Lufthansa, Austrian Airlines and Swissair all run frequent internal services, and there are generally good connections between the airport and downtown.

Tickets and reservations Flugtickets und Reservierungen

When is the … flight to Berlin?	**Wann geht der … Flug nach Berlin?** *van gayt dehr … floog naakh behrleen*
first/next/last	**erste/nächste/letzte** *ehrster/naikhster/letster*
I'd like 2 … tickets to …	**Ich hätte gern zwei … nach …** *ikh hetter gehrn tsvie … naakh*
one-way	**einfache Flugtickets** *ienfakher floogtikets*
round-trip	**Rückflugtickets** *rewkfloogtikets*
first class	**erste Klasse** *ehrster klasser*
business class	**Businessklasse** *biznessklasser*
economy class	**Touristenklasse** *tooristenklasser*
How much is a flight to …?	**Wie viel kostet ein Flug nach …?** *Vee feel kostet ien floog naakh*
Are there any supplements?	**Kommen da noch Zuschläge hinzu?** *kommen daa nokh tsooshlaiger hinntsoo*
I'd like to … my reservation for flight number LH123.	**Ich möchte meine Reservierung für Flugnummer LH123 …** *ikh murkhter miene rezehrveerung fewr floognummer el haa ien tsvie drie …*
cancel	**stornieren** *shtorneeren*
change	**ändern** *ehndern*
confirm	**bestätigen** *beshtaitigen*

Inquiries about the flight Fragen zum Flug

How long is the flight?	**Wie lange dauert der Flug?** *vee langer dowert dehr floog*
What time does the plane leave?	**Wann fliegt die Maschine ab?** *van fleegt dee masheener ap*
What time will we arrive?	**Wann kommen wir an?** *van kommen veer an*
What time do I have to check in?	**Wann muss ich einchecken?** *van muss ikh ientsheken*

NUMBERS ➤ 216; TIME ➤ 220

Checking in Einchecken

Where is the check-in desk for flight …?
Wo ist der Abfertigungs schalter für den Flug …?
voa ist dehr apfehrti- gungzshalter fewr dayn floog …

I have …
Ich habe … *ikh haaber*

3 cases to check in
drei Koffer für die Abfertigung
drie koffer fewr dee apfehrtigung

2 pieces of hand luggage
zwei Stück Handgepäck
tsvie shtewk hantgepehk

Ihr Flugticket/Ihren Pass, bitte.	Your ticket/passport please.
Möchten Sie am Fenster oder am Gang sitzen?	Would you like a window or an aisle seat?
Raucher oder Nichtraucher?	Smoking or non-smoking?
Bitte gehen Sie zur Abflughalle.	Please go through to the departure lounge.
Wie viele Gepäckstücke haben Sie?	How many pieces of baggage do you have?
Sie haben Übergepäck.	You have excess baggage.
Sie müssen pro Kilo Übergepäck einen Zuschlag von … Mark zahlen.	You'll have to pay a supplement of … Marks per kilo of excess baggage.
Das ist als Handgepäck zu schwer/groß.	That's too heavy/large for hand baggage.
Haben Sie diese Taschen selbst gepackt?	Did you pack these bags yourself?
Enthalten sie spitze Gegenstände oder Elektrogeräte?	Do they contain any sharp or electrical items?

ANKUNFT	arrivals
ABFLUG	departures
SICHERHEITSKONTROLLE	security check
LASSEN SIE IHR GEPÄCK	do not leave bags
NICHT UNBEWACHT	unattended

LUGGAGE/BAGGAGE ➤ 71

Information Auskunft

Is there any delay on the flight from ...? **Hat der Flug aus ... Verspätung?**
hat dehr floog owss ... fehrshpaitung

How late will it be? **Wie viel Verspätung hat er?**
Vee feel fehrshpaitung hat ehr

Has the flight from ... landed? **Ist der Flug aus ... gelandet?**
ist dehr floog owss ... gelandet

Which gate does the flight to ... leave from? **An welchem Flugsteig geht der Flug nach ...?**
an velkhem floogshtieg gayrt dehr floog naakh

Boarding/In-flight Einsteigen/Während des Fluges

Your boarding card, please. **Ihre Bordkarte, bitte.**
eerer bortkarter bitter

Could I have something to drink/eat, please? **Kann ich bitte etwas zu trinken/essen haben?**
kan ikh bitter etvass tsoo trinken/essen haaben

Please wake me for the meal. **Bitte wecken Sie mich zum Essen.**
bitter veken zee mikh tsum essen

What time will we arrive? **Wann kommen wir an?**
van kommen veer an

I feel airsick. **Ich bin luftkrank.** *ikh bin luftkrank*

A sick bag, please. **Eine Spucktüte, bitte.**
iener shpuktewter bitter

Arrival Ankunft

Where is/are ...? **Wo ist/sind ...?** *voa ist/zint*

bureau de change **die Wechselstube** *dee vekselshtoober*

buses **die Busse** *dee busser*

rental car **die Autovermietung** *dee owtofehrmeetung*

exit **der Ausgang** *dehr owsgang*

taxis **die Taxis** *dee taksiss*

telephone **das Telefon** *dass taylayfoan*

Is there a bus into town? **Gibt es einen Bus in die Stadt?**
gipt ess ienen buss in dee shtat

How do I get to the ... Hotel? **Wie komme ich zum ... Hotel?**
vee kommer ikh tsum ... hottel

Luggage/Baggage Gepäck

Where no porters are available, you should be able to find luggage carts (Kofferkulis) for passengers' use. In Germany they tend to be coin-operated (1–2 DM, returnable after use).

Porter! Excuse me!	**Gepäckträger! Entschuldigen Sie!** *gepehktraiger entshuldiggen zee*
Could you take my luggage …? *kurnen zee mien gepehk … traagen*	**Können Sie mein Gepäck … tragen?**
to a taxi/bus	**zu einem Taxi/Bus** *tsoo ienem taksi/buss*
Where is/are …?	**Wo ist/sind …?** *voa ist/zint*
luggage carts	**die Kofferkulis** *dee kofferkooliss*
luggage lockers	**die Schließfächer** *dee shleesfehkher*
baggage check	**die Gepäckaufbewahrung** *dee gepehkowfbevaarung*
baggage claim	**die Gepäckausgabe** *dee gepehkowsgaaber*
Where is the luggage from flight …?	**Wo ist das Gepäck vom Flug …?** *voa ist dass gepehk fom floog*

Loss and theft Verlust und Diebstahl

My luggage has been lost/stolen.	**Mein Gepäck ist verloren gegangen/ gestohlen worden.** *mien gepehk ist fehrloaren gegangen/geshtoalen vorden*
My suitcase was damaged in transit.	**Mein Koffer ist beim Transport beschädigt worden.** *mien koffer ist biem transpoart beshaidigt vorden*
Our luggage has not arrived.	**Unser Gepäck ist nicht angekommen.** *unzer gepehk ist nikht angekommen*

Wie sieht Ihr Gepäck aus?	What does your luggage look like?
Haben Sie den Gepäckschein?	Do you have the claim check?
Ihr Gepäck …	Your luggage …
könnte nach Frankfurt geschickt worden sein.	may have been sent to Frankfurt.
könnte heute noch ankommen.	may arrive later today.
Bitte kommen Sie morgen wieder.	Please come back tomorrow.
Rufen Sie diese Nummer an, um nachzufragen, ob Ihr Gepäck angekommen ist.	Call this number to check if your luggage has arrived.

POLICE ➤ 152; COLORS ➤ 143

Train Bahn

Children under 4 travel free on German railways (**Deutsche Bundesbahn**), and those aged 4–11 pay half fare. Children under 6 travel free in Austria.

On most trains you can book a parent-child compartment (**Baby-Kleinkindabteil**), which is designed especially for parents with young children and even has a changing table (**Wickeltisch**).

Check out the various discounts/reductions and travel cards available: For extensive travel within Europe (Eurailpass, Freedom Pass, Inter-Rail, Euro-Minigruppe); children (Puzzle-Ticket Junior); travel for a set number of days in one country (Euro-Domino, Swiss Flexipass, German Rail Pass); groups (Euro-Minigruppe); under 26 (Inter-Rail, Freedom).

InterCityExpress (ICE)	intersitee aykspress	high-speed InterCity within Germany; luxury facilities.
EuroCity/InterCity (EC/IC)	oyroasitee/intersitee	long-distance InterCity connecting German and other European cities.
InterRegio (IR)	inter-raygioa	local trains connecting with the **IC** train network.
Nahvekehrszug	naafehrkaytst-soog	local train, stopping at all stations; (Austria: **Personenzug**; Switzerland: **Regionalzug**).
RegionalExpress (RE)	raygioanaal aykspress	medium distance trains connecting outlying areas with the city.
RegionalBahn (RB)	raygionaalbaan	local train, stopping at all stations.
StadtExpress (SE)	shtataykspress	commuter trains connecting outlying communities to the city.
S-Bahn (S)	essbaan	fast commuter train covering a shorter distance than the **StadtExpress**.
Nachtzüge	nakht-tsewger	night trains with either sleeping-car compartments (**Schlafwagen**) or berths (**Liegewagen**); supplement payable for bedding; reservations are usually necessary.
Inter-City-Night (ICN)	"intercity night"	night train with the comfort of hotel-standard coaches; tourist class available with reclining seats (**Liegesessel**); cars, motorcycles, and bicycles are also transported by the **ICN**.
City-Night-Line (CNL)	("city nightline")	equivalent of the **ICN** running between Cologne and Vienna, Hamburg and Zurich.

To the station Unterwegs zum Bahnhof

How do I get to the rail station/ main rail station?	**Wie komme ich zum Bahnhof/Hauptbahnhof?** *vee kommer ikh tsum baanhoaf/howptbaanhoaf*
Do trains to Heidelberg leave from Mannheim Station?	**Fahren die Züge nach Heidelberg vom Mannheimer Bahnhof ab?** *faaren dee tsewger naakh hiedelbehrg fom manhiemer baanhoaf ap*
How far is it?	**Wie weit ist es?** *vee viet ist ess*
Can I leave my car there?	**Kann ich mein Auto dort stehen lassen?** *kan ikh mien owto dort shtayenlasen*

At the station Auf dem Bahnhof

Where is/are ...?	**Wo ist/sind ...?** *voa ist/zint*
currency exchange office	**die Wechselstube** *dee vekselshtoober*
information desk	**die Auskunft** *dee owskunft*
baggage check	**die Gepäckaufbewahrung** *dee gepehkowfbevaarung*
lost-and-found	**das Fundbüro** *dass funtbewroa*
luggage lockers	**die Schließfächer** *dee shleesfehkher*
platforms	**die Bahnsteige** *dee baanshtieger*
snack bar	**der Schnellimbiss** *dehr shnelimbiss*
ticket office	**der Fahrkartenschalter** *dehr faarkartenshalter*
waiting room	**der Wartesaal** *dehr vartezaal*

ABFAHRT	departures
ANKUNFT	arrivals
AUSGANG	exit
AUSKUNFT	information
EINGANG	entrance
RESERVIERUNG	reservations
ZU DEN BAHNSTEIGEN	to the platforms

DIRECTIONS ➤ 94

Tickets Fahrkarten

Where can I buy tickets?	**Wo kann ich Fahrkarten kaufen?** *voa kan ikh faarkarten kowfen*
I'd like a ... ticket to ...	**Ich hätte gerne ... nach ...** *ikh hetter gehrner ... naakh*
one-way	**eine einfache Fahrkarte** *iener ienfakher faarkarter*
round-trip	**eine Rückfahrkarte** *iener rewkfaarkarter*
first / second class	**eine Fahrkarte erster/zweiter Klasse** *iener faarkarter ehrster/tsvieter klasser*
I'd like to reserve a seat.	**Ich möchte einen Platz reservieren lassen.** *ikh murkhter ienen plats rezehrveeren lasser*
aisle seat	**einen Platz am Gang** *ienen plats am gang*
window seat	**einen Fensterplatz** *ienen fensterplats*
berth	**einen Liegewagenplatz** *ienen leegevaagenplats*
Is there a sleeper/sleeping car?	**Gibt es einen Schlafwagen?** *gipt ess ienen shlaafvaagen*
I'd like a(n) ... berth.	**Ich möchte ... schlafen.** *ikh murkhter ... shlaafen*
upper/lower	**oben/unten** *oaben/unten*
Could I change my reservation, please?	**Kann ich bitte meine Reservierung ändern?** *kan ikh bitter miener rezehrveerung ehndern*
Can I buy a ticket on board?	**Kann ich im Zug eine Fahrkarte lösen?** *kan ikh im tsoog iener faarkarter lurzen*

Price Preis

How much is that?	**Wie viel kostet das?** *vee feel kostet dass*
Is there a discount for ...?	**Gibt es eine Ermäßigung für ...?** *gipt ess iener ehrmaissigung fewr*
children/families	**Kinder/Familien** *kinder/fameelien*
senior citizens	**Senioren** *zenioaren*
students	**Studenten** *shtudentern*
There is a supplement of ...	**Sie müssen einen Zuschlag von ... zahlen.** *zee mewssen ienen tsooshlaag fon ... tsaalen*

Queries Fragen

Do I have to change trains? **Muss ich umsteigen?**
muss ikh umshtiegen

It's a direct train. **Der Zug fährt durch.**
dehr tsoog fairt doorkh

You have to change at … **Sie müssen in … umsteigen.**
zee mewssen in … umshtiegen

How long is this ticket valid for? **Wie lange ist diese Fahrkarte gültig?**
vee langer ist deezer faarkarter gewltikh

Can I take my bicycle on to the train? **Kann ich mein Fahrrad im Zug mitnehmen?**
kan ikh mien faarraat im tsoog mitnaymen

Can I return on the same ticket? **Kann ich mit derselben Fahrkarte zurückfahren?**
kan ikh mit dehrzelben faarkarter tsoorewkfaaren

Which car is my seat in? **In welchem Wagen ist mein Platz?**
in velkhem vaagen ist mien plats

Is there a dining car on the train? **Führt der Zug einen Speisewagen?**
fewrt dehr tsoog ienen shpiezevaagen

Train times Abfahrtszeiten der Züge

Could I have a timetable, please? **Kann ich bitte einen Fahrplan haben?**
kan ikh bitter ienen faarplaan haaben

When is the … train to Berne? **Wann fährt der … Zug nach Bern?**
van fairt dehr … tsoog naakh behrn

first/next/last **erste/nächste/letzte**
ehrster/naikhster/letster

There's a train to Vienna at … **Um … fährt ein Zug nach Wien.**
um … fairt ien tsoog naakh veen

How frequent are the trains to ... ?	**Wie oft fahren die Züge nach ...?** *vee oft faaren dee tsewger naakh*
once/twice a day	**einmal/zweimal am Tag** *ienmaal/tsviemaal am taag*
5 times a day	**fünfmal am Tag** *fewnfmaal am taag*
every hour	**jede Stunde** *yayder shtunder*
What time do they leave?	**Wann fahren sie ab?** *van faaren zee ap*
on the hour	**zur vollen Stunde** *tsoor follen shtunder*
20 minutes past the hour	**um zwanzig Minuten nach** *um tsvantsikh minooten naakh*
What time does the train stop at ...?	**Wann hält der Zug in ...?** *van hehlt dehr tsoog in*
What time does the train arrive in ...?	**Wann kommt der Zug in ... an?** *van komt dehr tsoog in ... an*
How long is the trip/journey?	**Wie lange dauert die Fahrt?** *vee langer dowert dee faart*
Is the train on time?	**Ist der Zug pünktlich?** *ist dehr tsoog pewnktlikh*

Departures Abfahrt

Which platform does the train to ... leave from?	**Auf welchem Bahnsteig fährt der Zug nach ... ab?** *owf velkhem baanshtieg fairt dehr tsoog naakh ... ap*
Where is platform 4?	**Wo ist Bahnsteig vier?** *voa ist baanshtieg feer*
over there	**dort drüben** *dort drewben*
on the left/right	**auf der linken/rechten Seite** *owf dehr linken/rekhten zieter*
under the underpass	**durch die Unterführung (hindurch)** *doorkh dee unterfewrung (hinndoorkh)*
Where do I change for ...?	**Wo muss ich nach ... umsteigen?** *voa muss ikh naakh ... umshtiegen*
How long will I have to wait for a connection?	**Wie lange muss ich auf einen Anschluss warten?** *vee langer muss ikh owf ienen anshluss varten*

Boarding Einsteigen

Is this the right platform for the train to …?	**Ist dies der richtige Bahnsteig für den Zug nach …?** *ist deez dehr rikhtiger baanshtieg fewr dayn tsoog naakh*
Is this the train to …?	**Ist dies der Zug nach …?** *ist deez dehr tsoog naakh*
Is this seat free?	**Ist dieser Platz frei?** *ist deezer plats frie*
I think that's my seat.	**Ich glaube, das ist mein Platz.** *ikh glowber dass ist mien plats*
Here's my reservation.	**Hier ist meine Platzkarte.** *heer ist miener platskarter*
Are there any seats/berths available?	**Sind noch Plätze/Schlafplätze frei?** *zint nokh plehtser/shlaafpletser frie*
Do you mind …?	**Stört es Sie, …?** *shturt ess zee*
if I sit here?	**wenn ich hier sitze?** *ven ikh heer zitser*
if I open the window?	**wenn ich das Fenster öffne?** *ven ikh dass fenster urfner*

On the journey Während der Fahrt

How long are we stopping here for?	**Wie lange halten wir hier?** *vee langer halten veer heer*
When do we get to …?	**Wann kommen wir in … an?** *van kommen veer in … an*
Have we passed …?	**Sind wir schon an … vorbeigekommen?** *zint veer shoan an … foarbiegekommen*
Where is the dining/ sleeping car?	**Wo ist der Speisewagen/Schlafwagen?** *voa ist dehr shpiezevaagen/ shlaafvaagen*
Where is my berth?	**Wo ist mein Schlafplatz?** *voa ist mien shlaafplats*
I've lost my ticket.	**Ich habe meine Fahrkarte verloren.** *ikh haaber miener faarkarter fehrloaren*

| **NOTBREMSE** | Emergency brake |
| **AUTOMATIKTÜREN** | Automatic doors |

Long-distance bus/Coach
Überlandbus

Where is the bus station?	**Wo ist der Busbahnhof?** *voa ist dehr bussbaanhoaf*
When's the next bus to …?	**Wann fährt der nächste Bus nach …?** *van fairt dehr naikhster buss naakh*
Which bay does it leave from?	**Von welcher Haltestelle fährt er ab?** *fon velkher haltesteler fairt ehr ap*
Where are the bus stops?	**Wo sind die Bushaltestellen?** *voa zint dee busshalteshtelen*
Does the bus/coach stop at …?	**Hält der Bus in …?** *hehlt dehr buss in*

Bus/Streetcar Bus/Straßenbahn

Look out for travel cards (for a day, week or month) valid on buses, trams and the subway. Booklets of 10 tickets **(10er Karten)** are another cheap way to travel and you must always validate your ticket in the machine marked with the sign **Hier Fahrschein entwerten.**

Where is the bus station/train depot?	**Wo ist der Busbahnhof/das Straßenbahn-depot?** *voa ist dehr bussbaanhoaf/dass shtraassenbaandepoa*
Where can I get a bus/tram to …?	**Wo hält der Bus/die Straßenbahn zum …?** *voa hehlt dehr buss/dee shtraassenbaan tsum*
the airport	**Flughafen** *flooghaafen*
the railway station	**Bahnhof** *baanhoaf*
the town center	**Stadtzentrum** *shtat-tsentrum*

Gehen Sie zu der Haltestelle dort drüben.	You need that stop over there.
Nehmen Sie die Linie zehn.	You need bus number 10
Sie müssen in … umsteigen.	You must change buses at …

◦	**BUSHALTESTELLE**	Bus stop	◦
	BEDARFSHALTESTELLE	Request stop	
	RAUCHEN VERBOTEN	No smoking	
◦	**NOTAUSGANG**	Emergency exit	◦

Buying tickets Fahrscheine kaufen

Where can I buy tickets?	**Wo kann ich Fahrscheine kaufen?** *voa kan ikh faarshiener kowfen*
A one-way ticket to…, please.	**Eine einfache Fahrt nach …, bitte.** *iener ienfakher faart naakh … bitter*
A round-trip ticket to …, please.	**Einmal nach … und zurück, bitte.** *ienmaal naakh … unt tsoorewk bitter*
A booklet of tickets, please.	**Ein Fahrscheinheft, bitte.** *ien faarshienheft bitter*
How much is the fare to …?	**Wie viel kostet die Fahrt nach …?** *vee feel kostet dee faart naakh*

Traveling Während der Fahrt

Is this the right bus to the town hall?	**Ist dies der richtige Bus zum Rathaus?** *ist deez dehr rikhtiger buss tsum raathowss*
Could you tell me when to get off?	**Können Sie mir sagen, wann ich aussteigen muss?** *kurnen zee meer zaagen van ikh ows-shtiegen muss*
Do I have to change buses?	**Muss ich umsteigen?** *muss ikh umshtiegen*
How many stops are there to …?	**Wie viele Haltestellen sind es bis …?** *vee feeler halteshtelen zint ess biss*
It's 3 stops from here.	**Es sind drei Haltestellen von hier.** *ess zint drie halteshtelen fon heer*
Next stop, please!	**Die nächste Haltestelle, bitte!** *dee naikhster halteshteler bitter*

⊘ **FAHRKARTE ENTWERTEN**　　　Validate your ticket　　⊘

– Entschuldigung, ist dies der richtige Bus zum Rathaus?
– *Nein. Nehmen Sie die Linie 8, dort drüben.*
– Danke. Einmal zum Rathaus, bitte.
– *Das macht 2 Mark 50.*
– Können Sie mir sagen, wann ich aussteigen muss?
– *Es sind vier Haltestellen von hier.*

NUMBERS ➤ 216; BUYING TICKETS (TRAIN) ➤ 74

Subway U-Bahn

There are excellent subway systems in Berlin,
Bonn, Düsseldorf, Cologne, Frankfurt, Hamburg and Munich
and a smaller system in Vienna. Large maps outside each station
make the systems easy to use. Tickets should be purchased from
the vending machines at all **U-Bahn** stations before you board a train. Ticket
inspection is common and there are large fines for invalid tickets.
Look out for multiple tickets and day or month passes that make
traveling cheaper.

General inquiries Allgemeine Fragen

Where's the nearest subway station?	**Wo ist die nächste U-Bahnstation?** *voa ist dee naikhster oo-baanshtatsioan*
Where do I buy a ticket?	**Wo kann ich eine Fahrkarte kaufen?** *voa kan ikh iener faarkarter kowfen*
Could I have a map of the subway?	**Kann ich einen Plan für die U-Bahn haben?** *kan ikh ienen plaan fewr dee oo-baan haaben*

Traveling Während der Fahrt

Which line should I take for the main station?	**Welche Linie fährt zum Hauptbahnhof?** *velkher leenier fairt tsum howptbaanhoaf*
Is this the right train for …?	**Ist dies die richtige U-Bahn nach …?** *ist deez dee rikhtigger oo-baan naakh*
Which stop is it for …?	**An welcher Haltestelle muss ich für … aussteigen?** *an velkher halteshteler muss ikh fewr … owsshtiegen*
How many stops is it to …?	**Wie viele Haltestellen sind es bis …?** *vee feeler halteshtelen zint ess biss*
Is the next stop …?	**Ist die nächste Haltestelle …?** *ist dee naikhster halteshteler*
Where are we?	**Wo sind wir?** *voa zint veer*
Where do I change for …?	**Wo muss ich nach … umsteigen?** *voa muss ikh naakh … umshtiegen*
What time is the last train to …?	**Wann fährt die letzte U-Bahn nach …?** *van fairt dee letster oo-baan naakh*

ANDERE LINIEN	to other lines/transfer

BUYING TICKETS (BUS) ➤ 79; (TRAIN) ➤ 74

Ferry Fähre

Ferry companies operating services from the UK to the Continent include Stena Sealink, Hoverspeed, Brittany Ferries, P&O, Sally Ferries, North Sea Ferries, Scandinavian Seaways. Ferry services to the islands of the North Sea and Baltic Sea are popular: advance reservation (through local travel agencies) is advisable.

first/next/last	**erste/nächste/letzte**
	ehrster/naikhster/letster
A round-trip ticket for …	**Eine Rückfahrkarte für …**
	iener rewkfaarkarter fewr
1 car and 1 trailer	**ein Auto und einen Wohnwagen**
	ien owto unt ienen voanvaagen
2 adults and 3 children	**zwei Erwachsene und drei Kinder**
	tsvie ehrvaksener unt drie kinder
I want to reserve a …	**Ich möchte eine … buchen.**
	ikh murkhter iener … bookhen
single/double cabin	**Einzelkabine/Doppelkabine**
	ientselkabeener/doppelkabeener

RETTUNGSRING	life preserver/life belt
RETTUNGSBOOT	life boat
SAMMELPLATZ	muster station
KEIN ZUGANG ZU DEN	no access to
AUTODECKS	car decks

Boat trips Schiffsfahrten

Is there a …?	**Gibt es …?** *gipt ess*
boat trip	**eine Schiffsfahrt** *iener shifsfaart*
river cruise	**eine Flussfahrt** *iener flusfaart*
What time does the boat leave?	**Wann fährt das Schiff ab?**
	van fairt dass shif ap
What time does the boat return?	**Wann kommt das Schiff wieder?**
	van komt dass shif veeder
Where does the boat stop?	**Wo hält das Schiff?** *voa hehlt dass shif*
Where can we buy tickets?	**Wo können wir Fahrkarten kaufen?**
	voa kurnen veer faarkarten kowfen

BUYING TICKETS (BUS) ➤ *79; (TRAIN) 74*

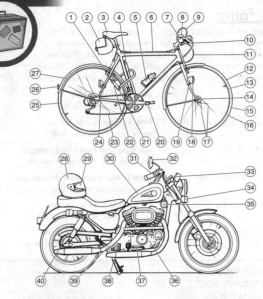

1 brake pad **Bremsbelag** m
2 bicycle bag **Fahrradtasche** f
3 saddle **Sattel** m
4 pump **Luftpumpe** f
5 water bottle **Wasserflasche** f
6 frame **Rahmen** m
7 handlebars **Lenker** m
8 bell **Klingel** f
9 brake cable **Bremskabel** nt
10 gear lever/shift **Schalthebel** m
11 gear/control cable **Schaltkabel** nt
12 inner tube **Schlauch** m
13 front/back wheel **Vorderrad** nt/
   Hinterrad nt
14 axle **Achse** f
15 tire/tyre **Reifen** m
16 wheel **Rad** nt
17 spokes **Speichen** fpl
18 bulb **Glühbirne** f
19 headlamp **Scheinwerfer** m
20 pedal **Pedal** nt20
21 lock **Schloss** nt

22 generator **Dynamo** m
23 chain **Kette** f
24 rear light **Rücklicht** nt
25 rim **Felge** f
26 reflectors **Rückstrahler** mpl
27 mudguard (fender) **Schutzblech** nt
28 helmet **Helm** m
29 visor **Visier** nt
30 fuel tank **Tank** m
31 clutch lever **Kupplungshebel** m
32 mirror **Spiegel** m
33 ignition switch **Zündung** f
34 turn switch (indicator) **Blinker** m
35 horn **Hupe** f
36 engine **Motor** m
37 gear stick/shift **Schalthebel** m
38 main stand **Ständer** m
39 exhaust pipe **Auspuff** m
40 chain **Kette** f

82

Bicycle/motorbike
Fahrrad/Motorrad

I'd like to rent a …	**Ich möchte … mieten.** *ikh murkhter … meeten.*
3/10 gear bicycle	**ein drei/zehn-Gang-Rad** *ien drie-/tsayn-gang-raat*
moped	**ein Moped** *ien moapet*
mountain bike	**ein Mountainbike** *ien "mountainbike"*
motorbike	**ein Motorrad** *ien moatorraat*
How much does it cost per day/week?	**Wie viel kostet es pro Tag/Woche?** *vee feel kostet ess proa taag/vokher*
Do you require a deposit?	**Muss ich eine Kaution hinterlegen?** *muss ikh iener kowtsioan hinterlaygern*
The brakes don't work.	**Die Bremsen funktionieren nicht.** *dee bremzen funktsionneeren nikht*
There are no lights.	**Die Beleuchtung fehlt.** *dee beloykhtung faylt*
The front/rear tire has a puncture.	**Der Vorderreifen/Hinterreifen hat einen Platten.** *dehr forder-riefen/hinter-riefen hat ienen platen*

Hitchhiking Trampen

Hitchhiking is permitted everywhere except on expressways/motorways and their access roads, but is not to be recommended for anyone. Alternatively, go to the **Mitfahrzentrale** (usually found in every town) that matches drivers with those looking for lifts; you pay a fee to the **Mitfahrzentrale** and make a contribution for the gas/petrol.

Where are you heading?	**Wohin fahren Sie?** *voahinn faaren zee*
I'm heading for …	**Ich fahre nach …** *ikh faarer naakh*
Is that on the way to …?	**Liegt das auf dem Weg nach …?** *leegt dass owf daym vayg naakh*
Could you drop me off …?	**Können Sie mich … absetzen?** *kurnen zee mikh … apzetsen*
here	**hier** *heer*
at the … exit	**an der … Ausfahrt** *an dehr … owsfaart*
in the center	**im Zentrum** *im tsentrum*
Thanks for the lift.	**Danke für das Mitnehmen.** *danker fewr dass mitnehmen*

DIRECTIONS ➤ 94; NUMBERS ➤ 216

Taxi/Cab Taxi

Catch a taxi at a rank (**Taxistand**) or phone from wherever you are; numbers are listed under **Taxi** in the local phone book or advertised in most telephone booths. Taxis in Germany are usually beige-colored Mercedes and all have meters. Tipping suggestions: Germany: round up bill; Austria: 10%; Switzerland: 15% (sometimes included).

Where can I get a taxi?	**Wo finde ich ein Taxi?** *voa finder ikh ien taksi*
Do you have the number for a taxi?	**Haben Sie die Nummer für ein Taxi?** *haaben zee dee nummer fewr ien taksi*
I'd like a taxi …	**Ich hätte gern … ein Taxi.** *ikh hetter gehrn … ien taksi*
now	**sofort** *zofoart*
in an hour	**in einer Stunde** *in iener shtunder*
for tomorrow at 9:00	**für morgen um neun Uhr** *fewr morgen um noyn oor*
The address is … going to …	**Die Adresse ist … nach …** *dee adresser ist … naakh*

◎	**FREI**	available/for hire ◎

Please take me to …	**Bitte bringen Sie mich …** *bitter bringen zee mikh*
airport	**zum Flughafen** *tsum flooghaafen*
railway station	**zum Bahnhof** *tsum baanhoaf*
the … Hotel	**zum … Hotel** *tsum … hottel*
this address	**zu dieser Adresse** *tsoo deezer adresser*
How much will it cost?	**Wie viel kostet das?** *vee feel kostet dass*
Please stop here.	**Bitte halten Sie hier.** *bitter halten zee heer*
How much is that?	**Was kostet das?** *vass kostet dass*
You said … marks.	**Sie sagten … Mark.** *zee zaagten … mark*
Keep the change.	**Der Rest ist für Sie.** *dehr rest ist fewr zee*

– Wie viel kostet das?
– *Vierzehn Mark, bitte.*
– Der Rest ist für Sie.

Car Auto

While driving, the following documents must be carried at all times: valid full driver's license (**Führerschein**), vehicle registration document (**Kraftfahrzeugzulassung**) and insurance documentation (**Versicherungsschein**). Insurance for minimum third-party risks is compulsory in Europe. It is recommended that you take out international motor insurance (for a "green card") through your insurer.

Conversion Chart

km.	1	10	20	30	40	50	60	70	80	90	100	110	120	130
miles	0.62	6	12	19	25	31	37	44	50	56	62	68	75	81

Road network

Germany/Austria	E – international expressway (green rectangle – no tolls); A (**Autobahn**) – national expressway (white numbers, blue background); B (**Bundesstraße**) – main road; L (**Landstraße**) – secondary road; G (**Gemeindestraße**) – local road
Switzerland	A – expressway/motorway (toll free); N – main road; E – secondary road

Speed limits mph (km/h)	Built-up area	Outside built-up area	motorway
Germany	31 (50)	62 (100)	81 (130)
Eastern Germany	31 (50)	50 (80)	62 (100)
Austria	31 (50)	62 (100)	81 (130)
Switzerland	31 (50)	50 (80)	62-74 (100-120)

Essential equipment: warning triangle, nationality plate and first-aid kit; headlight beams must be adjusted for right-hand drive vehicles; wearing seat belts is compulsory (front and back).

Minimum driving age:

Austria, Switzerland, Germany – 18; minimum rental age:

Germany – 18; Austria – 21; Switzerland – 21 (25 with some firms).

Tolls are payable on some Austrian roads, mainly mountain passes. All roads are toll free in Germany, but for travel on Swiss motorways, a pass/vignette is required – available from tourist offices, customs, post offices and garages. It is valid for 1 year, non-transferable and to be attached to your windshield. An additional pass/vignette is required for caravans or trailers. Vehicles "flash" to warn of their approach – it's not a signal for you to go. Note that the use of horns is prohibited in built-up areas. Alcohol limit in blood: max. 50mg/100ml. Note that any alcohol may impair concentration.

Car rental Autovermietung

You will need to produce a valid driver's license held for at least a year for Austria or Switzerland, or for 6 months for Germany.

Children's safety seats (**Kindersitze**) are compulsory for children under 12 and are available from car rental agencies; advance reservation is recommended.

Where can I rent a car?	**Wo kann ich ein Auto mieten?** *voa kan ikh ien owto meeten*
I'd like to rent a car.	**Ich möchte ein Auto mieten.** *ikh murkhter ien owto meeten*
a 2-/4-door car	**ein zweitüriges/viertüriges Auto** *ien tsvietewrigess/feertewriggess owto*
an automatic	**einen Automatikwagen** *ienen owtommaatikvaagen*
with 4-wheel drive	**mit Vierradantrieb** *mit feeraatantreeb*
with air conditioning	**mit Klimaanlage** *mit kleema-anlaager*
I'd like it for a day/a week.	**Ich möchte es für einen Tag/eine Woche.** *ikh murkhter ess fewr ienen taag/iener vokher*
How much does it cost per day/week?	**Wie viel kostet es pro Tag/Woche?** *vee feel kostet ess proa taag/vokher*
Is insurance included?	**Ist die Versicherung inbegriffen?** *ist dee fehrzikherung inbegriffen*
Are there special weekend rates?	**Gibt es Wochenendpauschalen?** *gipt ess vokhenentpowshaalen*
What sort of fuel does it take?	**Welchen Treibstoff braucht es?** *velkhen triebshtoff browkht ess*
Could I have full insurance, please?	**Kann ich bitte eine Vollkaskoversicherung haben?** *kan ikh bitter iener folkasko-fehrzikherung haaben*

Kann ich Ihren Führerschein sehen?	May I see your driver's license?
Wer fährt?	Who will be driving?
Bitte bringen Sie das Auto vor ... am ... zurück.	Please return the car by ... on ...

DAYS OF THE WEEK ➤ *218*; *PAYING* ➤ *89*

Gas station Tankstelle

Where's the next gas station, please?	**Wo ist die nächste Tankstelle, bitte?** *voa ist dee naikhster tankshteler bitter*
Is it self-service?	**Ist hier Selbstbedienung?** *ist heer zelbstbedeenung*
Fill it up, please.	**Volltanken, bitte.** *foltanken bitter*
… liters of gasoline, please.	**… Liter Benzin, bitte.** *… leeter bentseen bitter*
super/premium	**Super** *zooper*
regular	**Normal** *normaal*
lead-free	**bleifreies Benzin** *blie-frie-ess bentseen*
diesel	**Diesel** *deezel*
I'm pump number …	**Zapfsäule Nummer …** *tsapfzoyler nummer*
Where is the air pump/water?	**Wo ist die Luftpumpe/das Wasser?** *voa ist dee luftpumpe/dass vasser*

PREIS PRO LITER	price per liter

Parking Parken

In most Blue Zones, you may park free of charge for a limited period with a parking disk (available from tobacconists, gas stations, tourist offices and automobile clubs). Except for one-way streets, parking is only permitted on the right-hand side. No parking where you see these signs: **Halten verboten**; **Stationierungsverbot**. Vehicles that are illegally parked may be ticketed or booted; towing usually occurs only in cases of obstruction.

Is there a parking lot nearby?	**Gibt es hier in der Nähe einen Parkplatz?** *gipt ess heer in dehr naier ienen parkplats*
What's the charge per hour/per day?	**Wie viel kostet es pro Stunde/Tag?** *vee feel kostet ess proa shtunder/taag*
Where do I pay?	**Wo muss ich bezahlen?** *voa muss ikh betsaalen*
Do you have some change for the parking meter?	**Haben Sie Kleingeld für die Parkuhr?** *haaben zee kliengelt fewr dee parkoor*
My car has been booted. Who do I call?	**Mein Auto ist mit einer Parkkralle festgesetzt worden. Wen kann ich anrufen?** *mien owto ist mit iener park-kraler festgezetst vorden. vayn kan ikh anroofen*

NUMBERS ➤ 216; DIRECTIONS ➤ 94

Breakdown Panne

For help in the event of a breakdown: refer to your breakdow
assistance documents; or contact the breakdown service:
Germany: **ADAC** ☎ 01802/22 22 22; Austria: **ÖAMTC** ☎ 120
or **ARBÖ** ☎ 123; Switzerland: ☎ 140. On German autobahns, the
emergency phones connect you to the operator; ask for the **Pannendienst**.

Where is the nearest garage?	**Wo ist die nächste Reparaturwerkstatt?** *voa ist dee naikhster rayparatoorvehrkshto*
I've had a breakdown.	**Ich habe eine Panne.** *ikh haaber iener pane*
Can you send a mechanic/ tow truck?	**Können Sie einen Mechaniker/Abschlepp wagen schicken?** *kurnen zee ienen mekhanikker/apshlepvaagen shiken*
I'm a member of ...	**Ich bin Mitglied im ...** *ikh bin mitgleet im*
My registration number is ...	**Meine Mitgliedsnummer ist ...** *miener mitgleetsnummer ist*
The car is ...	**Das Auto steht ...** *dass owto shtayt*
on the highway/motorway	**auf der Autobahn** *owf dehr owtobaan*
2 km from ...	**zwei km von ... entfernt** *tsvie killommayter fon ... entfehrnt*
How long will you be?	**Wie lange dauert es, bis Sie kommen?** *vee langer dowert ess biss zee kommen*

What is wrong? Wo liegt der Fehler?

My car won't start.	**Mein Auto springt nicht an.** *mie owto shpringt nikht an*
The battery is dead.	**Die Batterie ist leer.** *dee batteree ist layr*
I've run out of gas/petrol.	**Ich habe kein Benzin mehr.** *ikh haaber kien bentseen mayr*
I have a flat/puncture.	**Ich habe einen Platten.** *ikh haaber ienen platen*
The ... doesn't work.	**... funktioniert nicht.** *... funktsioneert nikht*
I've locked the keys in the car.	**Ich habe die Schlüssel im Auto eingeschlossen.** *ikh haaber dee shlewssel im owto iengeshlossen*

epairs Reparaturen

Do you do repairs?

Führen Sie Reparaturen aus?
fewren zee rayparatooren owss

Could you have a look at my car?

Können Sie sich mein Auto ansehen?
kurnen zee zikh mien owto anzayen

Can you repair it (temporarily)?

Können Sie es (provisorisch) reparieren?
kurnen zee ess (provizoarish) raypareeren

Please make only essential repairs.

Bitte reparieren Sie nur das Nötigste.
bitter raypareeren zee noor dass nurtiggster

Can I wait for it?

Kann ich darauf warten?
kan ikh dahrowf varten

Can you repair it today?

Können Sie es heute reparieren?
kurnen zee ess hoyter raypareeren

When will it be ready?

Wann wird es fertig? *van veert ess fehrtikh*

How much will it cost?

Wie viel wird das kosten?
vee feel veert dass kosten

That's outrageous!

Das ist unverschämt! *dass ist unfehrshaimt*

Can I have a receipt for the insurance?

Kann ich eine Quittung für die Versicherung haben? *kan ikh iener kvittung fewr dee fehrzikherung haaben*

... funktioniert nicht.	The ... isn't working.
Ich habe die nötigen Ersatzteile nicht da.	I don't have the necessary parts.
Ich muss die Ersatzteile bestellen.	I will have to order the parts.
Ich kann es nur provisorisch reparieren.	I can only repair it temporarily.
Ihr Auto hat Totalschaden.	Your car is totaled.
Es kann nicht repariert werden.	It can't be repaired.
Es wird ... fertig.	It will be ready ...
heute noch	later today
morgen	tomorrow
in ... Tagen	in ... days

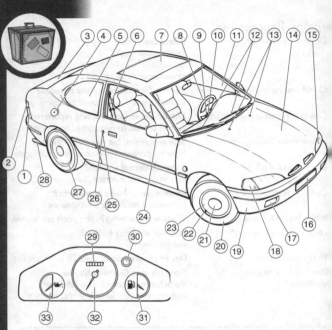

1	tail lights/back lights **Rücklichter** ntpl	17	fog lamp **Nebelscheinwerfer** m
2	brakelights **Bremslichter** ntpl	18	indicators/turn signals **Blinker** mpl
3	trunk/boot **Kofferraum** m	19	bumper **Stoßstange** f
4	petrol cap (gas tank door) **Tankdeckel** m	20	tires/tyres **Reifen** mpl
5	window **Fenster** nt	21	hubcap/wheel cover **Radkappe** f
6	seat belt **Sicherheitsgurt** m	22	valve **Ventil** nt
7	sunroof **Schiebedach** nt	23	wheels **Räder** ntpl
8	steering wheel **Lenkrad** nt	24	outside/wing mirror **Außenspiegel** m
9	starter/ignition **Zündung** f	25	central locking **Zentralverriegelung** f
10	ignition key **Zündschlüssel** m	26	lock **Schloss** nt
11	windscreen **Windschutzscheibe** f	27	wheel rim **Felge** f
12	windshield/windscreen wipers **Scheibenwischer** mpl	28	exhaust pipe **Auspuffrohr** nt
13	windshield/windscreen washer **Scheibenwaschanlage** f	29	odometer/milometer **Kilometerzähler** m
14	hood/bonnet **Motorhaube** f	30	warning light **Warnlampe** f
15	headlights **Scheinwerfer** mpl		
16	license plate **Nummernschild** nt		

90

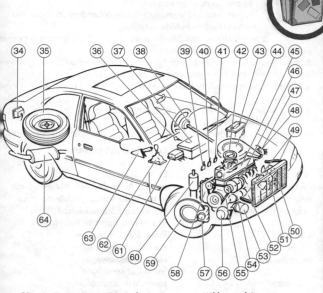

31	fuel pump/gauge **Benzinuhr** f
32	speedometer **Tachometer** m
33	oil gauge **Ölstandsanzeiger** m
34	tail lights **Rückfahrscheinwerfer** mpl
35	spare wheel **Ersatzrad** nt
36	choke **Choke** m
37	heater **Heizung** f
38	steering column **Lenksäule** f
39	accelerator **Gaspedal** nt
40	brake pedal **Bremspedal** nt
41	clutch **Kupplung** f
42	carburetor **Vergaser** m
43	battery **Batterie** f
44	air filter **Luftfilter** m
45	camshaft **Nockenwelle** f
46	alternator **Lichtmaschine** f
47	distributor **Verteiler** m
48	points **Unterbrecherkontakte** mpl
49	radiator hose (top/bottom) **Kühlwasserleitung** f
50	radiator **Kühler** m
51	fan **Ventilator** m
52	engine **Motor** m
53	oil filter **Ölfilter** m
54	starter motor **Anlasser** m
55	fan belt **Keilriemen** m
56	horn **Hupe** f
57	brake pads **Bremsbeläge** mpl
58	transmission/gearbox **Getriebe** nt
59	brakes **Bremsen** fpl
60	shock absorbers **Stoßdämpfer** mpl
61	fuses **Sicherungen** fpl
62	gear lever/shift **Schaltknüppel** m
63	handbrake **Handbremse** f
64	muffler **Auspufftopf** m

CAR REPAIRS ➤ *89*

Accidents Verkehrsunfälle

In the event of an accident:

1. put your red warning triangle (**Warndreieck**) about 100 meters / metres behind your car;

2. report the accident to the police (compulsory if there is person injury); don't leave before they arrive;

3. show your driver's license and "green card" (**grüne Karte**); and give you name, address, insurance company to the other party;

4. report to the appropriate insurance office of the third party and your ov company;

5. don't make any written statement without advice of a lawyer or automobile club official;

6. note all relevant details of the other party and any independent witness

There has been an accident.	**Es ist ein Unfall passiert.** *ess ist ien unfal passeert*
It's …	**Es ist …** *ess ist*
on the expressway	**auf der Autobahn** *owf dehr owtobaan*
near …	**in der Nähe von …** *in dehr naier fon*
Where's the nearest telephone?	**Wo ist das nächste Telefon?** *voa ist dass naikhster taylayfoan*
Call …	**Rufen Sie ..** *roofen zee*
the police	**die Polizei** *dee pollitsie*
an ambulance	**einen Krankenwagen** *ienen krankenvaagen*
a doctor	**einen Arzt** *ienen aartst*
the fire department	**die Feuerwehr** *dee foyervehr*
Could you help me please?	**Können Sie mir bitte helfen?** *kurnen zee meer bitter helfen*

Injuries Verletzungen

There are people injured.	**Es gibt Verletzte.** *ess gipt fehrletster*
No one is hurt.	**Es ist niemand verletzt.** *ess ist neemant fehrletst*
He is bleeding.	**Er blutet.** *ehr blootet*
She's unconscious.	**Sie ist bewusstlos.** *zee ist bevustloass*
He can't breathe.	**Er kann nicht atmen.** *ehr kan nikht aatmen*
Don't move him.	**Bewegen Sie ihn nicht.** *bevaygen zee een nikht*

What's your insurance company?	**Ihre Versicherungsge-sellschaft, bitte?** *eerer fehrzikherungzgezelshaft bitter*
What's your name and address?	**Ihr Name und Ihre Anschrift, bitte?** *eer naamer unt eerer anshrift bitter*
He ran into me.	**Er ist mit mir zusammengestoßen.** *ehr ist mit meer tsoozammengeshtoassen*
She was driving too fast.	**Sie ist zu schnell gefahren.** *zee ist tsoo shnel gefaaren*
I had right of way.	**Ich hatte Vorfahrt.** *ikh hater foarfaart*
I was (only) driving at … km/h.	**Ich bin (nur) … km/h gefahren.** *ikh bin (noor) … kilomayter proa shtunder gefaaren*
I'd like an interpreter.	**Ich möchte einen Dolmetscher haben.** *ikh murkhter ienen dolmecher haaben*
He/She saw it happen.	**Er/Sie hat gesehen, wie es passiert ist.** *ehr/zee hat gezayen vee ess passeert ist*
The registration number was …	**Das Kraftfahrzeugkennzeichen war …** *dass kraftfaartzoygkentsiekhen vaar*

Kann ich bitte Ihren … sehen?	Can I see your … please?
Führerschein	driver's license
Versicherungsschein	insurance certificate
Kraftfahrzeugschein	vehicle registration document
Wann ist es passiert?	What time did it happen?
Wo ist es passiert?	Where did it happen?
War jemand anders an dem Unfall beteiligt?	Was anyone else involved?
Gibt es Zeugen?	Are there any witnesses?
Sie haben die Geschwindigkeitsbegrenzung überschritten.	You were speeding.
Ihre Beleuchtung funktioniert nicht.	Your lights aren't working.
Sie müssen (sofort) ein Bußgeld bezahlen.	You'll have to pay a fine (on the spot).
Sie müssen auf der Wache eine Aussage machen	We need you to make a statement at the station.

Asking directions
Wegbeschreibung

Excuse me, please.	**Entschuldigen Sie bitte.** *entshuldigen zee bitter*
How do I get to …?	**Wie komme ich nach …?** *ve kommer ikh naakh*
Where is …?	**Wo ist …?** *voa ist*
Can you show me on the map where I am?	**Können Sie mir auf der Karte zeigen, wo ich bin?** *kurnen zee meer owf dehr karter tsiegen voa ikh bin*
I've lost my way.	**Ich habe mich verlaufen.** *ikh haaber mikh fehrlowfen*
Can you repeat that please?	**Können Sie das bitte wiederholen?** *kurnen zee dass bitter veederhoalen*
More slowly, please.	**Langsamer, bitte.** *langzaamer bitter*
Thanks for your help.	**Vielen Dank für Ihre Hilfe.** *feelen dank fewr eerer hilfer*

Traveling by car Im Auto unterwegs

Is this the right road for …?	**Ist dies die richtige Straße nach …?** *ist deez dee rikhtiger shtraasser naakh*
How far is it to … from here?	**Wie weit ist es von hier nach …?** *vee viet ist ess fon heer naakh*
Where does this road lead?	**Wohin führt diese Straße?** *voahinn fewrt deezer shtraasser*
How do I get onto the expressway?	**Wie komme ich auf die Autobahn?** *vee kommer ikh owf dee owtobaan*
What's the next town called?	**Wie heißt die nächste Stadt?** *vee hiest dee naikhster shtat*
What is causing the traffic jam?	**Warum ist hier Stau?** *varum ist heer shtow*
How long does it take by car?	**Wie lange dauert es mit dem Auto?** *vee langer dowert ess mit daym owto*

> – Entschuldigen Sie bitte. Wie komme ich zum Bahnhof?
> – *Nehmen Sie die dritte Straße links und gehen Sie dann geradeaus.*
> – Die dritte links. Ist es weit?
> – *Es sind 5 Minuten zu Fuß.*
> – Vielen Dank für Ihre Hilfe.
> – *Bitte schön.*

Location Lage

Es ist ...	It's ...
geradeaus	straight ahead
auf der linken Seite	on the left
auf der rechten Seite	on the right
am Ende der Straße	at the end of the street
an der Ecke	at the corner
um die Ecke	round the corner
in Richtung ...	in the direction of ...
gegenüber .../hinter ...	opposite .../behind ...
neben .../nach ...	next to .../after ...
Gehen Sie die ... entlang.	Go down the ...
Seitenstraße/Hauptstraße	side street/main street
Gehen Sie über ...	Cross the ...
den Platz/die Brücke	square/bridge
Nehmen Sie ..	Take the ...
die dritte Straße rechts	third turning to the right
Biegen Sie ... links ab.	Turn left ...
nach der ersten Ampel	after the first traffic light
an der zweiten Kreuzung	at the second intersection/crossroad

By car Im Auto

Es liegt ... von hier.	It's ... of here.
nördlich/südlich	north/south
östlich/westlich	east/west
Nehmen Sie die Straße nach ...	Take the road for ...
Sie sind auf der falschen Straße.	You're on the wrong road.
Sie müssen nach ... zurückfahren.	You'll have to go back to ...
Folgen Sie den Schildern nach ...	Follow the signs for ...

How far? Wie weit?

Es ist ...	It's ...
nah/nicht weit/weit	close/not far/a long way
fünf Minuten zu Fuß	5 minutes on foot
zehn Minuten im Auto	10 minutes by car
etwa zehn Kilometer entfernt	about 10 km away

TIME ➤ 220; NUMBERS ➤ 216

Road signs Verkehrszeichen

ANLIEGER FREI	access only
AUSWEICHSTRECKE	alternative route
EINBAHNSTRASSE	one-way street
EINORDNEN	stay in lane/get in lane
GESPERRT	road closed
LICHT AN	use headlights
NIEDRIGE BRÜCKE	low bridge
SCHULE	school
UMLEITUNG	detour
VORFAHRT GEWÄHREN	yield

Town plans Stadtpläne

Altstadt f	old town
Bahnhof m	station
Bushaltestelle f	bus stop
Buslinie f	bus route
Flughafen m	airport
Fußgängerüberweg m	pedestrian crossing
Fußgängerzone f	pedestrian zone
Hauptstraße f	main street
Kino nt	movie theater
Kirche f	church
öffentliches Gebäude nt	public building
Park m	park
Parkplatz m	parking lot
Polizeiwache f	police station
Postamt nt	post office
Sportplatz m	athletic field
Stadion nt	stadium
Standort m	you are here
Taxistand m	taxi rank
Theater nt	theater
Toiletten fpl	toilets
U-Bahnstation f	subway station
Unterführung f	underpass
Verkehrsbüro nt	information office

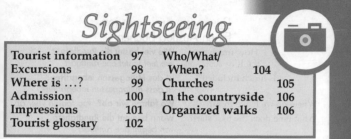

Sightseeing

Tourist information Fremdenverkehrsbüro

Tourist information offices are often situated in the town center; look for
Fremdenverkehrsamt or **Verkehrsbüro.**

Popular events to look out for are wine and beer festivals (e.g. **Oktoberfest** in Munich), **Fasching** (carnival time leading up to Ash Wednesday) and other local festivals.

Where's the tourist office?	**Wo ist das Fremdenverkehrsbüro?** *voa ist dass fremdenfehrkayrsbewroa*
What are the main points of interest?	**Welches sind die wichtigsten Sehenswürdigkeiten?** *velkhess zint dee vikhtiggsten zayenzvewrdikhkieten*
We're here for ...	**Wir sind ... hier.** *veer zint ... heer*
only a few hours	**nur ein paar Stunden** *noor ien paar shtunden*
a day	**einen Tag** *ienen taag*
a week	**eine Woche** *iener vokher*
Can you recommend ...?	**Können Sie ... empfehlen?** *kurnen zee ... empfaylen*
a sightseeing tour	**eine Stadtrundfahrt** *iener shtatruntfaart*
an excursion	**einen Ausflug** *ienen owsfloog*
a boat trip	**eine Schiffsfahrt** *iener shifsfaart*
Do you have any information on ...?	**Haben Sie Informationen über ...?** *haaben zee infoarmatsioanen ewber*
Are there any trips to ...?	**Gibt es Ausflüge nach ...?** *gipt ess owsflewger naakh*

NUMBERS ➤ 216; DIRECTIONS ➤ 94

Reserving an excursion
Einen Ausflug buchen

How much does the tour cost?	**Wie viel kostet die Rundfahrt?** *vee feel kostet dee runtfaart*
Is lunch included?	**Ist das Mittagessen inbegriffen?** *ist dass mittaagessen inbegriffen*
Where do we leave from?	**Wo fahren wir ab?** *voa faaren veer ap*
What time does the tour start?	**Wann beginnt die Rundfahrt?** *van begint dee runtfaart*
What time do we get back?	**Wann sind wir zurück?** *van zint veer tsoorewk*
Do we have free time in ...?	**Haben wir in ... Zeit zur freien Verfügung?** *haaben veer in ... tsiet tsoor frieen fehrfewgung*
Is there an English-speaking guide?	**Gibt es einen Englisch sprechenden Führer?** *gipt ess ienen english shprekhenden fewrer*

On tour Unterwegs

Are we going to see ...?	**Werden wir ... sehen?** *vehrden veer ... zayen*
We'd like to have a look at the ...	**Wir möchten ... sehen.** *veer murkhten ... zayen*
Can we stop here ...?	**Können wir hier anhalten, ...?** *kurnen veer heer anhalten*
to take photographs	**um Fotos zu machen** *um foatoas tsoo makhen*
to buy souvenirs	**um Reiseandenken zu kaufen** *um riezeandenken tsoo kowfen*
for the bathrooms/toilets	**um zur Toilette zu gehen** *um tsoor twoaletter tsoo gayen*
Would you take a photo of us, please?	**Würden Sie bitte ein Foto von uns machen?** *vewrden zee bitter ien foatoa fon uns makhen*
How long do we have here/in ...?	**Wie viel Zeit haben wir hier/in ... zur Verfügung?** *vee feel tsiet haaben veer heer/in ... tsoor fehrfewgung*
Wait! ... isn't back yet.	**Warten Sie! ... ist noch nicht da.** *varten zee ... ist nokh nikht daa*

Where is …? Wo ist …?

Town maps are on display in city centers, train, streetcar and many bus stations, and at tourist information offices.

Where is the …	**Wo ist …** *voa ist*
abbey	**die Abtei** *dee aptie*
art gallery	**die Kunstgalerie** *dee kunstgalehree*
battle site	**das Schlachtfeld** *dass shlakhtfelt*
botanical garden	**der Botanische Garten** *dehr botaanisher garten*
castle	**das Schloss** *dass shloss*
cathedral	**der Dom** *dehr doam*
cemetery	**der Friedhof** *dehr freet-hoaf*
church	**die Kirche** *dee keerkher*
city wall	**die Stadtmauer** *dee shtatmower*
downtown area	**die Innenstadt** *dee innenshtat*
fountain	**der Brunnen** *dehr brunnen*
harbor	**der Hafen** *dehr haafen*
market	**der Markt** *dehr markt*
monastery	**das Kloster** *dass kloaster*
museum	**das Museum** *dass muzayum*
old town	**die Altstadt** *dee altshtat*
opera house	**das Opernhaus** *dass oapernhowss*
palace	**der Palast** *dehr palast*
park	**der Park** *dehr park*
parliament building	**das Parlamentsgebäude** *dass parlamentsgeboyder*
shopping area	**das Geschäftsviertel** *dass geshehftsfeertel*
statue	**die Statue** *dee shtaatuer*
theater	**das Theater** *dass tayaater*
town hall	**das Rathaus** *dass raat-howss*
university	**die Universität** *dee unnivehrzitait*
Can you show me on the map?	**Können Sie es mir auf der Karte zeigen?** *kurnen zee ess meer owf dehr karter tsiegen*

DIRECTIONS ➤ 94

Admission Eintritt

Museums are usually closed on Mondays and on important holidays (Christmas, New Year's Day, and so on). Usual opening hours are from 9 a.m. to 4 p.m.

Is the … open to the public?	**Ist … der Öffentlichkeit zugänglich?** *ist … dehr urfentlikhkiet tsoogehnglikh*
Can we look around?	**Können wir uns umsehen?** *kurnen veer uns umzayen*
What are the opening hours?	**Was sind die Öffnungszeiten?** *vass zint dee urfnungztsieten*
When does it close?	**Wann schließt er/sie/es?** *van shleest ehr/zee/ess*
Is … open on Sundays?	**Ist … sonntags geöffnet?** *ist … zontaags geurfnet*
When is the next guided tour?	**Wann ist die nächste Führung?** *van ist dee naikhster fewrung*
Do you have a guidebook (in English)?	**Haben Sie einen Reiseführer (auf Englisch)?** *haaben zee ienen riezefewrer (owf ennglish)*
Can I take pictures?	**Darf ich fotografieren?** *darf ikh fottografeeren*
Is there access for the disabled?	**Ist es für Behinderte zugänglich?** *ist ess fewr behinderter tsoogehnglikh*
Is there an audio guide in English?	**Gibt es einen Audio-Führer auf Englisch?** *gipt ess ienen owdiofewrer owf ennglish*

Paying/Tickets Bezahlen/Eintrittskarten

How much is the entrance fee?	**Was kostet der Eintritt?** *vass kostet dehr eintri*
Are there discounts for …?	**Gibt es Ermäßigungen für …?** *gipt ess ehrmaissiggungen fewr*
children	**Kinder** *kinder*
disabled	**Behinderte** *behinderter*
groups	**Gruppen** *gruppen*
seniors	**Rentner** *rentner*
students	**Studenten** *shtuddenten*
1 adult and 2 children please.	**Ein Erwachsener und zwei Kinder, bitte.** *ien ehrvaksener unt tsvie kinder bitter*

- Fünf Eintrittskarten, bitte. Gibt es Ermäßigungen?
- *Ja. Kinder und Rentner zahlen sieben Mark fünfzig.*
- Zwei Erwachsene und drei Kinder, bitte.
- *Das macht achtundvierzig Mark fünfzig, bitte.*

EINTRITT FREI	Admission free
EINTRITT VERBOTEN	No entry
FOTOGRAFIEREN VERBOTEN	No photography
GEÖFFNET	Open
GESCHLOSSEN	Closed
GESCHENKLADEN	Gift shop
LETZER EINTRITT 17 UHR	Latest entry at 5 p.m.
NÄCHSTE FÜHRUNG UM …	Next tour at …
ÖFFNUNGSZEITEN	Visiting hours

Impressions Eindrücke

It's …	**Es ist …** *ess ist*
amazing	**erstaunlich** *ehrshtownlikh*
beautiful	**schön** *shurn*
bizarre	**merkwürdig** *mehrkvewrdikh*
boring	**langweilig** *langvielikh*
breathtaking	**atemberaubend** *atemberowbent*
brilliant	**großartig** *groassartikh*
It's great fun.	**Es macht Spaß.** *ess makht shpaass*
interesting	**interessant** *interessant*
magnificent	**großartig** *groassartikh*
pretty	**hübsch** *hewbsh*
romantic	**romantisch** *rommantish*
strange	**seltsam** *zeltzaam*
stunning	**hinreißend** *hinriessent*
superb	**phantastisch** *fantastish*
terrible	**schrecklich** *shreklikh*
ugly	**hässlich** *hesslikh*
It's good value.	**Es ist preiswert.** *ess ist priesvayrt*
It's a rip off.	**Es ist Wucher.** *ess ist vookher*
I like it.	**Es gefällt mir.** *ess gefehlt meer*
I don't like it.	**Es gefällt mir nicht.** *ess gefehlt meer nikht*

Tourist glossary
Sehenswürdigkeiten

Altarbild altarpiece
Altertum antiquity
Altertümer antiquities
Aquarell watercolor
ausgeliehen an on loan to
Ausgrabungen excavations
Ausstellung display, exhibition
Ausstellungsstück exhibit
Backsteingotik Gothic style brick buildings
Badeanlagen baths
... begonnen started in ...
Bernstein amber
Bibliothek library
Bild picture
Bildhauer(in) sculptor
Bogen arch
Bronzezeit bronze age
Bühne stage
Buntglasfenster stained glass window
Burg castle
Chor(stuhl) choir (stall)
Dach roof
darstellen represent
Dom cathedral
Druck print
Ebene 1 level 1
Edelstein gemstone
Ehrenmal cenotaph
Eingang doorway
Einzelheit detail
Elfenbein ivory
Empore/Galerie gallery
... entdeckt discovered in ...
entworfen von ... designed by ...
Entwurf design
... erbaut erected/built in ...
Erker oriel window
... fertiggestellt completed in ...

Fachwerk half-timber
Festung fort/fortress
Friedhof cemetery
Flohmarkt flea market
Flügel wing (of building)
Gartenanlage formal garden
Gasse alley
Gebäude building
Geburtshaus von ... birthplace of ...
... geboren born in ...
Gefäß vessel
... gegründet founded in ...
Gemächer apartments (*royal*)
Gemälde canvas (*painting*)
Gemälde painting
gemalt von ... painted by ...
gestiftet von ... donated by ...
... gestorben died in ...
Gewölbe vault
Grab grave
Grabmal tomb
Grabstein headstone
Gründerzeit Founders' Period
Grundriss plan
Hallenkirche hall church
Hauptschiff nave
Herrenhaus manor house
Herrschaft reign
Hof courtyard
im Stil des/der in the style of
in Auftrag gegeben von commissioned by
interaktives Ausstellungsstück interactive exhibit
Jahrhundert century
Jugendstil Art Nouveau
Jungsteinzeit Neolithic Period
Kaiser emperor
Kaiserin empress
Kanzel pulpit

Kapelle	chapel
Keramik	ceramics
König	king
Königin	queen
Kreuz	cross
Kreuzzug	crusade
Krone	crown
Kunst	art
Kunsthandwerk	crafts
Künstler(in)	artist
Kupferstich	etching
Kuppel	dome
Landschaft	landscape (*painting*)
lebte	lived
Leinwand	canvas (*material*)
Leuchtturm	lighthouse
Maler(in)	painter
Marmor	marble
Maßstab 1:100	scale 1:100
Mauer	wall
Meisterwerk	masterpiece
Mittelalter	Middle Ages
mittelalterlich	medieval
Mittelschiff	nave
Möbel	furniture
Münze	coin
Ölfarben	oils
Orgel	organ
Pfeiler	pillar
Plastik	sculpture
Platz	square
Portal	porch
Prunkzimmer	stateroom
Rathaus	town/city hall
Romanik	Romanesque
Römer	Romans
Querhaus	transept
Sammlung	collection
Säule	pillar
Schloss	castle
Schmuck	decoration, jewelry
Schiefer	slate
Schnitzerei	carving
Schule des/der	school of
Seitenschiffe	side aisles
silbern	silver
Sims	sill
Skizze	sketch
Sockel	base
Spätgotik	late Gothic
Stadtmauer	city wall
Stein	stone
Steinzeit	Stone Age
Stich	engraving
Stil	style
Strebepfeiler	buttress
Tafel	plaque
Taufstein	font
Ton	clay
Töpferwaren	pottery
Tor	gate
Treppe	staircase
Turm	tower, spire
Uhr	clock
vergoldet	gilded
Vierung	crossing (architecture)
von	by (person)
Vortrag	lecture
vorübergehendes Ausstellungsstück	temporary exhibit
Wachsfigur	waxwork
Waffe	weapon
Wand	wall
Wandgemälde	mural
Wandteppich	tapestry
Wassergraben	moat
Wasserleitung	aqueduct
Wasserspeier	gargoyle
... wieder aufgebaut in ...	rebuilt in ...
Zeichnung	drawing
zeitgenössische Kunst	contemporary art
zerstört von ...	destroyed by ...
Ziegel	brick
Zinne	battlement

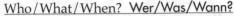

Who/What/When? Wer/Was/Wann?

What's that building?	**Was ist das für ein Gebäude?** *vass ist dass fewr ien geboyder*
Who was the ...?	**Wer war der ...?** *vayr var dehr*
architect/artist	**Architekt/Künstler** *arkhitekt/kewnstler*
When was it built/painted?	**Wann wurde es erbaut/gemalt?** *van voorder ess ehrbowt/gemaalt*
What style is that?	**Was ist das für ein Stil?** *vas ist das fewr ien stil?*
What period is that?	**Aus welcher Zeit ist das?** *owss velkher tsiet ist dass*

Karolinger/karolingisch   (mid ca. 8–10 century)
Pre-romanesque architectural style characterized by round and polygonal churches (e.g. the Palatine Chapel in Aachen Cathedral) and churches with two chancels (e.g. The Benedictine Abbey Church of Corvey).

Romanik   (mid ca. 11–mid ca. 13 century)
A somewhat geometric style evident in church architecture and sculpture and in manuscript illumination (e.g. the Cologne region, Speyer, and Mainz).

Gotik/Spätgotik   (mid ca. 13–mid ca. 16 century)
Characterized by slender towers, lofty pointed vaulting, flying buttresses and sculptural decoration (e.g. the cathedrals of Cologne, Regensburg and Freiburg-im-Breisgau).

Barock/Rokoko   (1630–1780)
The Baroque style was characterized by irregularity of form and great variety, aiming to give the overall effect of movement. The Rococo was the extreme form of this and resulted in elaborate decoration.

Biedermeier   (1816–1848)
Style of art and furniture design characterized by comfortable, cushioned, lightweight furniture with flowing lines and glass-fronted cupboards. Painters of this style were Ferdinand Waldmüller and Karl Spitzweg.

Jugendstil   (1890–1905)
The German equivalent of Art Nouveau, Jugendstil developed in Germany and Austria as a reaction against the extravagance of contemporary interior decoration. It first appeared in art and later in furniture, vases and building façades. An example 0used in interior design is at the Schauspielhaus in Munich. Architects: Peter Behrens, Hans Poelzig; painter: Gustav Klimt.

Bauhaus   (1920–1930)
Architectural school inspired in its style by the fundamental theme of the marriage of art and technique (e.g. the Bauhaus, Dessau; sections of the Weissenhof Siedlung; the Hauptbahnhof in Stuttgart; Chilehaus, Hamburg).

Rulers Herrscher

das Fränkische Reich (481–919)

Frankish dynasty, founded by Clovis I, saw the development of
Christianity amid a period of colonization. In 800 Charlemagne
was crowned Emperor of the Holy Roman Empire and he
expanded the Empire over Europe.

die Reformation (1500–1550)

In 1517, Martin Luther published his "95 theses" in Wittenberg.

Friedrich der Große (1740–1786)

Under Frederick the Great, Prussia's borders were expanded.

das Deutsche Reich (1871–1918)

This period was characterized by Prussian domination and struggles
between church and state. The First World War was the culmination
and downfall of this empire.

Weimarer Republik (1918–1933)

After the abdication of the Kaiser, Germany adopted a Republican
Constitution and made its first attempt at democracy.

das Dritte Reich (1933–1945)

Hitler founded a totalitarian state, led by his dictatorship, or Third Reich,
the aim of which was world domination. Defeat for Germany in the Second
World War finally resulted in Hitler's fall from power.

Wiedervereinigung (1989–90)

The Berlin Wall opened in 1989 and in March 1990 East Germans held free
elections for the first time. The re-unification treaty was signed by East and
West Germany in August 1990 and took effect in October 1990.

Churches/Religious services Kirchen/Gottesdienste

Although large churches are normally open to the public during the day,
services should be respected and most churches request that bare shoulders
are covered before entering.

Catholic church	**katholische Kirche** _katoalisher keerkher_
Protestant church	**evangelische Kirche** _evangaylisher keerkher_
mosque	**Moschee** _moshay_
synagogue	**Synagoge** _zewnagoager_
What time is …?	**Wann ist …?** _van ist_
mass/the service	**die Messe/der Gottesdienst** _dee messer/dehr gottesdeenst_

I'd like a map of …	**Ich hätte gern eine Karte …** *ikh hetter gehrn iener karter*
this region	**von dieser Gegend** *fon deezer gaygent*
walking routes	**mit Wanderwegen** *mit vandervaygen*
bicycle routes	**mit Radwegen** *mit raatvaygen*
How far is it to …?	**Wie weit ist es nach …?** *vee viet ist ess naakh*
Is there a right of way?	**Darf man dort hingehen?** *darf man dort heengayen*
Is there a trail to …?	**Gibt es einen Wanderweg nach …?** *gipt ess ienen vandervayk naakh*
Can you show me on the map?	**Können Sie es mir auf der Karte zeigen?** *kurnen zee ess meer owf dehr karter tsiegen*
I'm lost (on foot/driving).	**Ich habe mich verlaufen/verfahren.** *ikh haaber mikh fehrlowfen/fehrfaaren*

Organized walks/hikes Organisierte Wanderungen

When does the guided walk/hike start?	**Wann beginnt die geführte Wanderung?** *van begint dee gefewrter vanderung*
When will we return?	**Wann kommen wir zurück?** *van kommen veer tsoorewk*
What is the walk/hike like?	**Wie ist die Wanderung?** *vee ist dee vanderung*
gentle/medium	**leicht/mittel** *liekht/mittel*
tough	**anstrengend** *anshtrengent*
I'm exhausted.	**Ich bin erschöpft.** *ikh bin ehrshurpft*
How high is that mountain?	**Wie hoch ist dieser Berg?** *vee hoakh ist deezer behrg*
What kind of … is that?	**Was für … ist das?** *vass fewr … ist dass*
animal/bird	**ein Tier/ein Vogel** *ien teer/ien foagel*
flower/tree	**eine Blume/ein Baum** *iener bloomer/ien bowm*

Geographic features
Geographische Gegebenheiten

bridge	**die Brücke** *dee brewker*
cave	**die Höhle** *dee hurler*
cliff	**die Klippe** *dee klipper*
field	**das Feld** *dass felt*
footpath	**der Fußweg** *dehr foosvayg*
forest	**der Wald** *dehr valt*
glacier	**der Gletscher** *dehr glecher*
gorge	**die Schlucht** *dee shlukht*
hill	**der Hügel** *dehr hewgel*
lake	**der See** *dehr zay*
mountain	**der Berg** *dehr berg*
mountain range	**das Gebirge** *dass gebeerger*
nature reserve	**das Naturschutzgebiet**
	dass natoorshutsgebeet
panorama	**das Panorama** *dass panoraama*
park	**der Park** *dehr park*
pass	**der Pass** *dehr pass*
path	**der Weg** *dehr vayg*
peak	**der Gipfel** *dehr gipfel*
picnic area	**der Picknickplatz** *dehr piknikplats*
pond	**der Teich** *dehr tiekh*
rapids	**die Stromschnellen**
	dee shtroamshnellen
river	**der Fluss** *dehr fluss*
sea	**das Meer** *dass mayr*
spa	**die Heilbad** *dee hielbahd*
spring	**die Quelle** *dee kweller*
stream	**der Bach** *dehr bakh*
track	**der Weg** *dehr vayg*
valley	**das Tal** *das taal*
viewpoint	**der Aussichtspunkt**
	dehr owssikhtspunkt
vineyard	**der Weinberg** *dehr vienbehrg*
waterfall	**der Wasserfall** *dehr vasserfal*
wood	**der Wald** *dehr valt*

Leisure

Events Veranstaltungen

Local papers and, in large cities, weekly entertainment guides will tell you what's on. In many larger cities such as Berlin, Frankfurt, and Munich, you'll even find publications in English.

Do you have a program of events?	**Haben Sie einen Veranstaltungskalender?** *haaben zee ienen fehranshtaltungzkalender*
Can you recommend a …?	**Können Sie … empfehlen?** *kurnen zee … empfaylen*
Is there a … on somewhere?	**Wird irgendwo … gegeben?** *veert eergentvoa … gegayben*
ballet	**ein Ballett** *ien ballet*
concert	**ein Konzert** *ien kontsehrt*
Is there a movie on somewhere?	**Wird irgendwo ein Film gezeigt?** *veert eergentvoa ien film getsiegt*
opera	**eine Oper** *iener oaper*

Tickets for concerts, theater, and other cultural events are on sale at special ticket agencies. In small towns these may be in kiosks, book or music stores ask at the local tourist office.

Availability Erhältlichkeit

Where can I get tickets?	**Wo kann ich Karten kaufen?** *voa kan ikh karten kowfen*
Are there any seats for tonight?	**Gibt es für heute Abend noch Karten?** *gip ess fewr hoyter aabent nokh karten*
There are … of us.	**Wir sind … Personen.** *veer zint … pehrzoanen*
When does it start/end?	**Wann fängt es an/hört es auf?** *van fehngt ess an/hurt ess owf*

Tickets Eintrittskarten

How much are the seats?	**Wie viel kosten diese Plätze?** *vee feel kosten deezer plehtser*
Do you have anything cheaper?	**Haben Sie etwas Billigeres?** *haaben zee etvass billigeress*
I'd like to reserve …	**Ich möchte … vorbestellen.** *ikh murkhter … foarbeshtelen*
3 for Sunday evening	**drei für Sonntagabend** *drie fewr sontaagaabent*
1 for Friday matinée	**eine Karte für die Nachmittagsvorstellung am Freitag** *iener karter fewr dee naakhmittaags foarstehlung am frietaag*
Where's the coat check?	**Wo ist die Garderobe?** *voa ist dee garderoaber*

Ihre Kreditkartennummer, bitte.	What's your credit card number?
Welche Kreditkarte ist es?	What's your credit card type?
Bis wann ist Ihre Kreditkarte gültig?	What's your credit card expiration date?
Bitte holen Sie die Karten … ab.	Please pick up the tickets …
vor neunzehn Uhr	by 7 p.m.
an der Vorverkaufskasse	at the box office

– *Goethe Theater, guten Tag.*
– Guten Tag. Ich hätte gern 2 Karten für "Doktor Faust" heute abend, bitte.
– *Natürlich. Ihre Kreditkartennummer, bitte.*
– Ja, 050 365 7854.
– *Welche Kreditkarte ist es?*
– VISA. Nehmen Sie VISA?
– *Ja, natürlich. Bis wann ist Ihre Kreditkarte gültig?*
– Juli achtundneunzig.
– *Danke. Bitte holen Sie die Karten an der Vorverkaufskasse ab.*

VORVERKAUF	Advance reservations
AUSVERKAUFT	Sold out
KARTEN FÜR HEUTE	Tickets for today

NUMBERS ➤ 216

109

Movies Kino

Foreign films are usually dubbed into German, but more and more cinemas are showing at least one film in the original English

Is there a multiplex cinema near here?	**Gibt es hier in der Nähe ein Multiplex-Kino?** *gipt ess heer in dehr naier ien multipleks-keeno*
What's playing at the movies?	**Was läuft heute abend im Kino?** *vass loyft hoyter aabent im keeno*
Is the film dubbed?	**Ist der Film synchronisiert?** *ist dehr film zewnkronizeert*
Is the film subtitled?	**Hat der Film Untertitel?** *hat dehr film unterteetel*
Is the film in the original English?	**Ist der Film in der englischen Originalfassung?** *ist dehr film in dehr englishen originaalfassung*
Who's the main actor?	**Wer spielt die Hauptrolle?** *vayr shpeelt dee howptroler*
A ..., please.	**..., bitte.** *... bitter*
box of popcorn	**Eine Schachtel Popcorn** *iener shakhtel "popcorn"*
chocolate ice cream	**Ein Schokoladeneis** *ien shokkolaadenies*
hot dog	**Ein heißes Würstchen** *ien hiessess vewrstkhen*
soft drink/soda	**Ein Erfrischungsgetränk** *ien ehrfrishungzgetrehnk*
small/regular/large	**klein/mittel/groß** *klien/mittel/groass*

Theater Theater

What's playing at the ... Theater?	**Was wird im ...-Theater gegeben?** *vass veert im ... -tayaater gegayben*
Who's the playwright?	**Wer ist der Autor?** *vayr ist dehr owtor*
Do you think I'd enjoy it?	**Glauben Sie, dass es mir gefallen würde?** *glowben zee dass ess meer gefallen vewrder*
I don't know much German.	**Ich spreche nicht viel Deutsch.** *ikh shprekher nikht feel doych*

Opera/Ballet/Dance Oper/Ballett/Tanz

The German-speaking countries have a strong music tradition: each major city has an opera house and you'll find concerts going on in even the smallest towns. The annual **Bayreuther Festspiele** (Wagner operas) is a spectacular event.

Who's the composer?	**Wer ist der Komponist?** *vayr ist dehr komponist*
Who's the soloist?	**Wer ist der Solist/die Solistin?** *vayr ist dehr zollist/dee zollistin*
Is formal dress expected?	**Wird Abendgarderobe erwartet?** *veert aabentgarderoaber ehrvartet*
Where's the opera house?	**Wo ist das Opernhaus?** *voa ist dass oapernhowss*
Who's dancing?	**Wer tanzt?** *vayr tantst*
I'm interested in contemporary dance.	**Ich interessiere mich für modernen Tanz.** *ikh interesseerer mikh fewr modehrnen tants*

Music/Concerts Musik/Konzerte

Where's the concert hall?	**Wo ist die Konzerthalle?** *voa ist dee kontsehrthaller*
Which orchestra/band is playing?	**Welches Orchester/Welche Band spielt?** *velkhess orkester/velkher bant shpeelt*
What are they playing?	**Was wird gespielt?** *vass veert geshpeelt*
Who is the conductor?	**Wer ist der Dirigent?** *vayr ist dehr dirigent*
Who is the soloist?	**Wer ist der Solist/die Solistin?** *vayr ist dehr zolist/dee zolistin*
I really like …	**Ich höre gern …** *ikh hurrer gehrn*
country music	**Countrymusik** *countrymuzeek*
folk music	**Volksmusik** *folksmuzeek*
jazz	**Jazz** *dzhaiss*
music of the 60s	**Musik aus den Sechzigern** *muzeek owss dayn zekhtsiggern*
rock music	**Rockmusik** *rokmuzeek*
soul music	**Soul** *"soul"*
Are they popular?	**Sind sie beliebt?** *zint zee beleebt*

111

Nightlife Nachtleben

What is there to do in the evenings?	**Was kann man abends unternehmen?** *vass kan man aabents unternaymen*
Can you recommend a ...?	**Können Sie ein ... empfehlen?** *kurnen zee ien ... empfaylen*
Is there a ... in town?	**Gibt es in der Stadt ...?** *gipt ess in dehr shtat*
bar	**eine Bar** *iener baar*
casino	**ein Spielkasino** *ien shpeelkazeeno*
disco	**eine Diskothek** *iener diskotayk*
gay club	**ein Gay Club** *ien gayklub*
nightclub	**einen Nachtklub** *ienen nakhtklub*
restaurant	**ein Restaurant** *ien restorahng*
Is there a floor show/cabaret?	**Wird dort eine Show/ein Varieté gezeigt?** *veert dort iener shoa/ien variaytay getsiegt*
What type of music do they play?	**Welche Art von Musik wird dort gespielt?** *velkher aart fon muzeek veert dort geshpeelt*
How do I get there?	**Wie komme ich dahin?** *vee kommer ikh dahin*

Admission Einlass

What time does the show start?	**Wann fängt die Show an?** *van fehngt dee shoa an*
Is evening dress required?	**Wird Abendgarderobe verlangt?** *veert aabentgarderoaber fehrlangt*
Is there a cover charge?	**Muss man Eintritt bezahlen?** *muss man ientrit bertsaalen*
Is a reservation necessary?	**Muss man reservieren?** *muss man rezehrveeren*
Do we need to be members?	**Müssen wir Mitglieder sein?** *mewssen veer mitgleeder zien*
How long will we have to stand in line?	**Wie lange müssen wir Schlange stehen?** *vee langer mewssen veer shlanger shtayer*
I'd like a good table.	**Ich hätte gern einen guten Tisch.** *ikh hetter gehrn ienen gooten tish*

Children Kinder

Can you recommend something for the children?	**Können Sie etwas für die Kinder empfehlen?** *kurnen zee etvass fewr dee kinder empfaylen*
Can I take a baby carriage in?	**Kann ich mit einem Kinderwagen hinein?** *kan ikh mit ienem kindervaagen hinien*
Are there changing facilities here for babies?	**Gibt es hier einen Wickelraum für Babys?** *gipt ess heer ienen vikkelrowm fewr baybis*
game/amusement arcade	**die Spielhalle** *dee shpeelhaller*
fairground	**der Festplatz** *dehr festplats*
kiddie pool	**das Planschbecken** *dass planshbeken*
playground	**der Spielplatz** *dehr shpeelplats*
play group	**die Spielgruppe** *dee shpeelgrupper*
puppet show	**das Puppenspiel** *dass puppenshpeel*
zoo	**der Zoo** *dehr tsoa*

Baby-sitting Kinderbetreuung

Can you recommend a reliable babysitter?	**Können Sie eine zuverläßige Kinderbetreuung empfehlen?** *kurnen zee iener tsoofehrlehssiger kinderbetroyung empfaylen*
Is there constant supervision?	**Werden die Kinder ständig beaufsichtigt?** *vayrden dee kinder shtehndikh beowfzikhtigt*
Are the helpers properly trained?	**Sind die Helfer richtig ausgebildet?** *zint dee helfer rikhtikh owsgebildet*
When/Where can I drop them off?	**Wann/Wo kann ich sie abliefern?** *vann/voa kan ikh zee apleefern*
I'll pick them up at …	**Ich hole sie um … ab.** *ikh hoaler zee um … ap*
We'll be back by …	**Wir sind spätestens um … wieder da.** *veer zint shpaitestenss um … veeder daa*
What age is he/she?	**Wie alt ist er/sie?** *vee alt ist ehr/zee*
She's 3 and he's 18 months.	**Sie ist drei Jahre und er ist achtzehn Monate alt.** *zee ist drie jaarer unt ehr ist akhtsayn moanaater alt*

Sports Sport

Soccer/football is by far the most popular spectator sport, though you'll find almost all sports well represented. Hiking and cycling are the two most popular actitivites: in most rural areas there are **Wanderwege** (marked paths) and there are designated bicycle paths alongside most roads. Water sports, golf, tennis, fishing and horse back riding are also popular and skiing conditions can be among the best in the world (➤ 117).

Watching Zuschauer

Is there a football game/ soccer match this Saturday?	**Findet diesen Samstag ein Fußballspiel statt?** *findet deezen zamstaag ien foosbalshpeel shtat*
Which teams are playing?	**Welche Mannschaften spielen?** *velkher manshaften shpeelen*
Can you get me a ticket?	**Können Sie mir eine Karte besorgen?** *kurnen zee meer iener karter bezoargen*
What's the admission charge?	**Was kostet der Eintritt?** *vass kostet dehr ientrit*
Where's the racetrack/course?	**Wo ist die Pferderennbahn?** *voa ist dee pfayrderenbaan*
Where can I place a bet?	**Wo kann ich eine Pferdewette abschließen?** *voa kan ikh iener pfayrdevetter apshleesen*
What are the odds on ...?	**Wie stehen die Chancen für ...?** *vee shtayen dee shangsen fewr*

athletics	**Leichtathletik** *liekhtatlayteek*
basketball	**Basketball** *baasketbal*
cycling	**Rad fahren** *raat faaren*
soccer/football	**Fußball** *foosbal*
golf	**Golf** *golf*
horse racing	**Pferderennen** *pfayrderenen*
swimming	**Schwimmen** *shvimmen*
tennis	**Tennis** *tenniss*
volleyball	**Volleyball** *vollibal*

aying Sport treiben

Where's the nearest …?	**Wo ist der nächste …?** *voa ist dehr naikhster*
golf course	**Golfplatz** *golfplats*
sports club	**Sportverein** *shportfehrien*
Where are the tennis courts?	**Wo sind die Tennisplätze?** *voa zint dee tennisplehtser*
What's the charge per …?	**Wie viel kostet es pro …?** *vee feel kostet ess proa*
day / round / hour	**Tag/Runde/Stunde** *taag/runder/shtunder*
Do I need to be a member?	**Muss man Mitglied sein?** *muss man mitgleet zien*
Where can I rent / hire …?	**Wo kann ich … mieten?** *voa kan ikh … meeten*
shoes	**Schuhe** *shooer*
clubs	**Schläger** *shlayger*
equipment	**die Ausrüstung** *dee owsrewstung*
a racket	**einen Schläger** *ienen shlayger*
Can I get tuition?	**Kann ich Stunden nehmen?** *kan ikh shtunden naymen*
Is there an aerobic class?	**Gibt es einen Aerobic-Kurs?** *gipt ess ienen ayrobbik-koors*
Do you have a fitness room?	**Haben Sie einen Fitness-Raum?** *haaben zee ienen fitness-rowm*
Can I join in?	**Kann ich mitspielen?** *kan ikh mitshpeelen*

Wir sind leider ausgebucht.	I'm sorry, we're booked up.
Sie müssen eine Kaution von … hinterlegen.	There is a deposit of …
Welche Größe haben Sie?	What size are you?
Sie brauchen ein Passbild.	You need a passport-size photo.

UMKLEIDERÄUME	Changing rooms
ANGELN VERBOTEN	No fishing
ANGELN NUR MIT	Fishing for permit
ANGELSCHEIN	holders only

At the beach Am Strand

Try the North Sea and Baltic coast for swimming and sailing
the Frisean and Baltic Islands offer quieter beaches for those
not bothered by a brisk wind.

The lakes in the area surrounding the Alps provide good sailing
and fishing and will often have small secluded beaches.

Is the beach pebbly/sandy?	**Ist es ein Kiesstrand/Sandstrand?** *ist ess ien kees-shtrant/zantshtrant*
Is there a … here?	**Gibt es hier …?** *gipt ess heer*
children's pool	**ein Kinderbecken** *ien kinderbekken*
swimming pool	**ein Schwimmbad** *ien shvimbaat*
indoor/open-air pool	**ein Hallenbad/Freibad** *ien hallenbaat/friebaat*
Is it safe to swim/dive here?	**Kann man hier gefahrlos baden/tauche** *kan man heer gefaarloass baaden/towkhen*
Is it safe for children?	**Ist es für Kinder ungefährlich?** *ist ess fewr kinder ungefairlikh*
Is there a lifeguard?	**Gibt es einen Rettungsschwimmer?** *gipt ess ienen rettungzshvimmer*
I want to rent/hire a/some …	**Ich möchte … mieten.** *ikh murkhter … meeten*
deck chair	**einen Liegestuhl** *ienen leegeshtool*
jet ski	**Jet-Ski** *jet-ski*
motorboat	**ein Motorboot** *ien moatorboat*
rowboat	**ein Ruderboot** *ien rooderboat*
sailboat	**ein Segelboot** *ien zaygelboat*
skin-diving equipment	**eine Taucherausrüstung** *iener towkherowsrewstung*
umbrella/sunshade	**einen Sonnenschirm** *ienen zonnenshirm*
surfboard	**ein Surfbrett** *ien "surf"bret*
waterskis	**Wasserskier** *vassershee-er*
windsurfer	**einen Windsurfer** *ienen vint"surfer"*
For … hours.	**Für … Stunden.** *fewr … shtunden*

Skiing   Ski fahren

Austria and Switzerland are at the heart of Europe's skiing, with excellent slopes and usually a traditional atmosphere. Resorts vary from the very fashionable and expensive to the cozy conviviality often found in small resorts; the choice is yours!

Is there much snow?	**Liegt viel Schnee?** *leegt veel shnay*
What's the snow like?	**Wie ist der Schnee?** *vee ist dehr shnay*
I'd like to rent/hire …	**Ich möchte … mieten.** *ikh murkhter … meeten*
poles	**Skistöcke** *sheeshturker*
skates	**Schlittschuhe** *shlitshooer*
ski boots	**Skischuhe** *sheeshooer*
skis	**Skier** *shee-er*
These are too …	**Sie sind zu …** *zee zint tsoo*
big/small	**groß/klein** *groass/klien*
loose/tight	**locker/eng** *loker/eng*
uncomfortable	**unbequem** *unbekvaym*
A lift pass for a day/5 days, please.	**Eine Liftkarte für einen Tag/fünf Tage, bitte.** *iener liftkarter fewr ienen taag/fewnf taager bitter*
I'd like to join the ski school. I'm …	**Ich möchte Skiunterricht nehmen. Ich bin …** *ikh murkhter sheeunterikht naymen. ikh bin*
a beginner	**Anfänger** *anfehnger*
experienced	**fortgeschritten** *fortgeshritten*

DRAHTSEILBAHN/GONDEL	cable car/gondola
SESSELLIFT	chair lift
SCHLEPPLIFT	drag lift

Making Friends

Introductions Vorstellung

Greetings vary according to how well you know someone.
The following is a guide:
It's polite to shake hands, both when you meet and say good-bye; when being introduced into a group, men will shake hands first with women and then with men.
In German, there are three forms for "you" (taking different verb forms):
du (informal/singular) and **ihr** (informal/plural) are used when talking to relatives, close friends, colleagues and children (and between young people);
Sie (formal) is used in all other cases (singular and plural). It's polite to address adults as Mr. and Mrs. **(Herr and Frau)** and to speak to them using the formal form of "you" **(Sie)** until you are asked to use the familiar form **(du)**.

Hello, we haven't met.	**Guten Tag, wir kennen uns nicht.** *gooten taag veer kennen uns nikht*
My name is …	**Ich heiße …** *ikh hiesser*
May I introduce …?	**Darf ich … vorstellen?** *darf ikh … foarshtehlen*
John, this is …	**John, das ist …** *John dass ist*
Pleased to meet you.	**Sehr angenehm.** *zayr angenaym*
What's your name?	**Wie heißen Sie?** *vee hiessen zee*
I'm sorry, I didn't catch your name.	**Es tut mir leid, ich habe Ihren Namen nicht verstanden.** *ess toot meer liet ikh haaber eeren naamen nikht fehrshtanden*
How are you?	**Wie geht es Ihnen?** *vee gayt ess eenen*
Fine, thanks. And you?	**Danke, gut. Und Ihnen?** *danker goot. unt eenen*

> – Guten Tag.
> – *Guten Tag, wie geht es Ihnen?*
> – Danke, sehr gut. Und Ihnen?
> – *Danke, gut.*

here are you from? Woher kommen Sie?

Where do you come from?	**Woher kommen Sie?** *voahayr kommen zee*
Where were you born?	**Wo sind Sie geboren?** *voa zint zee geboaren*
I'm from ...	**Ich komme aus ...** *ikh kommer owss*
Australia	**Australien** *owstraalien*
Britain	**Großbritannien** *groasbritanien*
Canada	**Kanada** *kanada*
England	**England** *englant*
Ireland	**Irland** *eerlant*
New Zealand	**Neuseeland** *noyzaylant*
Scotland	**Schottland** *shotlant*
U.S.	**den USA** *dayn oo-ess-aa*
Wales	**Wales** *"Wales"*
Where do you live?	**Wo wohnen Sie?** *voa voanen zee*
What part of ... are you from?	**Aus welchem Teil von ... kommen Sie?** *owss velkhem tiel fon ... kommen zee*
Austria	**Österreich** *ursteriekh*
Germany	**Deutschland** *doychlant*
Switzerland	**der Schweiz** *dehr shviets*
We come here every year.	**Wir kommen jedes Jahr hierher.** *veer kommen yaydess yaar heerhayr*
It's my/our first visit.	**Ich bin/Wir sind zum ersten Mal hier.** *ikh bin/veer zint tsum ehrsten maal heer*
Have you ever been to Britain/ the U.S.?	**Sind Sie schon einmal in Großbritannien/in den USA gewesen?** *zint zee shoan ienmaal in groasbritanien/in dayn oo-ess-aa gevayzen*
I love (the) ... here.	**... hier gefällt mir sehr gut.** *heer gefehlt meer zayr goot*
I don't care for (the) ... here.	**... hier gefällt mir nicht besonders gut.** *heer gefehlt meer nikht bezonders goot*
countryside	**die Landschaft** *dee lantshaft*
cuisine	**die Küche** *dee kewkher*

119

Who are you with? Mit wem sind Sie hi

I'm on my own.	**Ich bin allein hier.** *ikh bin alien heer*
I'm with a friend.	**Ich bin mit einem Freund/einer Freundin** *ikh bin mit ienem froynt/iener froyndin hee*
I'm with my ...	**Ich bin mit ... hier.** *ikh bin mit ... heer*
wife	**meiner Frau** *miener frow*
husband	**meinem Mann** *mienem man*
family	**meiner Familie** *miener fameelier*
children	**meinen Kindern** *mienen kindern*
parents	**meinen Eltern** *mienen eltern*
boyfriend/girlfriend	**meinem Freund/meiner Freundin** *mienem froynt/miener froyndin*
father/mother	**der Vater/die Mutter** *dehr faater/dee mutter*
son/daughter	**der Sohn/die Tochter** *dehr zoan/dee tokhter*
brother/sister	**der Bruder/die Schwester** *dehr brooder/dee shvester*
uncle/aunt	**der Onkel/die Tante** *dehr onkel/dee tanter*
What's your son's/wife's name?	**Wie heißt Ihr Sohn/Ihre Frau?** *vee hiesst eer zoan/eerer frow*
I'm ...	**Ich bin ...** *ikh bin*
married/single	**verheiratet/unverheiratet (ledig)** *fehrhieraatet/unfehrhieraatet (lehdikh)*
divorced	**geschieden** *gesheeden*
I'm separated.	**Ich lebe getrennt.** *ikh layber getrent*
We live together.	**Wir leben zusammen.** *veer layben tsoozamen*
Do you have any children?	**Haben Sie Kinder?** *haaben zee kinder*
2 boys and a girl.	**zwei Jungen und ein Mädchen.** *tsvie yungen unt ien maitkhen*
How old are they?	**Wie alt sind sie?** *vee alt zint zee*
They're ten and twelve.	**Sie sind zehn und zwölf.** *zee zint tsayn unt tsvurlf*

What do you do?
Was machen Sie beruflich?

What are you studying?	**Was studieren Sie?** *vass shtuddeeren zee*
I'm studying …	**Ich studiere …** *ikh shtudeerer*
sciences	**Naturwissenschaften** *natoorvissenshaften*
the arts	**Geisteswissenschaften** *giestesvissenshaften*
I'm in business.	**Ich bin Geschäftsmann/Geschäftsfrau.** *ikh bin geshehftsman/geshehftsfrow*
I'm in …	**Ich bin im … tätig.** *ikh bin im … taitikh*
engineering	**Ingenieurwesen** *insheniurvayzen*
retail	**Einzelhandel** *ientselhandel*
sales	**Verkauf** *fehrkowf*
Who do you work for?	**Bei welcher Firma arbeiten Sie?** *bie velkher feerma aarbieten zee*
I work for …	**Ich arbeite bei …** *ikh aarbieter bie*
I'm a/an …	**Ich bin …** *ikh bin*
accountant [*fem.*]	**Buchhalter[in]** *bookhhalter[in]*
housewife	**Hausfrau** *howsfrow*
student [*fem.*]	**Student[in]** *shtudent[in]*
I'm …	**Ich bin …** *ikh bin*
retired	**pensioniert** *pensioaneert*
self-employed	**selbständig** *zelbshtehndikh*
What are your hobbies?	**Was haben Sie für Hobbys?** *vass haaben zee fewr hobbiss*
I like music.	**Ich höre gern Musik.** *ikh hurer gehrn muzeek*
I like reading.	**Ich lese gern.** *ikh layzer gehrn*
I like sport.	**Ich treibe gern Sport.** *ikh trieber gehrn shport*
I play …	**Ich spiele …** *ikh shpeeler*
chess/cards	**Schach/Karten** *shakh/karten*

What weather! Was für ein Wetter!

What a lovely day!	**Was für ein herrlicher Tag!** *vass fewr ien hehrlikker taag*
What awful weather!	**Was für ein schreckliches Wetter!** *vass fewr ien shreklikhess vetter*
Isn't it cold/hot today!	**Was für eine Kälte/Hitze heute!** *vass fewr iener kehlter/hitser hoyter*
Is it usually as warm/cold as this?	**Ist es immer so warm/kalt?** *ist ess immer zoa varm/kalt*
Do you think it's going to … tomorrow?	**Glauben Sie, es wird morgen …?** *glowben zee ess veert morgen*
be a nice day	**schön** *shurn*
rain	**regnen** *raygnen*
snow	**schneien** *shnieen*
What is the weather forecast?	**Was sagt der Wetterbericht?** *vass zaagt dehr vetterberikht*
It's …	**Es ist …** *ess ist*
cloudy	**bewölkt** *bevurlkt*
foggy	**neblig** *nayblikh*
frosty	**frostig** *frostikh*
icy	**eisig** *iezikh*
rainy	**regnerisch** *raygnerish*
windy	**windig** *vindikh*
thundery	**gewitterig** *gevitterikh*
It's snowy.	**Es schneit.** *ess shniet*
Has the weather been like this for long?	**Ist das Wetter schon lange so?** *ist dass vetter shoan langer zoa*
What's the pollen count?	**Wie hoch ist der Pollenflug?** *vee hoakh ist dehr pollenfloog*
high/medium/low	**hoch/mittel/niedrig** *hoakh/mittel/needrikh*
What's the forecast for skiing?	**Wie ist der Wintersportbericht?** *vee ist dehr vintershportberikht*

Enjoying your trip?
Gefällt Ihnen Ihre Reise?

Sind Sie im Urlaub?	Are you on vacation?
Wie sind Sie hergekommen?	How did you get here?
Wie war die Fahrt?	How was the journey?
Wo wohnen Sie?	Where are you staying?
Wie lange sind Sie schon hier?	How long have you been here?
Wie lange bleiben Sie?	How long are you staying?
Wohin fahren Sie als nächstes?	Where are you going next?
Gefällt Ihnen Ihr Urlaub?	Are you enjoying your vacation?

I'm here on ...	**Ich bin ... hier.** *ikh bin ... heer*
a business trip	**geschäftlich** *geshehftlikh*
vacation/holiday	**im Urlaub** *im oorlowp*
We came by ...	**Wir sind mit ... gekommen.** *veer zint mit ... gekomen*
train/bus/plane	**der Bahn/dem Bus/dem Flugzeug** *dehr baan/daym buss/daym floogtsoyg*
car/ferry	**dem Auto/der Fähre** *daym owto/dehr fairer*
We're staying in ...	**Wir wohnen ...** *veer voanen*
an apartment	**in einer Ferienwohnung** *in iener fayrienvoanung*
a hotel	**in einem Hotel** *in ienem hottel*
with friends	**bei Freunden** *bie froynden*
We're staying on a campsite.	**Wir sind auf einem Campingplatz.** *veer zint owf ienem kempingplats*
We've visited ...	**Wir haben ... besichtigt.** *veer haaben ... bezikhtiggt*
Can you suggest ...?	**Können Sie vorschlagen, ...?** *kurnen zee foarshlaagen*
things to do	**was wir unternehmen können** *vass veer unternaymen kurnen*
places to eat	**wo wir essen können** *voa veer essen kurnen*
places to visit	**was wir besichtigen können** *vass veer bezikhtigen kurnen*
We're having a great/ awful time.	**Es gefällt uns sehr gut/überhaupt nicht.** *ess gefehlt uns zayr goot/ ewberhowpt nikht*

Invitations Einladungen

Would you like to have dinner with us on …?	**Möchten Sie am … mit uns zu Abend essen?** *murkhten zee am … mit uns tsoo aabent essen*
May I invite you to lunch?	**Darf ich Sie zum Mittagessen einladen?** *darf ikh zee tsum mittaagessen ienlaaden*
Can you come for a drink this evening?	**Kommen Sie heute Abend auf ein Gläsche** *kommen zee hoyter aabent owf ien glaiskhen*
We are having a party. Can you come?	**Wir geben eine Party. Können Sie komme** *veer gayben iener paartee. kurnen zee kommen*
May we join you?	**Dürfen wir uns zu Ihnen setzen?** *dewrfen veer uns tsoo eenen zetsen*
Would you like to join us?	**Möchten Sie sich zu uns setzen?** *murkhten zee zikh tsoo uns zetsen*

Going out Ausgehen

What are your plans for …?	**Was haben Sie … vor?** *vass haaben zee … foar*
today / tonight	**heute/heute Abend** *hoyter/hoyter aabent*
tomorrow	**morgen** *morgen*
Are you free this evening?	**Sind sie heute Abend frei?** *zint zee hoyter aabent frie*
Would you like to …?	**Möchten Sie gern …?** *murkhten zee gehrn*
go dancing	**tanzen gehen** *tantsen gayen*
go for a drink	**ein Gläschen trinken gehen** *ien glaiskhen trinken gayen*
go for a meal	**essen gehen** *essen gayen*
go for a walk	**spazieren gehen** *shpatseeren gayen*
go shopping	**einkaufen gehen** *ienkowfen gayen*
Where would you like to go?	**Wohin möchten Sie gehen?** *voahin murkhten zee gayen*
Do you enjoy …?	**Gehen Sie gern …?** *gayen zee gehrn*
shopping / dancing	**einkaufen/tanzen** *ienkowfen/tantsen*
I'd rather …	**Ich würde lieber …** *ikh vewrder leeber*
go to the movies	**ins Kino gehen** *ins keeno gayen*
go for a walk	**spazieren gehen** *shpatseeren gayen*

ccepting/Declining
nnehmen–Ablehnen

Great. I'd love to.	**Danke, sehr gern.** *danker zayr gehrn*
Thank you, but I'm busy.	**Vielen Dank, aber ich habe keine Zeit.** *feelen dank aaber ikh haaber kiener tsiet*
May I bring a friend?	**Darf ich einen Freund/eine Freundin mitbringen?** *darf ikh ienen froynt/iener froyndin mitbringen*
Where shall we meet?	**Wo treffen wir uns?** *voa treffen veer uns*
I'll meet you …	**Wir treffen uns …** *veer treffen uns*
in the bar	**in der Bar** *in dehr baar*
in front of your hotel	**vor Ihrem Hotel** *foar eerem hottel*
I'll pick you up at 8.	**Ich hole Sie um acht Uhr ab.** *ikh hoaler zee um akht oor ap*
Could we make it a bit later/earlier?	**Geht es etwas später/früher?** *gayt ess etvass shpaiter/frewer*
How about another day?	**Vielleicht ein andermal?** *feelliekht ien andermaal*
That will be fine.	**Das ist in Ordnung.** *dass ist in ordnung*

ining out/in Eine Einladung zum Essen

If you are invited home for a meal, always take a gift – a bottle of wine, sparkling wine, chocolates or flowers.

Let me buy you a drink.	**Möchten Sie etwas trinken?** *murkhten zee etvass trinken*
Do you like …?	**Mögen Sie …?** *murgen zee*
What are you going to have?	**Was nehmen Sie?** *vass naymen zee*
Are you enjoying your meal?	**Schmeckt Ihnen das Essen?** *shmekt eenen dass essen*
That was a lovely meal.	**Das war ein herrliches Essen.** *dass vaar ien hehrlikhess essen*

Socializing Begegnungen

Are you waiting for someone?	**Warten Sie auf jemanden?** *vaarten zee owf yaymanden*
Do you mind if I …?	**Stört es Sie, wenn ich …?** *shturt ess zee ven ikh*
sit here/smoke	**hier sitze/rauche** *heer zitser/rowkher*
Can I get you a drink?	**Möchten Sie etwas trinken?** *murkhten zee etvass trinken*
I'd love to have some company.	**Ich hätte gern Gesellschaft.** *ikh hetter gehrn gezelshaft*
Why are you laughing?	**Warum lachen Sie?** *varum lakhen zee*
Is my German that bad?	**Ist mein Deutsch so schlecht?** *ist mien doych zoa shlekht*
Shall we go somewhere quieter?	**Sollen wir irgendwohin gehen, wo es ruhiger ist?** *zollen veer eergentvoahin gayen voa ess roo-iger ist*
Leave me alone, please!	**Lassen Sie mich bitte in Ruhe!** *lassen zee mikh bitter in rooer*
I'm not ready for that.	**Das möchte ich nicht.** *dass murkhter ikh nikht*
You look great!	**Du siehst wunderbar aus!** *doo zeest vunderbaar owss*
I'm afraid we've got to leave now.	**Wir müssen jetzt leider gehen.** *veer mewssen yetst lieder gayen*
Thanks for the evening.	**Danke für den Abend.** *danker fewr dayn aabent*
Can I see you again tomorrow?	**Kann ich Sie morgen wiedersehen?** *kan ikh zee morgen veederzayen*
See you soon.	**Bis bald.** *biss balt*
Can I have your address?	**Kann ich Ihre Adresse haben?** *kan ikh eerer adresser haaben*

Telephoning Telefonieren

Public telephone booths take either phonecards or coins. Phonecards (**Telefonkarten**) are available at the post office, some newsstands and currency exchange offices.

To phone home from German-speaking countries, dial 00 followed by: Australia 61; Canada 1; Ireland 353; New Zealand 64; South Africa 27; UK 44; U.S. 1.

Phone numbers are given in pairs, and note that in telephoning **zwei** becomes **zwo**.

Can I have your telephone number?	**Kann ich Ihre Telefonnummer haben?** *kan ikh eerer taylayfoan-numer haaben*
Here's my number.	**Das ist meine Nummer.** *dass ist miener numer*
Please call me.	**Bitte rufen Sie mich an.** *bitter roofen zee mikh an*
I'll give you a call.	**Ich rufe Sie an.** *ikh roofer zee an*
Where's the nearest telephone booth?	**Wo ist die nächste Telefonzelle?** *voa ist dee naikhster taylayfoantseler*
May I use your phone?	**Darf ich Ihr Telefon benutzen?** *darf ikh eer taylayfoan benutsen*
It's an emergency.	**Es handelt sich um einen Notfall.** *ess handelt zikh um ienen noatfal*
I'd like to call someone in England/U.S./Canada.	**Ich möchte nach England/USA/Kanada. telefonieren** *ikh murkhter naakh englant/ oo-es-aa/kanada taylay-foneeren*
What's the area code for …?	**Was ist die Vorwahl von …?** *vass ist dee foarvaal fon*
I'd like a phonecard, please.	**Ich hätte gern eine Telefonkarte.** *ikh hetter gehrn iener taylayfoankarter*
What's the number for Directory Assistance?	**Welche Nummer hat die Auskunft?** *velkher nummer hat dee owskunft*
I'd like the number for …	**Ich möchte die Nummer für …** *ikh murkhter dee nummer fewr*
I'd like to call collect/reverse the charges.	**Ich möchte ein R-Gespräch anmelden.** *ikh murkhter ien ehr-geshpraikh anmelden*

Speaking Am Apparat

Hello. This is …	**Hallo. Hier spricht …** *halloa. heer shprikht*
I'd like to speak to … please.	**Ich möchte … sprechen.** *ikh murkhter … shprekhen*
Extension …	**Apparat …** *aparaat*
Speak louder/more slowly,	**Sprechen Sie bitte etwas lauter/langsame** *shprekhen zee bitter etvass lowter/langzaamer*
Could you repeat that, please.	**Können Sie das bitte wiederholen.** *kurnen zee dass bitter veederhoalen*
I'm afraid he/she's not in.	**Er/Sie ist leider nicht da.** *ehr/zee ist lieder nikht daa*
You've got the wrong number.	**Sie sind falsch verbunden.** *zee zint falsh fehrbunden*
Just a moment.	**Einen Augenblick, bitte.** *ienen owgenblik bitter*
When will he/she be back?	**Wann ist er/sie wieder da?** *van ist ehr/zee veeder daa*
Will you tell him/her that I called?	**Würden Sie ihm/ihr sagen, dass ich angerufen habe?** *vewrden zee eem/eer zaagen dass ikh angeroofen haaber*
My name is …	**Mein Name ist …** *mien naamer ist*
Would you ask him/her to phone me?	**Würden Sie ihn/sie bitten, mich anzurufen** *vewrden zee een/zee bitten mikh antsooroofen*
Would you take a message, please?	**Würden Sie bitte etwas ausrichten?** *vewrden zee bitter etvass owsrikhten*
I must go now.	**Ich muss jetzt aufhören.** *ikh muss yetst owfhuren*
Nice to speak to you.	**Es war nett, mit Ihnen zu sprechen.** *ess vaar net mit eenen tsoo shprekhen*
I'll be in touch.	**Ich melde mich wieder.** *ikh melder mikh veeder*
Bye.	**Auf Wiederhören.** *owf veederhuren*

Stores & Services

Germany still places the emphasis on small, traditional specialist shops, offering a more personal experience, although modern shopping malls (**Einkaufszentrum**) are to be found on the outskirts of most towns; these types of shops often accept credit cards.

Local markets can be found everywhere, from big cities to the smallest regional towns.

While shopping, why not take time out to head to a **Café** or **Kaffeehaus** to enjoy the traditional afternoon coffee break (**Kaffee und Kuchen**).

ESSENTIAL

I'd like …	**Ich hätte gern …** *ikh hetter gehrn*
Do you have …?	**Haben Sie …?** *haaben zee*
How much is that?	**Was kostet das?** *vass kostet dass*
Thank you.	**danke** *danker*

Stores and services
Geschäfte und Dienstleistungen

Where is …? Wo ist …?

Where's the nearest …? **Wo ist der/die/das nächste …?**
voa ist dehr/dee/dass naikhster

Where's there a …? **Wo gibt es einen/eine/ein …?**
voa gipt ess ienen/iener/ien

Where's the main shopping mall? **Wo ist das Haupteinkaufszentrum?**
voa ist dass howptienkowfstsentrum

Is it far from here? **Ist es weit von hier?** *ist ess viet fon heer*

How do I get there? **Wie komme ich dorthin?**
vee kommer ikh dorthin

Stores Geschäfte

antique store	**das Antiquitätengeschäft** *dass antikvitaitengesheft*
bakery	**die Bäckerei** *dee behkerie*
bank	**die Bank** *dee bank*
bookstore	**die Buchhandlung** *dee bookhhandlung*
butcher shop	**die Fleischerei/Metzgerei** *dee fliesherie/metsgerie*
camera shop	**das Fotogeschäft** *dass foatogeshehft*
clothing store	**das Bekleidungsgeschäft** *dass bekliedungzgeshehft*
delicatessen	**das Feinkostgeschäft** *dass fienkostgeshef...*
department store	**das Kaufhaus** *dass kowfhowss*
drugstore	**die Apotheke** *dee apotayker*
fish store	**das Fischgeschäft** *dass fishgeshehft*
florist's	**das Blumengeschäft** *dass bloomengesheh...*
gift shop	**der Geschenkladen** *dehr geshenklaaden*
grocery store	**das Lebensmittelgeschäft** *dass laybensmittelgeshehft*
health food store/shop	**der Naturkostladen** *dehr natoorkostlaade...*
hardware store	**die Eisenwarenhandlung** *dee iezenvaarenhandlung*

130

jewelry store	**der Juwelier** *dehr yuveleer*
market	**der Markt** *dehr markt*
pastry shop	**die Konditorei** *dee konditorrie*
produce store	**die Gemüsehandlung** *dee gemewzehandlung*
record (music) store	**das Plattengeschäft** *dass plattengesehft*
shoe store	**das Schuhgeschäft** *dass shoogesehft*
shopping mall/center	**das Einkaufszentrum** *dass ienkowfstsentrum*
souvenir store	**der Andenkenladen** *dehr andenkenlaaden*
sporting goods store	**das Sportgeschäft** *dass shportgesehft*
supermarket	**der Supermarkt** *dehr zoopermarkt*
tobacconist's/tobacco store	**das Tabakgeschäft** *dass tabakgesehft*
toy store	**das Spielwarengeschäft** *dass shpeelvaarengesehft*
liquor store	**die Wein und Spirituosenhandlung** *dee vien- unt shpiritoo-oazenhandlung*

Services Dienstleistungen

dentist	**der Zahnarzt** *dehr tsaanaartst*
doctor	**der Arzt** *dehr aartst*
dry-cleaner's	**die Reinigung** *dee rienigung*
fax bureau	**das Telefaxbüro** *dass taylayfaksbewroa*
hairdresser's (ladies/men)	**der Friseur (Damen/Herren)** *dehr frizur (daamen-/hehren-)*
hospital	**das Krankenhaus** *dass krankenhowss*
laundromat	**der Waschsalon** *dehr vashzalong*
library	**die Bücherei** *dee bewkherie*
optician	**der Optiker** *dehr optiker*
police station	**die Polizei** *dee pollitsie*
polyclinic	**die Poliklinik** *dee polikleenik*
post office	**das Postamt** *dass posstamt*
travel agency	**das Reisebüro** *dass riezebewroa*
ticket agency	**die Kartenvorverkaufsstelle** *dee kartenforfehrkowfs-shteler*

Opening hours Öffnungszeiten

When does the ... open/shut?	**Wann öffnet/schließt ...?** *van urfnet/shleest*
Are you open in the evening?	**Haben Sie abends geöffnet?** *haaben zee aabents geurfnet*
Do you close for lunch?	**Haben Sie mittags geschlossen?** *haaben zee mittaags geshlossen*

General times for:	Opening	Closing	Lunch break	closed
stores	8/9 (8)	6:30(8.30 Thu) (6) [6.30]	12-1/2	Sat (from 2 p.m) except first Sat of month, Sun
post office	8 (7.30) [9]	6 (5) (6.30) [6]	none (12-2) 12-2 [1.45]	Sat p.m., Sun weekend
banks	8.30 (9) [8.30]	4 (5.30 Thu) (3.30/4) [4.30–5.30]	1-2.30 12.30–1.30	weekend weekend

Where is the ...	**Wo ist ...?** *voa ist*
cashier	**die Kasse** *dee kasser*
escalator	**die Rolltreppe** *dee roltreper*
elevator	**der Fahrstuhl/Lift** *dehr faarshtool/lift*
store guide	**der Kaufhaus-Wegweiser** *dehr kowfhowss-vaygviezer*
It's on the ...	**Er/sie/es ist im ...** *ehr/zee/ess ist im*
ground (*U.S.* first) floor	**Erdgeschoss** *ehrdgeshoss*
first (*U.S.* second) floor	**ersten Stock** *ehrsten shtok*

GESCHÄFTSZEITEN	business hours
GESCHLOSSEN	closed
DURCHGEHEND GEÖFFNET	open all day
AUSGANG	exit
EINGANG	entrance
FAHRSTUHL	elevator
NOTAUSGANG	(emergency/fire) exit
ROLLTREPPE	escalator
STANDORT	you are here
TREPPE	stairs

Service Bedienung

Can you help me?	**Können Sie mir helfen?** *kurnen zee meer helfen*
I'm looking for …	**Ich suche …** *ikh zookher*
I'm just browsing.	**Ich sehe mich nur um.** *ikh zayer mikh noor um*
It's my turn.	**Ich bin an der Reihe.** *ikh bin an dehr rie-er*
Do you have any …?	**Haben Sie …?** *haaben zee*
I'd like …	**Ich hätte gern …** *ikh hetter gehrn*
I'd like to buy …	**Ich möchte … kaufen.** *ikh murkhter … kowfen*
Could you show me …?	**Können Sie mir … zeigen?** *kurnen zee meer … tsiegen*
How much is this/that?	**Was kostet dies/das?** *vass kostet deez/dass*
That's all, thanks.	**Danke, das ist alles.** *danker dass ist alless*

Guten Morgen/Guten Tag.	Good morning/afternoon.
Werden Sie schon bedient?	Are you being served?
Kann ich Ihnen helfen?	Can I help you?
Wer ist der Nächste?	Who's next?
Was wünschen Sie?	What would you like?
Da muss ich eben nachsehen.	I'll just check that for you.
Ist das alles?	Is that everything?
Sonst noch etwas?	Anything else?

– *Kann ich Ihnen helfen?*
– Nein, danke. Ich sehe mich nur um.
– *Bitte.*
– Entschuldigen Sie.
– *Ja, kann ich Ihnen helfen?*
– Was kostet das?
– *Moment, da muss ich eben*
nachsehen … achtundneunzig Mark.

Preference Vorliebe

GRAMMAR

Comparatives and superlatives of adjectives are formed by adding **-er** (**-r**) and **-est** (**-st**) respectively, very often together with an **Umlaut**.

alt (old)   **älter** (older)   **ältest** (oldest)
kurz (short)   **kürzer** (shorter)   **kürzest** (shortest)
See also page 169 for an explanation of the agreement of adjectives.

Welche … möchten Sie?	What … would you like?
Farbe/Form	color/shape
Qualität/Menge	quality/quantity
Welche Art möchten Sie?	What sort would you like?
An welche Preislage haben Sie gedacht?	What price range are you thinking of?

I don't want anything too expensive.	**Ich möchte nichts allzu Teures.** *ikh murkhter nikhts altsoo toyress*
In the region of … DM.	**Um die … Mark.** *um dee … mark*
It must be …	**Es muss … sein.** *ess muss … zien*
big/small	**groß/klein** *groass/klien*
cheap/expensive	**preiswert/teuer** *priesvayrt/toyer*
dark/light	**dunkel/hell** *dunkel/hell*
light/heavy	**leicht/schwer** *liekht/shvayr*
oval/round/square	**oval/rund/quadratisch** *oavaal/runt/kvadraatish*
genuine/imitation	**echt/imitiert** *ekht/imiteert*
Do you have anything …?	**Haben Sie etwas …?** *haaben zee etvass*
larger/smaller	**Größeres/Kleineres** *grursseress/klieneress*
better quality	**Besseres** *besseress*
cheaper	**Preiswerteres** *priesvayrteress*
Can you show me …?	**Können Sie mir … zeigen?** *kurnen zee meer … tsiegen*
that/this one/these/those ones	**das da/dieses hier/diese da/diese dort** *dass daa/deezess heer/deezer daa/deezer dort*

134   COLORS ➤ 143

Conditions of purchase Kaufbedingungen

Is there a warranty? **Ist darauf Garantie?**
ist darowf garantee

Are there any instructions with it? **Ist eine Gebrauchsanweisung dabei?**
ist iener gebrowkhsanviezung dabie

Out of stock Nicht vorrätig

Es tut mir leid, wir haben keine.	I'm sorry, we haven't any.
Wir haben es nicht vorrätig.	We're out of stock.
Können Sie mir etwas anderes/ein anderes Modell zeigen?	Can I show you something else/a different sort?
Sollen wir es Ihnen bestellen?	Shall we order it for you?

Can you order it for me? **Können Sie es mir bestellen?**
kurnen zee ess meer beshtelen

How long will it take? **Wie lange dauert das?**
vee langer dowert dass

Where else might I get ...? **Wo sonst könnte ich ... bekommen?**
voa zonst kurnter ikh ... bekommen

Decision Entscheidung

That's not quite what I want. **Es ist nicht ganz das, was ich möchte.**
ess ist nikht gants dass vass ikh murkhter

No, I don't like it. **Nein, das gefällt mir nicht.**
nien dass gefehlt meer nikht

That's too expensive. **Das ist zu teuer.** *dass ist tsoo toyer*

I'd like to think about it. **Ich muss es mir überlegen.**
ikh muss ess meer ewberlaygen

I'll take it. **Ich nehme es.** *ikh naymer ess*

– Können Sie mir bitte
diesen Hut dort zeigen?
– *Selbstverständlich. Ich hole ihn eben herunter.*
– Danke ... Hm, es ist nicht
ganz das, was ich suche.
– *Also, wir haben auch anderes
Modelle und verschiedene Farben.*
– Nein, danke. Trotzdem vielen Dank.

Paying Bezahlen

VAT or sales tax (**MwSt**) is imposed on almost all goods and services. Tax can be reclaimed on larger purchases when returning home (outside the EU).

Small businesses tend not to accept credit cards and cash is much more widely used. However, large stores, restaurants and hotels often accept major credit cards – look out for the signs on the door.

Where do I pay?	**Wo kann ich bezahlen?** *voa kan ikh betsaalen*
How much is that?	**Was kostet das?** *vass kostet dass*
Could you write it down, please?	**Können Sie das bitte aufschreiben?** *kurnen zee dass bitter owfshrieben*
Do you accept …?	**Nehmen Sie …?** *naymen zee*
this credit card	**diese Kreditkarte** *deezer kredeetkarter*
traveler's checks	**Reiseschecks** *riezesheks*
I'll pay …	**Ich bezahle …** *ikh betsaaler*
in cash	**bar** *baar*
by credit card	**mit Kreditkarte** *mit kredeetkarter*
Sorry, I don't have enough money.	**Es tut mir leid, ich habe nicht genug Geld dabei.** *ess toot meer liet ikh haaber nikht genoog gelt dabie*

Wie bezahlen sie?	How are you paying?
Diese Transaktion ist nicht akzeptiert worden.	This transaction has not been approved.
Diese Karte ist nicht gültig.	This card is not valid.
Darf ich Ihren Ausweis sehen?	May I have further identification?

Could I have a receipt please?	**Kann ich bitte eine Quittung haben?** *kan ikh bitter iener kvittung haaben*
I think you've given me the wrong change.	**Ich glaube, Sie haben mir falsch herausgegeben.** *ikh glowber zee haaben meer falsh hayrowsgegayben*
May I have a carrier bag, please?	**Kann ich bitte eine Tragetasche haben?** *kan ikh bitter iener traagetasher haaben*

KASSE	cashier

Complaints Beschwerden

This doesn't work.	**Das ist nicht in Ordnung.** *dass ist nikht in ordnung*
Can you exchange this, please?	**Können Sie das bitte umtauschen?** *kurnen zee dass bitter umtowshen*
I'd like a refund.	**Ich hätte gern mein Geld zurück.** *ikh hetter gehrn mien gelt tsoorewk*
Here's the receipt.	**Hier ist die Quittung.** *heer ist dee kvittung*
I don't have the receipt.	**Ich habe die Quittung nicht.** *ikh haaber dee kvittung nikht*
I'd like to see the manager.	**Ich möchte mit dem Geschäftsführer sprechen.** *ikh murkhter mit daym geshehftsfewrer shprekhen*

A **Reinigung** is a dry-cleaner, sometimes with a rapid service (**Schnellreinigung**). If you want a self-service laundromat, look for a **Waschsalon**.

Repairs/Cleaning Reparaturen/Reinigung

This is broken. Can you repair it?	**Das ist kaputt. Können Sie es reparieren?** *dass ist kaput. kurnen zee ess repareeren*
Do you have … for this?	**Haben Sie … hierfür?** *haaben zee … heerfewr*
a battery	**eine Batterie** *iener battehree*
replacement parts	**Ersatzteile** *ehrzatstieler*
There's something wrong with …	**Mit … stimmt etwas nicht.** *mit … shtimt etvass nikht*
I'd like this …	**Können Sie das bitte …?** *kurnen zee dass bitter*
cleaned/pressed	**reinigen/bügeln** *rieniggen/bewgeln*
Can you … this?	**Können Sie das …?** *kurnen zee dass*
alter/mend/patch	**ändern/reparieren/flicken** *ehndern/repareeren/flikken*
When will it/they be ready?	**Wann ist es/sind sie fertig?** *van ist ess/zint zee fehrtikh*
This isn't mine.	**Das gehört mir nicht.** *dass gehurt meer nikht*
There's … missing.	**Es fehlt …** *ess faylt*

Bank / Currency Exchange Office
Bank/Wechselstube

Currency	100 Pfennig (Pf) = 1 Deutsche Mark (DM)
	100 Groschen (g.) = 1 Austrian Schilling (ÖS)
	100 Rappen (Rp) = 1 Swiss Franc (Fr.)
Germany	Coins: 1, 2, 5, 10, 50 Pf.; 1, 2, 5, 10 DM
	Notes: 5, 10, 20, 50, 100, 500, 1,000 DM
Austria	Coins: 2, 5, 10, 20 g.; 1, 5, 10, 20 ÖS
	Notes: 20, 50, 100, 500, 1,000, 5,000 ÖS
Switzerland	Coins: 5, 10, 20 Rp; 1/2, 1, 2, 5 Fr.
	Notes: 10, 20, 50, 100, 500, 1000 Fr.

At some banks, cash can be obtained from ATMs with Visa, Eurocard, American Express and many other international cards. Instructions are often given in English. You can also change money at travel agencies and hotels, but the rate will not be as good. Remember your passport when you want to change money.

Where's the nearest …?	**Wo ist die nächste …?**
	voa ist dee naikhster
bank	**Bank** *bank*
bureau de change	**Wechselstube** *vekselshtoober*

Changing money Geldwechsel

Can I exchange foreign currency here?	**Kann ich hier Devisen wechseln?** *kan ikh heer dayveezen vekseln*
I'd like to change some dollars/pounds into DM.	**Ich möchte Dollar/Pfund in DM wechseln.** *ikh murkhter dollar/pfunt in day mark vekseln*
I want to cash some traveler's checks.	**Ich möchte Reiseschecks einlösen.** *ikh murkhter riezesheks ienlurzen*
What's the exchange rate?	**Wie ist der Wechselkurs?** *vee ist dehr vekselkoors*
How much commission do you charge?	**Welche Gebühr nehmen Sie?** *velkher gebewr naymen zee*
Could I have some small change, please.	**Kann ich bitte Kleingeld haben?** *kan ikh bitter kliengeld haaben*

DEVISEN	foreign currency
BANKGEBÜHREN	bank charges
ALLE TRANSAKTIONEN	all transactions
DRÜCKEN/ZIEHEN/DRÜCKEN	push/pull/press
KASSEN	cashiers
WECHSELSTUBE	bureau de change
GELDAUTOMAT	ATM/cash machine

Security Sicherheit

Kann ich … sehen?	Could I see …?
Ihren Pass	your passport
Ihren Ausweis	some identification
Ihre Scheckkarte	your bank card
Ihre Adresse, bitte.	What's your address?
Wo wohnen Sie?	Where are you staying?
Füllen Sie bitte dieses Formular aus.	Fill in this form, please.
Bitte unterschreiben Sie hier.	Please sign here.

Cash machines/ATMs Geldautomaten

Can I withdraw money on my credit card here?

Kann ich hier mit meiner Kreditkarte Geld abheben? *kan ikh heer mit miener kredeetkarter gelt aphayben*

Where are the ATMs/cash machines?

Wo sind die Geldautomaten? *voa zint dee geltowtomaaten*

Can I use my … card in the cash machine?

Nimmt der Geldautomat meine … Karte? *nimt dehr geltowtomaat miener … karter*

The cash machine has eaten my card.

Der Geldautomat hat meine Karte einbehalten. *dehr geltowtomaat hat miemer karter ienbehalten*

Pharmacy Apotheke

Pharmacies are easily recognized by their sign: a green cross, usually lit up. If you are looking for a pharmacy at night, on Sundays or holidays, you'll find the address of duty pharmacies **(Apotheken-Notdienst)** listed in the newspaper or displayed in any pharmacy windows.

Where's the nearest (all-night) pharmacy?	**Wo ist die nächste Apotheke (mit Nachtdienst)?** *voa ist dee naikhster apottayker (mit nakhtdeenst)*
What time does the pharmacy open/close?	**Wann öffnet/schließt die Apotheke?** *van urfnet/shleest dee apottayker*
Can you make up this prescription for me?	**Können Sie mir diese Medizin zubereiten?** *kurnen zee meer deezer meditseen tsooberieten*
Shall I wait?	**Soll ich darauf warten?** *zoll ikh darowf varten*
I'll come back for it.	**Ich hole es später ab.** *ikh hoaler ess shpaiter ap*
I am …	**Ich bin …** *ikh bin*
diabetic	**Diabetiker** *dee-abaytiker*
epileptic	**Epileptiker** *epileptiker*
I am on the pill.	**Ich nehme die Pille.** *ikh naymer dee piller*

Dosage instructions Dosierung

How much should I take?	**Wie viel soll ich einnehmen?** *vee feel zoll ikh iennaymen*
How often should I take it?	**Wie oft soll ich es einnehmen?** *vee oft zoll ikh ess iennaymen*
Is it suitable for children?	**Ist es für Kinder geeignet?** *ist ess fewr kinder geiegnet*

Nehmen Sie zwei Tabletten/ Teelöffel … ein.	Take 2 tablets/teaspoons …
vor/nach dem Essen	before/after meals
mit etwas Wasser	with water
ganz	whole
morgens/abends	in the morning/at night
… Tage lang	for … days

Asking advice Beratung

What would you recommend for …?	**Was empfehlen Sie gegen …?** *vass empfaylen zee gaygen*
a cold	**eine Erkältung** *iener ehrkehltung*
a cough	**Husten** *hoosten*
diarrhea	**Durchfall** *doorkhfal*
a hangover	**einen Kater** *ienen kaater*
hayfever	**Heuschnupfen** *hoyshnupfen*
insect bites	**Insektenstiche** *inzektenshtikher*
a sore throat	**Halsschmerzen** *hals-shmehrtsen*
sunburn	**Sonnenbrand** *zonnenbrant*
travel sickness	**Reisekrankheit** *riezekrankhiet*
an upset stomach	**Magenverstimmung** *maagenfehrstimmung*
Can I get it without a prescription?	**Kann ich das ohne Rezept bekommen?** *kan ikh dass oaner retsept bekommen*

Over-the-counter treatment Rezeptfreie Mittel

Can I have …?	**Ich hätte gern …** *ikh hetter gehrn*
antiseptic cream	**eine Wundsalbe** *iener vuntzalber*
(soluble) aspirin	**(lösliches) Aspirin** *(lurzlikhess) aspireen*
bandage	**einen Verband** *ienen fehrbant*
condoms	**Kondome** *kondoamer*
cottonballs	**Watte** *vatter*
insect repellent/spray	**ein Insektenschutzmittel/Insektenspray** *ien inzektenshutsmittel/inzektenshpray*
pain killers	**ein Schmerzmittel** *ien shmehrtsmittel*
vitamin tablets	**Vitamintabletten** *vittameentabletten*

Toiletries Toilettenartikel

I'd like ...	**Ich hätte gern ...**	*ikh hetter gehrn*
after shave	**ein Rasierwasser**	*ien razeervasser*
after sun lotion	**After-Sun-Creme**	*"after sun" kraym*
deodorant	**ein Deodorant**	*ien deh-odoarant*
lip salve	**einen Lippenbalsam**	*ienen lipernbalzaam*
moisturizing cream	**Feuchtigkeitscreme**	*foykhtikhkietskraym*
razor blades	**Rasierklingen**	*razeerklingen*
sanitary napkins	**Damenbinden**	*daamenbinden*
soap	**eine Seife**	*iener ziefer*
sun block	**einen Sonnenblocker**	*ienern zonnenblokker*
suntan cream/lotion	**Sonnencreme/Sonnenmilch**	*zonnenkraym/zonnenmilkh*
factor ...	**Lichtschutzfaktor ...**	*likhtshutsfaktor*
tampons	**Tampons**	*tampongs*
tissues	**Papiertaschentücher**	*papeertashentewkher*
toilet paper	**Toilettenpapier**	*twalettenpapeer*
toothpaste	**Zahnpasta**	*tsaanpasta*

For the baby Für das Baby

baby food	**Babynahrung**	*baybinaarung*
diapers	**Windeln**	*vindeln*
sterilizing solution	**Sterilisierlösung**	*shterilizeerlurzung*

Haircare Haarpflege

comb	**einen Kamm**	*ienen kam*
conditioner	**eine Spülung**	*iener shpewlung*
hair brush	**eine Haarbürste**	*iener haarbewrster*
hair mousse	**einen Schaumfestiger**	*ienen showmfestiger*
hair spray	**ein Haarspray**	*ien haarshpray*
shampoo	**ein Haarwaschmittel**	*ien haarvashmittel*

Clothing Bekleidung

Traditional national costume is still worn for special occasions in most parts of Germany, Austria and Switzerland but tends to look out of place elsewhere! If you want to buy a traditional costume as a gift, look for **Lederhosen** (knee-length leather trousers) for boys.

General Allgemeines

I'd like … **Ich hätte gern …** *ikh hetter gehrn*

Do you have any …? **Haben Sie …?** *haaben zee*

DAMENBEKLEIDUNG	ladies wear
HERRENBEKLEIDUNG	menswear
KINDERKLEIDUNG	children's wear

Color Farbe

I'm looking for something in … **Ich suche etwas in …**
ikh zookher etvass in

beige **beige** *bayzh*

black **schwarz** *shvarts*

blue **blau** *blow*

brown **braun** *brown*

green **grün** *grewn*

gray **grau** *grow*

orange **orange** *orrangzh*

pink **rosa** *roaza*

purple **violett** *viollet*

red **rot** *roat*

white **weiß** *viess*

yellow **gelb** *gelp*

light … **hell…** *hell*

dark … **dunkel…** *dunkel*

I want a darker/lighter shade. **Ich möchte einen dunkleren/helleren Farbton.** *ikh murkhter ienen dunkleren/helleren farbtoan*

Do you have the same in …? **Haben Sie das Gleiche in …?** *haaben zee dass gliekher in*

Clothes and accessories
Kleidungsstücke und Accessoires

I'd like ...	**Ich hätte gern ...** *ikh hetter gehrn*
belt	**einen Gürtel** *ienen gewrtel*
bikini	**einen Bikini** *ienen bikeeni*
blouse	**eine Bluse** *iener bloozer*
bra	**einen BH** *ienen bayhaa*
coat	**einen Mantel** *ienen mantel*
dress	**ein Kleid** *ien kliet*
handbag	**eine Handtasche** *iener hanttasher*
hat	**einen Hut** *ienen hoot*
jacket	**eine Jacke** *iener yaker*
jacket (of suit)	**ein Jackett** *ien zhakett*
jeans	**Jeans** *"jeans"*
leggings	**Leggings** *"leggings"*
pants	**eine Hose** *iener hoazer*
panty hose	**eine Strumpfhose** *iene shtrumpfhoazer*
pullover	**einen Pullover** *ienen pulloaver*
raincoat	**einen Regenmantel** *ienen raygenmantel*
scarf	**ein Halstuch** *ien halstookh*
shirt	**ein Hemd** *ien hemt*
shorts	**Shorts** *"shorts"*
shorts/briefs	**eine Unterhose** *iener unterhoazer*
skirt	**einen Rock** *ienen rok*
socks	**Socken** *zokken*
stockings	**Strümpfe** *shtrewmpfer*
suit	**einen Anzug** *ienen antsoog*
sunglasses	**eine Sonnenbrille** *iener zonnenbriller*
sweatshirt	**ein Sweatshirt** *ien "sweatshirt"*
swimming trunks	**eine Badehose** *iener baadehoazer*
swimsuit	**einen Badeanzug** *ienen baade-antsoog*
tie	**eine Krawatte** *iener kravatter*
tights	**eine Strumpfhose** *iener shtrumpfhoazer*
underpants	**eine Unterhose** *iener unterhoazer*
with long/short sleeves	**mit langen/kurzen Ärmeln** *mit langen/kurtsen ehrmeln*

Shoes Schuhe

I'd like a pair of ...   **Ich möchte ein Paar ...**
ikh murkhter ien paar

boots	**Stiefel** *shteefel*
thongs	**Badelatschen** *baadelachen*
sandals	**Sandalen** *zandaalen*
shoes	**Schuhe** *shooer*
slippers	**Hausschuhe** *hows-shooer*
sneakers	**Turnschuhe** *toornshooer*

Walking/hiking gear Wanderausrüstung

knapsack/backpack	**einen Rucksack** *ienen rukzak*
walking boots	**Wanderschuhe** *vandershooer*
waterproof jacket	**eine Regenjacke** *iener raygenyakker*
windbreaker	**einen Anorak** *ienen annorak*

Fabric Stoff

I want something in ...   **Ich möchte etwas in ...**
ikh murkhter etvass in

cotton	**Baumwolle** *bowmvoller*
denim	**Jeansstoff** *dzeens-shtof*
lace	**Spitze** *shpitser*
leather	**Leder** *layder*
linen	**Leinen** *lienen*
wool	**Wolle** *voller*
Is this ...?	**Ist das ...?** *ist dass*
pure cotton	**reine Baumwolle** *riener bowmvoller*
synthetic	**Synthetik** *zewntaytik*
Is it hand washable/machine washable?	**Kann man es von Hand/in der Maschine waschen?** *kan man ess fon hant/in dehr masheener vashen*

VON HAND WASCHEN	handwash only
NICHT BÜGELN	do not iron

145

Does it fit? Passt es?

Can I try this on?	**Kann ich es anprobieren?**	
	kan ikh ess anprobbeeren	
Where's the fitting room?	**Wo ist die Anprobekabine?**	
	voa ist dee anproabekabeener	
It fits well. I'll take it.	**Es passt gut. Ich nehme es.**	
	ess past goot. ikh naymer ess	
It doesn't fit.	**Es passt nicht.** *ess past nikht*	
It's too…	**Es ist zu …** *ess ist tsoo*	
short/long	**kurz/lang** *kurts/lang*	
tight/loose	**eng/weit** *eng/viet*	
Do you have this in size …?	**Haben Sie das in Größe …?**	
	haaben zee dass in grursser	
What size is this?	**Welche Größe ist das?**	
	velkher grursser ist dass	
Could you measure me, please?	**Können Sie bitte bei mir Maß nehmen?**	
	kurnen zee bitter bie meer maass naymen	
I don't know German sizes.	**Ich kenne die deutschen Größen nicht.**	
	ikh kenner dee doychen grurssen nikht	

Size Größe

	Dresses/Suits						Women's shoes			
American	8	10	12	14	16	18	6	7	8	9
British	10	12	14	16	18	20	$4^{1}/2$	$5^{1}/2$	$6^{1}/2$	$7^{1}/2$
Continental	36	38	40	42	44	46	37	38	40	41

	Shirts				Men's shoes							
American)												
British)	15	16	17	18	5	6	7	8	$8^{1}/2$	9	$9^{1}/2$	10 11
Continental	38	41	43	45	38	39	41	42	43		43 44	44 45

EXTRA GROSS	extra large (XL)
GROSS	large (L)
MITTEL	medium (M)
KLEIN	small (S)

1 centimeter (cm.) = 0.39 in.	1 inch = 2.54 cm.
1 meter (m.) = 39.37 in.	1 foot = 30.5 cm.
10 meters = 32.81 ft.	1 yard = 0.91 m.

Health and beauty Schönheitspflege

Tipping: Germany: 10–15%; Austria: 10–15%;
Switzerland: included.

I'd like to make an appointment.	**Ich hätte gern für morgen einen Termin.** *ikh hetter gehrn fewr morgen ienen tehrmeen*
I'd like a …	**Ich möchte …** *ikh murkhter*
facial	**eine Gesichtsbehandlung** *iener gezikhtsbehandlung*
manicure	**eine Maniküre** *iener manikewrer*
massage	**eine Massage** *iener masaazher*
waxing	**eine Wachsbehandlung** *iener vaksbehandlung*

Hairdresser Friseur

I'd like a …	**Bitte … Sie mir die Haare.** *bitter … zee meer dee haarer*
cut and blow-dry	**schneiden und fönen** *shnieden unt furnen*
shampoo and set	**waschen und legen** *vashen unt laygen*
I'd like a trim.	**Nur nachschneiden, bitte.** *noor naakhshnieden bitter*
I'd like my hair colored/tinted.	**Bitte färben/tönen Sie mein Haar.** *bitter fehrben/turnen zee mien haar*
I'd like my hair with a fringe.	**Bitte schneiden Sie mir einen Pony.** *bitter shnieden zee meer ienen ponni*
I'd like my hair highlighted/permed.	**Bitte machen Sie mir Strähnchen/eine Dauerwelle.** *bitter makhen zee meer shtrainkhen/iener dowerveller*
Don't cut it too short.	**Nicht zu kurz schneiden.** *nikht tsoo kurts shnieden*
A little more off the …	**Bitte … etwas kürzer.** *bitter … etvass kewrtser*
back/front	**hinten/vorne** *hinten/forner*
neck/sides	**im Nacken/an den Seiten** *im nakken/an dayn zieten*
top	**oben** *oaben*
That's fine, thanks.	**Das ist gut so, danke.** *dass ist goot zoa danker*

Household articles Haushaltsartik

	I'd like …	**Ich hätte gern …** *ikh hetter gehrn*
	adapter	**einen Adapter** *ienen adapter*
	aluminum foil	**Alufolie** *aaloofoalier*
bottle-opener		**einen Flaschenöffner** *ienen flashenurfner*
can opener		**einen Büchsenöffner** *ienen bewksenurfner*
candles		**Kerzen** *kehrtsen*
clothes pins		**Wäscheklammern** *vehsheklammern*
corkscrew		**einen Korkenzieher** *ienen korkentsee-er*
lightbulb		**eine Glühbirne** *iener glewbeerner*
matches		**Streichhölzer** *shtriekh-hultser*
paper napkins		**Papierservietten** *papeerzehrvietten*
plastic wrap		**Klarsichtfolie** *klaarzikhtfoalier*
plug (electrical)		**einen Stecker** *ienen shtekker*
plug (for sink)		**einen Stöpsel** *ienen shturpsel*
scissors		**eine Schere** *iener shayrer*
screwdriver		**einen Schraubenzieher** *ienen shrowbentse*

Cleaning products Putzmittel

bleach	**Bleichmittel** *bliekhmittel*
dish cloth	**einen Spüllappen** *ienen shpewl-lappen*
dishwashing detergent	**Spülmittel** *shpewlmittel*
garbage bags	**Müllbeutel** *mewllboytel*
laundry detergent	**Waschpulver** *vashpulver*
sponge	**einen Schwamm** *ienen shvam*

China/Cutlery Geschirr/Besteck

cups	**Tassen** *tassen*
forks	**Gabeln** *gaabeln*
glasses	**Gläser** *glaizer*
knives	**Messer** *messer*
mugs	**Becher** *bekher*
plates	**Teller** *teller*
spoons	**Löffel** *lurfel*
teaspoons	**Teelöffel** *taylurfel*

eweler Juwelier

Could I see …?	**Könnte ich … sehen?** *kurnter ikh … zayen*
this/that	**dies/das** *deez/dass*
It's in the window/ display cabinet.	**Es ist im Schaufenster/in der Vitrine.** *ess ist im shaoofenster/in dehr vitreener*
I'd like …	**Ich hätte gern …** *ikh hetter gehrn*
alarm clock	**einen Wecker** *ienen vekker*
battery	**eine Batterie** *iener battehree*
bracelet	**ein Armband** *ien armbant*
brooch	**eine Brosche** *iener brosher*
chain	**eine Kette** *iener ketter*
clock	**eine Uhr** *iener oor*
earrings	**Ohrringe** *oar-ringer*
necklace	**eine Halskette** *iener halsketter*
ring	**einen Ring** *ienen ring*
watch	**eine Uhr** *iener oor*

Materials Material

Is this real silver/gold?	**Ist das echt Silber/Gold?** *ist dass ekht zilber/golt*
Is there any certification for it?	**Gibt es eine Bescheinigung dazu?** *gipt ess iener beshieniggung datsoo*
Do you have anything in …?	**Haben Sie etwas in …?** *haaben zee etvass in*
copper	**Kupfer** *kupfer*
crystal	**Kristall** *kristal*
diamond	**Diamant** *diamant*
enamel	**Email** *ayma-ee*
gold	**Gold** *golt*
pearl	**Perle** *pehrler*
pewter	**Zinn** *tsin*
platinum	**Platin** *plaateen*
silver	**Silber** *zilber*
stainless steel	**Edelstahl** *aydelshtaal*
Do you have anything …?	**Haben Sie etwas …?** *haaben zee etvass*
gold plated	**vergoldet** *fehrgoldet*
silver plated	**versilbert** *fehrzilbert*

Newsstand / Bookstore
Zeitungskiosk/Buchhandlung

Foreign newspapers can usually be found at railway stations airports, or at newsstands in major cities.

Cigarettes can be bought from specialist tobacco shops, vending machines restaurants and supermarkets.

Do you sell English language books/newspapers?	**Verkaufen Sie englische Bücher/Zeitungen** *fehrkowfen zee englisher bewkher/ tsietungen*
I'd like …	**Ich hätte gern …** *ikh hetter gehrn*
book	**ein Buch** *ien bookh*
candy/sweets	**Süßigkeiten** *zewssikhkieten*
chewing gum	**Kaugummi** *kowgummi*
chocolate bar	**einen Schokoladenriegel** *ienen shokollaadenreegel*
cigarettes (packet of)	**eine Schachtel Zigaretten** *iener shakhtel tsigaretten*
cigars	**Zigarren** *tsigaren*
dictionary	**ein Wörterbuch** *ien vurterbookh*
German-English	**Deutsch-Englisch** *doych-english*
envelopes	**Briefumschläge** *breefumshlaiger*
guidebook of …	**einen Reiseführer von …** *ienen riezefewrer fon*
lighter	**ein Feuerzeug** *ien foyertsoyg*
magazine	**eine Zeitschrift** *iener tsietshrift*
map of the town	**einen Stadtplan** *ienen shtatplaan*
road map of …	**eine Straßenkarte von …** *iener shtraassenkarter fon*
matches	**Streichhölzer** *shtriekh-hultser*
newspaper	**eine Zeitung** *iener tsietung*
pen	**einen Kugelschreiber** *ienen koogelshrieber*
postcard	**eine Postkarte** *iener posstkarter*
stamps	**Briefmarken** *breefmarken*
tobacco	**Tabak** *tabak*

Photography Fotografie

I'm looking for a/an ...	**Ich suche ...** *ikh zookhe*
automatic camera	**eine Automatikkamera** *iener owtomateekameraa*
compact camera	**eine Kompaktkamera** *iener kompaktkameraa*
disposable camera	**eine Einwegkamera** *iener ienvaygkameraa*
I'd like a ...	**Ich hätte gern ...** *ikh hetter gehrn*
battery	**eine Batterie** *iener battehree*
camera case	**eine Fototasche** *iener foatotasher*
(electronic) flash	**einen (Elektronen)blitz** *ienen (aylektroanen)blits*
filter	**einen Filter** *ienen filter*
lens	**ein Objektiv** *ien obyekteef*
lens cap	**einen Objektivdeckel** *ienen obyekteefdekel*

Film/Processing Filme/Entwickeln

I'd like a ... for this camera.	**Ich hätte gern einen ... für diesen Fotoapparat.** *ikh hetter gehrn ienen ... fewr deezen foato-apparaat*
black and white film	**Schwarzweißfilm** *shvartsviesfilm*
color film	**Farbfilm** *farpfilm*
24/36 exposures	**vierundzwanzig/sechsunddreißig Aufnahmen** *feerunttsvantsikh/zeksuntdriessikh owfnaamen*
I'd like this film developed, please.	**Bitte entwickeln Sie diesen Film.** *bitter entvikeln zee deezen film*
Would you enlarge this, please?	**Können Sie das bitte vergrößern?** *kurnen zee dass bitter fehrgrurssern*
When will the photos be ready?	**Wann sind die Fotos fertig?** *van zint dee foatoss fehrtikh*
I'd like to pick up my photos. Here's the receipt.	**Ich möchte meine Fotos abholen. Hier ist der Schein.** *ikh murkhter miener foatoss aphoalen. heer ist dehr shien*

Police Polizei

Crime, theft, accidents or lost property should be reported to the nearest police department (**Polizei**).

To get the police in an emergency dial, ☎ 110 in Germany, ☎ 133 in Austria, ☎ 117 in Switzerland.

Where's the nearest police station?	**Wo ist die nächste Polizeiwache?** *voa ist dee naikhster pollitsievakher*
Does anyone here speak English?	**Spricht hier jemand Englisch?** *shprikht heer yaymant english*
I want to report …	**Ich möchte … melden.** *ikh murkhter … melden*
an accident	**einen Unfall** *ienen unfal*
an attack	**einen Überfall** *ienen ewberfal*
a mugging/rape	**einen Straßenraub/eine Vergewaltigung** *ienen shtraassenrowp/iener fehrgevaltigung*
My child is missing.	**Mein Kind ist verschwunden.** *mien kint ist fehrshvunden*
Here's a photo of him/her.	**Hier ist ein Foto von ihm/ihr.** *heer ist ien foato fon eem/eer*
Someone's following me.	**Ich werde verfolgt.** *ikh vayrder fehrfolgt*
I need an English-speaking lawyer.	**Ich brauche einen Englisch sprechenden Anwalt.** *ikh browkher ienen english shprekhenden anvalt*
I need to make a phone call.	**Ich muss telefonieren.** *ikh muss taylayfoneeren*
I need to contact the … Consulate.	**Ich muss mich mit dem … Konsulat in Verbindung setzen.** *ikh muss mikh mit daym … konsulaat in fehrbindung zetsen*
American/British	**amerikanischen/britischen** *amerikaanishen/brittishen*

Können Sie ihn/sie beschreiben?	Can you describe him/her?
männlich/weiblich	male/female
blond/brünett	blonde/brunette
rothaarig/grau	redheaded/gray
kurzes/langes/schütteres Haar	short/long hair/balding
ungefähre Größe …	approximate height …
(ungefähres) Alter …	aged (approximately) …
er/sie trug …	he/she was wearing …

CLOTHES ➤ 144; COLORS ➤ 143

Lost property/Theft Fundsachen/Diebstahl

I want to report a theft/break-in.	**Ich möchte einen Diebstahl/Einbruch melden.** *ikh murkhter ienen deepshtaal/ienbrukh melden*
I've been robbed/mugged.	**Ich bin bestohlen worden/auf der Straße überfallen worden.** *ikh bin beshtoalen vorden/owf dehr shtrasser ewberfallen vorden*
I've lost my …	**Ich habe … verloren.** *ikh haaber … fehrloaren*
Someone stole my …	**Jemand hat … gestohlen** *yemant hat … geshtoalen*
bicycle	**mein Fahrrad** *mien faaraat*
camera	**meine Kamera** *miener kameraa*
(rental) car	**meinen (Miet)wagen** *mienen (meet)vaagen*
credit cards	**meine Kreditkarten** *miener kredeetkarten*
handbag	**meine Handtasche** *miener hant-tasher*
money	**mein Geld** *mien gelt*
passport	**meinen Reisepass** *mienen riezepass*
purse	**meine Handtasche** *miener hanttasher*
ticket	**meine Fahrkarte** *miener faarkarter*
wallet	**meinen Geldbeutel** *mienen geltboytel*
watch	**meine Uhr** *miener oor*
What shall I do?	**Was soll ich tun?** *vass zoll ikh toon*
I need a police report for my insurance.	**Ich brauche eine polizeiliche Bescheinigung für meine Versicherung.** *ikh browkher iener pollitsielikher beshienigung fewr miener fehrzikherung*

Was fehlt?	What's missing?
Wann ist es passiert?	When did it happen?
Wo wohnen Sie?	Where are you staying?
Wo ist es gestohlen worden?	Where was it taken from?
Wo waren Sie zu der Zeit?	Where were you at the time?
Wir besorgen Ihnen einen Dolmetscher.	We're getting an interpreter for you.
Wir werden die Sache verfolgen.	We'll look into the matter.
Bitte füllen Sie dieses Formular aus.	Please fill in this form.

Post office Postamt

Swiss post offices are recognized by the **PTT** sign and in Aus
and Germany they are marked **Post.**

Mail boxes are yellow in Germany and Switzerland and blue
in Austria. They may have separate slots for postcards **(Postkarten**
letters **(Briefe)** and abroad **(Ausland)** or, in Switzerland **A** (first class) or **B**
(second class). Stamps can be bought from vending machines near mail
boxes, from some tobacconists and stationers, as well as from the post off

General queries Allgemeine Fragen

Where is the nearest/main post office?	**Wo ist das nächste Postamt/die Hauptpo** *voa ist dass naikhster posstamt/ dee howptposst*
What time does the post office open/close?	**Wann öffnet/schließt das Postamt?** *van urfnet/shleest dass posstamt*
Does it close for lunch?	**Ist es mittags geschlossen?** *ist ess mittaags geshlossen*
Where's the mailbox?	**Wo ist der Briefkasten?** *voa ist dehr breefkasten*
Where's the general delivery?	**Wo ist der Schalter für postlagernde Sendungen?** *voa ist dehr shalter fewr posstlaagernder zendungen*
Is there any mail for me? My name is ...	**Ist Post für mich da? Ich heiße ...** *ist posst fewr mikh daa? ikh hiesser ...*

Buying stamps Briefmarken kaufen

A stamp for this postcard/ letter, please.	**Eine Briefmarke für diese Postkarte/dies Brief, bitte.** *iener breefmarker fewr deezer posstkarter/deezen breef bitter*
A ...-Mark/-Pfennig stamp, please.	**Eine Briefmarke zu ... Mark/Pfennig, bit** *iener breefmarker tsoo ... mark/pfennikh*
What's the postage for a post ...? card/letter to ...?	**Was kostet eine Postkarte/ein Brief nach** *vass kostet iener posstkarter/ien breef naak*

> – Guten Tag. Ich möchte diese
> Postkarten in die USA schicken.
> – *Wie viele?*
> – Neun, bitte.
> – *Das ist neun mal eine Mark*
> *zwanzig: zehn Mark achtzig bitte.*

...nding parcels Pakete schicken

...want to send this parcel/ | **Ich möchte dieses Paket**
...ackage by ... | **per ... schicken.**
| *ikh murkhter deezess pakayt*
| *pehr ... shikken*

...rmail | **Luftpost** *luftposst*

...xpress | **Express** *ekspress*

...gistered mail | **Einschreiben** *ienshrieben*

...contains ... | **Es enthält ...** *ess enthehlt*

> **Bitte füllen Sie die** | Please fill in the customs
> **Zollerklärung aus.** | declaration.
> **Wie hoch ist der Wert?** | What is the value?
> **Was ist darin?** | What's inside?

...ecommunications Fernmeldeverkehr

...d like a phonecard, please. | **Ich hätte gern eine Telefonkarte.**
| *ikh hetter gehrn iener taylayfoankarter*

.../20/50 units. | **zehn/zwanzig/fünfzig Einheiten.**
| *tsayn/tsvantsikh/fewnftsikh ienhieten*

...o you have a photocopier/ | **Haben Sie hier ein Fotokopiergerät/Telefax?**
...x machine here? | *haaben zee her ien foatokopeergerait/*
| *taylayfaks*

...d like ... copies. | **Ich hätte gern ... Kopien.**
| *ikh hetter gehrn ... kopee-en*

...d like to send a message... | **Ich möchte gern eine Nachricht ... schicken.**
| *ikh murkhter gehrn iener nakhrikht ... shikken*

...y E-mail/fax | **per E-mail/Fax**
| *pehr elektronisher post/fax*

...hat's your E-mail address? | **Wie ist Ihre E-mail Adresse?**
| *vee ist eerer elektronisher postadresser*

...an I access the Internet here? | **Kann ich auf das Internet zugreifen?**
| *kan ikh awf dass internet tsoogriefen*

...hat are the charges per hour? | **Wie viel kostet es pro Stunde?**
| *vee feel kostet es pro shtunder*

...ow do I log on? | **Wie logge ich ein?**
| *vee logger ikh ien*

155

Souvenirs Andenken

Here are some suggestions for souvenirs.

Germany: beer mugs (**Bierkrüge**)
wooden toys (**Holzspielwaren**)
cuckoo clocks (**Kuckucksuhren**)
furs (**Pelze**)

Austria: petit-point embroidery and linen goods (**Stickerei**)
jewelry (**Schmuck**)
chocolate marzipan balls (**Mozartkugeln**)
pottery (**Töpferei**)

Switzerland: watches (**Armbanduhren**)
cuckoo clocks (**Kuckucksuhren**)
cheese (**Käse**)
chocolate (**Schokolade**)
Swiss Army knives (**Taschenmesser**)
wooden products (**Holzartikel**)

Gifts Geschenke

I'd like ...	**Ich hätte gern ...** *ikh hetter gehrn ...*
bottle of wine	**eine Flasche Wein** *iener flasher vien*
box of chocolates	**eine Schachtel Pralinen** *iener shakhtel praleenen*
calendar	**einen Kalender** *ienen kalender*
key ring	**einen Schlüsselanhänger** *ienen shlewsselanhehnger*
postcard	**eine Postkarte** *iener posstkarter*
souvenir guide	**einen Andenkenbildband** *ienen andenkenbiltbant*
T-shirt	**ein T-Shirt** *ien "T-shirt"*
tea towel	**ein Geschirrtuch** *ien geshirtookh*

Music Musik

I'd like a ...	**Ich hätte gern ...** *ikh hetter gehrn*
cassette	**eine Kassette** *iener kassetter*
compact disc	**eine CD** *iener tsayday*
record	**eine Schallplatte** *iener shalplatter*
videocassette	**eine Videokassette** *iener veedayoakassetter*
Who are the popular native singers/bands?	**Welche einheimischen Sänger/Gruppen sind beliebt?** *velkher ienhiemishen zehnger/gruppen zint beleebt*

Toys and games Spielzeug und Spiele

I'd like a toy/game ...	**Ich hätte gern ein Spielzeug/Spiel ...** *ikh hetter gehrn ien shpeeltsoyg/shpeel*
for a boy	**für einen Jungen** *fewr ienen yungen*
for a 5-year-old girl	**für ein fünfjähriges Mädchen** *fewr ien fewnfjairigess maitkhen*
bucket and shovel	**Eimer und Schaufel** *iemer unt showfel*
chess set	**Schachspiel** *shakhshpeel*
doll	**Puppe** *pupper*
electronic game	**Elektronikspiel** *aylektroaneekshpeel*
teddy bear	**Teddybär** *teddibair*

Antiques Antiquitäten

How old is this?	**Wie alt ist das?** *vee alt ist dass*
Do you have anything of the ... era?	**Haben Sie etwas aus der ... Zeit?** *haaben zee etvass owss dehr ... tsiet*
Can you send it to me?	**Können Sie es mir schicken?** *kurnen zee ess meer shikken*
Will I have problems with customs?	**Bekomme ich Schwierigkeiten mit dem Zoll?** *bekommer ikh shveerikhkieten mit daym tsol*
Is there a certificate of authenticity?	**Ist eine Echtheitsurkunde vorhanden?** *ist iener ekhthietsoorkunder forhanden*

ARTISTIC PERIODS ➤ 104

157

Supermarket/foodstore
Supermarkt/Lebensmittelgeschäft

Supermarkets such as **Tengelmann**, **HL** and **Minimal** can be fou
in town centers, as can discount grocery stores such as
Lidl, **Penny** and **Aldi**; **Toom**, **Wertkauf** and **Real** are large supermarkets with
widest selection of food items and international specialties.

At the supermarket Im Supermarkt

Excuse me. Where can I find …? **Entschuldigen Sie. Wo finde ich …?**
entshuldigen zee. voa finder ikh

Do I pay for this here or at the **Muss ich das hier oder an der Kasse**
checkout? **bezahlen?**
*muss ikh dass heer oader an dehr
kasser betsaalen*

Where are the shopping carts/ **Wo sind die Einkaufswagen/Einkaufskörbe**
baskets? *voa zint dee ienkowfsvaagen/ienkowfskurbe*

Is there a … here? **Gibt es hier …?** *gipt ess heer*

bakery **eine Bäckerei** *iener behkerie*

fish counter **eine Fischtheke** *iener fishtayker*

BROT UND KUCHEN	bread and cakes
FRISCHES GEMÜSE	fresh produce
FRISCHFISCH	fresh fish
FRISCHFLEISCH	fresh meat
GEFLÜGEL	poultry
HAUSHALTSWAREN	household goods
MILCHPRODUKTE	dairy products
OBST/GEMÜSE IN DOSEN	canned fruit/vegetables
PUTZMITTEL	cleaning products
SONDERANGEBOT	special offer
TIEFKÜHLKOST	frozen foods
WEIN UND SPIRITUOSEN	wines and spirits

Weights and Measures

- 1 kilogram or kilo (kg.) = 1000 grams (g.)
  100g. = 3.5 oz. **1 kg.** = 2.2 lb **1 oz.** = 28.35g. **1 lb.** = 453.60g.
- **1 liter (l.)** = 1.06 U.S. quart **1 U.S. quart** = 0.95 l. **1 U.S. gallon** = 3.8 l.
  1 U.S. pint = 0.47 l.

Food hygiene Lebensmittel-Aufbewahrung

FÜR MIKROWELLE GEEIGNET	microwaveable
FÜR VEGETARIER GEEIGNET	suitable for vegetarians
KÜHL AUFBEWAHREN	keep refrigerated
MINDESTENS HALTBAR BIS ...	sell by ...

At the grocery store   Im Lebensmittelgeschäft

Do you have any ...?	**Haben Sie ...?** *haaben zee*
I'd like some of that/those.	**Ich hätte gern etwas davon.** *ikh hetter gehrn etvass dafon*
That's all, thanks.	**Danke, das ist alles.** *danker dass ist alless*
I'd like ...	**Ich hätte gern ...** *ikh hetter gehrn*
kilo of apples	**ein Kilo Äpfel** *ien keelo epfel*
half-kilo of tomatoes	**ein halbes Kilo Tomaten** *ien halbess keelo tomaaten*
100 grams of cheese	**hundert Gramm Käse** *hundert gram kaizer*
liter of milk	**einen Liter Milch** *ienen leeter milkh*
half-dozen eggs	**ein halbes Dutzend Eier** *ien halbess dutsent ieer*
piece of cake	**ein Stück Kuchen** *ien shtewk kookhen*
bottle of wine	**eine Flasche Wein** *iener flasher vien*
can of Coke	**eine Dose Cola** *iener doazer kohla*
carton of milk	**eine Tüte Milch** *iener tewter milkh*
jar of jam	**ein Glas Marmelade** *ien glaass marmelaader*
packet of chips	**eine Packung Chips** *iener pakkung cheeps*
tube of mustard	**eine Tube Senf** *iener toober zenf*

Provisions/picnic Proviant/Picknick

apples	**Äpfel** epfel
butter	**Butter** butter
candy/sweets	**Süßigkeiten** zewssikhkieten
cheese	**Käse** kaizer
chips	**Chips** cheeps
cookies	**Kekse** kekser
eggs	**Eier** ieer
French fries	**Pommes frites** pom frit
grapes	**Weintrauben** vientrowben
ice cream	**Eis** iess
instant coffee	**Pulverkaffee** pulferkafay
jam	**Marmelade** marmelaader
loaf of bread	**Brot** broat
margarine	**Margarine** margareener
milk	**Milch** milkh
mustard	**Senf** zenf
oranges	**Orangen** orrangzhen
rolls	**Brötchen** brurtkhen
sausages	**Würstchen** vewrstkhen
six pack of beer	**ein Sechserpack Bier** ien zekserpak beer
soft drink	**Erfrischungsgetränk** ehrfrishungzgetrehnk
sugar	**Zucker** tsukker
tea bags	**Teebeutel** tayboytel
wine	**Wein** vien
yogurt	**Jogurt** yoagoort

VEGETABLES ➤ 47; FRUIT ➤ 48

Health

Before you leave, make sure your health insurance policy covers any illness or accident while on vacation.

In Germany, EU citizens with a Form E111 are eligible for free medical treatment. However, it is still advisable to take out travel insurance. Switzerland is not part of the EU and health care is very expensive there – so insurance is strongly recommended as you'll be expected to pay for any medical treatment you receive.

German doctors tend to be titled according to their specialties.

For a GP you should look for a **praktischer Arzt.**

Staff at a pharmacy/chemist can recommend a nurse if you need injections or other care.

In an emergency call the Red Cross **(Rotes Kreuz)** or the medical emergency service **(Ärztlicher Notfalldienst),** which will give you a list of doctors (see the telephone directory for the number).

Ambulance: Germany ☎ 115, Austria ☎ 144, Switzerland ☎ 114 (most areas).

Doctor/General Arzt/Allgemeines

Where can I find a doctor/ dentist?	**Wo finde ich einen Arzt/Zahnarzt?** *voa finder ikh ienen aartst/ tsaanaartst*
Where is there a doctor who speaks English?	**Wo gibt es einen Arzt, der Englisch spricht?** *voa gipt ess ienen aartst dehr english shprikht*
Where's the doctor's office?	**Wo ist die Arztpraxis?** *voa ist dee aartstpraksiss*
What are the office hours?	**Wann ist Sprechstunde?** *van ist shprekhshtunde*
Could the doctor come to see me here?	**Könnte der Arzt mich hier besuchen?** *kurnter dehr aartst mikh heer bezookhen*
Can I make an appointment for …?	**Kann ich … einen Termin bekommen?** *kan ikh … ienen tehrmeen bekommen*
today/tomorrow	**heute/morgen** *hoyter/morgen*

TIME ➤ *220; DATE* ➤ *218*

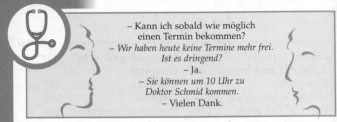

Accident and injury Unfall und Verletzung

My ... is hurt/injured.	**... ist verletzt.** *ist fehrletst*
husband/wife	**mein Mann/meine Frau** *mien man/miener frow*
son/daughter	**mein Sohn/meine Tochter** *mien zoan/miener tokhter*
friend (m/f)	**mein Freund/meine Freundin** *mien froynt/miener froyndin*
baby	**mein Baby** *mien "baby"*
He/She is ...	**Er/Sie ...** *ehr/zee*
unconscious	**ist bewusstlos** *ist bevustloass*
bleeding (heavily)	**blutet (schwer)** *blootet (shvayr)*
(seriously) injured	**ist (schwer) verletzt** *ist (shvayr) fehrletst*
I've got ...	**Ich habe ...** *ikh haaber*
blister	**eine Blase** *iener blaazer*
boil	**einen Furunkel** *ienen foorunkel*
bruise	**eine Quetschung** *iener kvechung*
burn	**eine Verbrennung** *iener fehrbrennung*
cut	**eine Schnittwunde** *iener shnitvunder*
graze	**eine Schürfwunde** *iener shewrfvunder*
insect bite	**einen Insektenstich** *ienen inzektenshtikh*
lump	**einen Knoten** *ienen knoaten*
rash	**einen Ausschlag** *ienen ows-shlaag*
sting	**einen Stich** *ienen shtikh*
strained muscle	**eine Muskelzerrung** *iener muskeltserung*
swelling	**eine Schwellung** *iener shvellung*
wound	**eine Wunde** *iener vunder*
My ... hurts.	**Mein/Meine ... tut weh.** *mien/miener ... toot vay*

hort-term symptoms
urzfristige Symptome

I've been feeling ill for … days.	**Ich fühle mich seit … Tagen nicht wohl.** *ikh fewler mikh ziet … taagen nikht voal*
I feel faint	**Mir ist schwindelig** *meer ist shvinderleik*
I feel feverish/shivery.	**Ich habe Fieber/Schüttelfrost.** *ikh haaber feeber/shewttelfrost*
I've been vomiting.	**Ich habe mich übergeben.** *ikh haaber mikh ewbergayben*
I've got diarrhea.	**Ich habe Durchfall.** *ikh haaber doorkhfal*
It hurts here.	**Es tut hier weh.** *ess toot heer vay*
I've have (a/an) …	**Ich habe …** *ikh haaber*
backache	**Rückenschmerzen** *rewkenshmehrtsen*
cold	**eine Erkältung** *iener ehrkehltung*
cramps	**Krämpfe** *krehmpfer*
earache	**Ohrenschmerzen** *oarenshmehrtsen*
headache	**Kopfschmerzen** *kopfshmehrtsen*
sore throat	**Halsschmerzen** *hals-shmehrtsen*
stiff neck	**einen steifen Nacken** *ienen stiefen nakken*
stomachache	**Magenschmerzen** *maagenshmehrtsen*
sunstroke	**einen Sonnenstich** *ienen zonnenshtikh*

ealth conditions Gesundheitszustand

I am …	**Ich bin …** *ikh bin*
deaf	**taub** *towp*
diabetic	**Diabetiker** *deeabaytiker*
epileptic	**Epileptiker** *epileptiker*
handicapped	**behindert** *behindert*
(… months) pregnant	**(im … Monat) schwanger** *(im … moanat) shvanger*
I am arthritic/asthmatic.	**Ich habe Arthritis/Asthma.** *ikh haaber aartreetiss/astma*
I have a heart condition/high blood pressure.	**Ich habe ein Herzleiden/zu hohen Blutdruck.** *ikh haaber ien hehrtslieden/tsoo hoaen blootdruk*
I had a heart attack … years ago.	**Ich hatte vor … Jahren einen Herzanfall.** *ikh hatter foar … yaaren ienen hehrtsanfal*

Doctor's inquiries Fragen des Arztes

Wie lange fühlen Sie sich schon so?	How long have you been feeling like this?
Haben Sie das zum ersten Mal?	Is this the first time you've had this?
Nehmen Sie noch andere Medikamente?	Are you taking any other medications?
Sind Sie gegen irgendetwas allergisch?	Are you allergic to anything?
Sind Sie gegen Wundstarrkrampf geimpft?	Have you been vaccinated against tetanus?
Leiden Sie an Appetitlosigkeit?	Have you lost your appetite?

Examination Untersuchung

Ich werde Ihre Temperatur/Ihren Blutdruck messen.	I'll take your temperature/ blood pressure.
Bitte streifen Sie den Ärmel hoch.	Roll up your sleeve, please.
Bitte machen Sie den Oberkörper frei.	Please undress to the waist.
Bitte legen Sie sich hin.	Please lie down.
Machen Sie den Mund auf.	Open your mouth.
Atmen Sie tief durch.	Breathe deeply.
Husten Sie, bitte.	Cough, please.
Wo tut es weh?	Where does it hurt?
Tut es hier weh?	Does it hurt here?

Diagnosis Diagnose

Sie müssen geröntgt werden.	I want you to have an X-ray.
Ich brauche eine Blutprobe/ Stuhlprobe/Urinprobe von Ihnen.	I want a specimen of your blood/stool/urine.
Ich überweise Sie an einen Facharzt.	I want you to see a specialist.
Ich überweise Sie ins Krankenhaus.	I want you to go to the hospital.
gebrochen/verstaucht	broken/sprained
verrenkt/gerissen	dislocated/torn
Sie haben ...	You've got (a/an) ...
eine Blinddarmentzündung	appendicitis
eine Blasenentzündung	cystitis

Grippe	flu
eine Lebensmittelvergiftung	food poisoning
eine Fraktur	fracture
eine Magenschleimhautentzündung	gastroenteritis
einen Bruch	hernia
eine ... Entzündung	inflammation of ...
Masern	measles
eine Lungenentzündung	pneumonia
Ischias	sciatica
eine Mandelentzündung	tonsilitis
einen Tumor	tumor
eine Geschlechtskrankheit	venereal disease
Es ist entzündet.	It's infected.
Es ist ansteckend.	It's contagious.

Treatment Behandlung

Ich gebe Ihnen ...	I'll give you ...
ein Antiseptikum	an antiseptic
ein Schmerzmittel	a pain killer
Ich verschreibe Ihnen ...	I'm going to prescribe ...
Antibiotika	a course of antibiotics
Zäpfchen	some suppositories
Sind Sie gegen bestimmte Medikamente allergisch?	Are you allergic to any medication?
Nehmen Sie 2 Tabletten/Teelöffel ... alle vier Stunden	Take 2 tablets/teaspoons ... every 4 hours
vor den Mahlzeiten	before meals
Kommen Sie in ... Tagen wieder.	I'd like you to come back in ... days.
Gehen Sie zum Arzt, wenn Sie wieder zu Hause sind.	Consult a doctor when you get home.

Parts of the body Körperteile

appendix	**der Blinddarm**	*dehr blintdarm*
arm	**der Arm**	*dehr arm*
back	**der Rücken**	*dehr rewken*
bladder	**die Blase**	*dee blaazer*
bone	**der Knochen**	*dehr knokhen*
breast	**die Brust**	*dee brust*
chest	**der Brustkorb**	*dehr brustkorp*
ear	**das Ohr**	*dass oar*
eye	**das Auge**	*dass owger*
face	**das Gesicht**	*dass gezikht*
finger	**der Finger**	*dehr finger*
foot	**der Fuß**	*dehr fooss*
gland	**die Drüse**	*dee drewzer*
hand	**die Hand**	*dee hant*
head	**der Kopf**	*dehr kopf*
heart	**das Herz**	*dass hehrts*
jaw	**der Kiefer**	*dehr keefer*
joint	**das Gelenk**	*dass gelenk*
kidney	**die Niere**	*dee neerer*
knee	**das Knie**	*dass knee*
leg	**das Bein**	*dass bien*
lip	**die Lippe**	*dee lipper*
liver	**die Leber**	*dee layber*
mouth	**der Mund**	*dehr munt*
muscle	**der Muskel**	*dehr muskel*
neck	**der Hals**	*dehr hals*
nerve	**der Nerv**	*nehrf*
nervous system	**das Nervensystem**	*dass nehrfenzewstaym*
nose	**die Nase**	*dee naazer*
rib	**die Rippe**	*dee ripper*
shoulder	**die Schulter**	*dee shulter*
skin	**die Haut**	*dee howt*
stomach	**der Magen**	*dehr maagen*
thigh	**der Oberschenkel**	*dehr oabershenkel*
throat	**der Hals**	*dehr hals*
thumb	**der Daumen**	*dehr dowmen*
toe	**die Zehe**	*dee tsayer*
tongue	**die Zunge**	*dee tsunger*
tonsils	**die Mandeln**	*dee mandeln*

Gynecologist Beim Frauenarzt

I have …	**Ich habe …** *ikh haaber*
abdominal pains	**Unterleibsschmerzen** *unterliebs-shmehrtsen*
period pains	**Menstruationsbeschwerden** *menstruatsioansbeshvayrden*
a vaginal infection	**eine Scheidenentzündung** *iener shieden-entsewndung*
I haven't had my period for … months.	**Ich habe seit … Monaten meine Periode nicht mehr gehabt.** *ikh haaber ziet … moanaten miener perioader nikht mayr gehapt*
I'm on the pill.	**Ich nehme die Pille.** *ikh naymer dee piller*

Hospital Krankenhaus

Please notify my family.	**Benachrichtigen Sie bitte meine Familie.** *benaakhrikhtiggen zee bitter miener fameelier*
What are the visiting hours?	**Wann ist Besuchszeit?** *van ist bezookhs-tsiet*
I'm in pain.	**Ich habe Schmerzen.** *ikh haaber shmehrtsen*
I can't eat/sleep.	**Ich kann nicht essen/schlafen.** *ikh kan nikht essen/shlaafen*
When will the doctor come?	**Wann kommt der Arzt?** *van komt dehr aartst*
Which ward is … in?	**Auf welcher Station liegt …?** *owf velkher shtatsioan leegt*
I'm visiting …	**Ich besuche …** *ikh bezookher*

Optician Optiker

I'm nearsighted/farsighted.	**Ich bin kurzsichtig/weitsichtig.** *ikh bin kurtszikhtikh/vietzikhtikh*
I've lost …	**Ich habe … verloren.** *ikh haaber … fehrloaren*
one of my contact lenses	**eine meiner Kontaktlinsen** *iener miener kontaktlinzen*
my glasses	**meine Brille** *miener briller*
a lens	**ein Brillenglas** *ien brillenglaass*
Could you give me a replacement?	**Können Sie es ersetzen?** *kurnen zee /ess ehrzetsen*

167

Dentist Zahnarzt

If you need to see a dentist, you'll probably have to pay the bill on the spot; save all receipts for reimbursement. EU nationals should obtain the E111 form before leaving home.

I have a toothache.	**Ich habe Zahnschmerzen.** *ikh haaber tsaanshmehrtsen*
This tooth hurts.	**Dieser Zahn tut weh.** *deezer tsaan toot ve*
I've broken a tooth/crown.	**Mir ist ein Zahn/eine Krone abgebrochen** *meer ist ien tsaan/iener kroaner apgebrokh*
I've lost a filling.	**Ich habe eine Füllung verloren.** *ikh haaber iener fewllung fehrloaren*
Can you repair this denture?	**Können Sie dieses Gebiss reparieren?** *kurnen zee deezess gebiss repareeren*
I don't want it extracted.	**Ich möchte ihn nicht ziehen lassen.** *ikh murkhter een nikht tsee-en lassen*

Ich gebe Ihnen eine Spritze/eine örtliche Betäubung.	I'm going to give you an injection/a local anesthetic.
Sie brauchen eine Füllung/Krone.	You need a filling/crown.
Ich muss ihn ziehen.	I'll have to take it out.
Ich kann es nur provisorisch behandeln.	I can only fix it temporarily.
Kommen Sie in … Tagen wieder.	Come back in … days.
Essen Sie … Stunden nichts.	Don't eat anything for … hours.

Payment/Insurance Bezahlung/Versicherung

How much do I owe you?	**Wie viel bin ich Ihnen schuldig?** *vee feel bin ikh eenen shuldikh*
Do you have health insurance?	**Sind Sie krankenversichert?** *zint zee krankenfehrzikhert*
I have insurance.	**Ich bin versichert.** *ikh bin fehrzikhert*
Can I have a receipt for my health insurance?	**Kann ich eine Quittung für meine Krankenkasse haben?** *kan ikh iener kvittung fewr miener krankenkasser haabe*
Would you fill in this health insurance form, please?	**Würden Sie bitte dieses Krankenkassen- formular ausfüllen?** *vewrden zee bitter deezess krankenkassen-formulaar owsfew*
Do you have Form E111?	**Haben Sie das Formular E-Hundertelf?** *haaben dass formullaar ay-hundertelf*

Many of the terms in this dictionary are cross-referenced to pages where the word appears in a full phrase. In addition, the notes below provide some basic grammar guidelines.

Nouns and Adjectives

All nouns in German are written with a capital letter. They are either masculine (*m*), feminine (*f*) or neuter (*nt*), and are classified by the article that precedes them. The rules for constructing the plural are rather complex.

According to their use in the sentence, German articles, nouns and modifying adjectives undergo related changes. The tables below show the declension of all three parts of speech.

	masc. sing.	*masc. plur.*
subject	**der reiche Mann**	**die reichen Männer**
direct object	**den reichen Mann**	**die reichen Männer**
possessive	**des reichen Mannes**	**der reichen Männer**
indirect object	**dem reichen Mann**	**den reichen Männern**

	fem. sing.	*fem. plur.*
subject	**die schöne Frau**	**die schönen Frauen**
direct object	**die schöne Frau**	**die schönen Frauen**
possessive	**der schönen Frau**	**der schönen Frauen**
indirect object	**der schönen Frau**	**den schönen Frauen**

	neuter sing.	*neuter plur.*
subject	**das kleine Kind**	**die kleinen Kinder**
direct object	**das kleine Kind**	**die kleinen Kinder**
possessive	**des kleinen Kindes**	**der kleinen Kinder**
indirect object	**dem kleinen Kind**	**den kleinen Kindern**

Verbs

Here are the infinitives and present tense of two important auxiliary verbs (**sein** and **haben**) and a regular (weak) verb (**lieben**):

	sein	**haben**	**lieben**
	(to be)	*(to have)*	*(to love)*
ich *(I)*	**bin** *(am)*	**habe**	**liebe**
du *(you informal)*	**bist** *(are)*	**hast**	**liebst**
er/sie/es/man *(he/she/it/one)*	**ist** *(is)*	**hat**	**liebt**
wir *(we)*	**sind** *(are)*	**haben**	**lieben**
ihr(*you informal*)	**seid** *(are)*	**habt**	**liebt**
sie *(they)*	**sind** *(are)*	**haben**	**lieben**
Sie(*you formal*)	**sind** *(are)*	**haben**	**lieben**

a few einige 15
a little ein wenig 15
a lot viel (-e, -en, -es, -er) 15
a.m. vormittags
A.P. Vollpension f 24
abdominal pains Unterleibsschmerzen pl 167
able, to be *(also ➤ can, could)* können
about *(approximately)* etwa 15
above *(place)* über 12
abroad im Ausland
abscess Abszess m
accept, to akzeptieren 136
access *(n)* Zugang m; Zutritt m
accessories Zubehör nt *sing* 144
accident Unfall m 152; *(road)* 92
accidentally versehentlich 28
accompany, to begleiten 65
accountant Buchhalter(in) m/f
ace *(cards)* As nt
acrylic Acryl nt
activities Aktivitäten fpl
actor/actress Schauspieler/Schauspielerin 110
adapter Adapter m 148
address Adresse f 84, 126
adjoining nebeneinander liegend 22;
~ room Nebenzimmer nt
admission charge Eintritt m 114
adult Erwachsene m/f 81, 100
advance: in advance im voraus
after *(place)* nach 95; *(time)* 13
afternoon, in the nachmittags 221
after shave Rasierwasser nt 142
aftersun lotion After-Sun-Creme f 142
age- what age? wie alt? 113
aged: ... Alter: ... nt 152
ago: 10 minutes ago vor 10 Minuten 13
agree: I agree ich bin einverstanden
air Luft f;
~ conditioning Klimaanlage f 22, 25; **~ freshener** Raumspray nt; **~ mattress** Luftmatratze f 31; **~ pump** Luftpumpe f 87
airline Fluggesellschaft f
airmail Luftpost f 155
airplane Flugzeug nt
airport Flughafen m 96
aisle Gang m 69
alcoholic *(drink)* alkoholisch

all alle, alles
allergic, to be allergisch sein 164
allergy Allergie f
allowance erlaubte Menge f 67
allowed: is it allowed? ist es erlaubt?
almost fast
alone allein 120
already schon 28
also auch
alter, to ändern 137
always immer 13
am: I am ich bin
ambassador Botschafter(in) m/f
ambulance Krankenwagen m 92
American *(adj)* amerikanisch 152; *(n)* Amerikaner(in) m/f;
~ football Football m
amount Betrag m 42
amusement arcade Spielhalle f 113
anchor, to vor Anker gehen
and und
anesthetic Betäubungsmittel nt
angling Angeln nt
animal Tier nt 106
another noch ein;
~ time ein andermal 125
antacid Antazidum m
antenna *(car/tv)* Antenne f
antibiotics Antibiotika pl
antifreeze Frostschutzmittel nt
antiques Antiquitäten pl 157;
~ store Antiquitätengeschäft nt 130
antiseptic Antiseptikum nt 165;
~ cream Wundsalbe f 141
any: any more noch mehr
anything else? sonst noch etwas?
apartment Wohnung f
apologize: I apologize es tut mir leid
apple Apfel m 160
appointment Termin m 147, 161
approximately ungefähr 152
April April m 218
archery Bogenschießen nt
architect Architekt(in) m/f 104
architecture Architektur f
are you ...? sind Sie ...?
area Gegend f
~ code Vorwahl f
arm Arm m 166
around *(place)* um ... herum *(time)* gegen 13, *(town)* durch 12
arrange: can you arrange it? können Sie dafür sorgen?

arrest, to be under festgenommen werden

arrive, to ankommen 68, 70, 71, 76

art Kunst f

art gallery Kunstgalerie f 99

artery Arterie f

arthritic, to be Arthritis haben 163

artificial sweetener Süßstoff m 38

artist Künstler(in) m/f 104

as soon as possible so bald wie möglich

ashore, to go an Land gehen

ashtray Aschenbecher m 39

ask, to: please ask her to call me back würden Sie sie bitten, mich zurückzurufen

asleep, to be schlafen

aspirin Aspirin m 141

asthmatic, to be Asthma haben 163

at *(place)* an 12; *(time)* um 13

at least mindestens 23

attack Überfall m 152; *(medical)* Anfall m

attendant *(museum)* Aufseher(in) m/f

attractive attraktiv

August August m 218

aunt Tante f 120

Australia Australien nt 119

Australian *(n)* Australier(in) m/f

Austria Österreich nt 119

Austrian *(n)* Österreicher(in) m/f

automated teller Geldautomat m 139

automatic *(car)* Automatikwagen m 86

automatic camera Automatikkamera f 151

automobile Auto m 86

autumn Herbst m 219

avalanche Lawine f

away weg

awful scheußlich

B

baby Baby nt 39, 113, 162;
~ bag Babytragetasche f
~ bottle Fläschchen nt;
~ food Babynahrung f 142;
~ seat Babysitz m; **~sitter** Babysitter m;
~ wipes Öltücher ntpl 142

back Rücken m 166

backache Rückenschmerzen pl 163

backpacking Rucksackwandern nt

bad schlecht 14

baggage Gepäck nt 69, 71;
~ allowance Freigepäck nt; **~ check** Gepäckaufbewahrung f 71, 73; **~ claim** Gepäckausgabe f 71 **~ tag** Gepäckschein m 71

baked gebacken

bakery Bäckerei f 130, 158

balcony Balkon m 29;
(theater) oberster Rang m

ball Ball m

ballet Ballett nt 108, 111

banana Banane f 52

band *(musical group)* Band f 111;
Gruppe f 157

bandage Verband m 141

bank Bank f 130, 138;
~ account Bankkonto nt;
~ card Scheckkarte f 139;
~ loan Darlehen nt

bar Bar f 112; *(hotel)* Bar f 26

barber Friseur m

basin Becken nt

basket: shopping basket Einkaufskorb m 158

basketball Basketball m 114

bath: to take a bath baden;
~ room Bad nt 26; Badezimmer nt 29;
~ towel Badetuch nt 27; Badehandtuch nt

battery Batterie f 88, 137, 151

battle site Schlachtfeld nt 99

beach Strand m 116

beard Bart m

beautiful schön 14, 101

because weil;
~ of wegen

bed Bett nt 21;
~ and breakfast Übernachtung f mit Frühstück 24; **~ I'm going to** ich gehe ins Bett; **~ room** Schlafzimmer nt 29

bedding Bettzeug nt 29

bee Biene f

beer Bier nt 40

before *(time)* vor 13, 221

begin, to *(also ➤ to start)* beginnen, anfangen

beginner Anfänger m 117

beginning Anfang m

beige beige 143

Belgian *(adj)* belgisch; *(n)* Belgier(in) m/f

Belgium Belgien nt

below 15°C unter 15 Grad

belt Gürtel m 144

beneath unter

berth Liegewagenplatz m 74; Schlafplatz m 77

best beste

better besser 14
between zwischen
bib Lätzchen nt
bicycle Fahrrad nt 75, 83, 153
~ **helmet** Fahrradhelm m
~ **path** Radweg m
bicycle rental Fahrradvermietung f 83
big groß 14, 117, 134
bikini Bikini m 144
bill Rechnung f 32, 42;
~ **put it on the** setzen Sie es auf die Rechnung
binoculars Fernglas nt sing
bird Vogel m 106
birthday Geburtstag m 219
bishop (chess) Läufer m
bite (insect) Stich m
bitten: I've been bitten by a dog ich bin von einem Hund gebissen worden
bitter bitter 41
black schwarz 143;
~ **and white film** (camera) Schwarzweißfilm m 151
blanket Decke f 27
bleeding, to be bluten 162
bless you! Gesundheit!
blind (n) Rollo nt 25
blister Blase f 162
blocked, to be verstopft sein 25;
the road is ~ die Straße ist blockiert
blood Blut nt 164;
~ **group** Blutgruppe f;
~ **pressure** Blutdruck m 163, 164
blouse Bluse f 144
blue blau 143
blusher (rouge) Rouge nt
board, on (bus) im Bus
boarding; ~ **card** Bordkarte f 70
boat Schiff nt 81; (small) Boot nt 81;
~ **trip** Schiffsfahrt f 81
body: parts of the body 166
boil Furunkel m 162
boiled gekocht
boiler Boiler m 29
bone Knochen m 166
book Buch nt 150;
~ **store** Buchhandlung f 130, 150
book, to reservieren 21; reservieren lassen 74; buchen 81, 98;
~ **I'd like to book ...** ich möchte ... reservieren lassen 74
booking Reservierung f 22; (restaurant) Tischbestellung f 36;

boots Stiefel mpl 145; (for sport) Schuhe mpl 115
border (country) Grenze f
boring langweilig 101
born: I was born in ... ich bin (year) in (place) geboren
borrow: may I borrow your ...? darf ich Ihren/Ihre/Ihr ... leihen?
botanical garden Botanischer Garten m 99
bottle Flasche f 37, 159;
~ **bank** Altglascontainer m;
~ **opener** Flaschenöffner m 148
bow (ship) Bug m
box of chocolates Schachtel f Pralinen 156
box office Kasse f
boxing Boxen nt
boy Junge m 120, 157;
~ **friend** Freund m 120
bra BH m 144
brass Messing nt
bread Brot nt 38
breakdown kaputtgehen 28
break, to zerbrechen 28; (journey) unterbrechen
breakage Bruch m
breakdown Panne f 88;
~ **to have a** eine Panne haben 88
breakfast Frühstück nt 26, 27
break-in Einbruch m 153
breast Brust f 166
breathe, to atmen 164
bridge Brücke f 107; (cards) Bridge nt
briefcase Aktenkoffer m
briefs Unterhose f 144
brilliant großartig 101
bring, to bringen
Britain Großbritannien nt 119
British (adj) britisch 152
Briton Brite m, Britin f
brochure Broschüre f;
broken (bone) gebrochen sein 164
bronchitis Bronchitis f
bronze (adj) Bronze-
brother Bruder m 120
brown braun 143
browse, to sich umsehen 133
bruise Quetschung f 162
brush Bürste f
bubble bath Schaumbad nt
bucket Eimer m
build, to bauen
building Gebäude nt

built erbaut 104
bureau de change Wechselstube f 70, 138
burger Hamburger m 40
burglary *(also ▶theft)* Einbruch m
burn Verbrennung f 162
burn: it's burnt es ist verbrannt
burnt, to be *(food)* angebrannt sein
bus Bus m 70, 78, 79;
~ **route** Buslinie f 96; ~ **station**
Busbahnhof m 78; ~ **stop** Bushaltestelle f
65, 96
business Geschäft nt;
~ **class** Businessklasse f 68;
~ **man** Geschäftsmann m;
~ **trip** Geschäftsreise f;
~ **woman** Geschäftsfrau f;
on ~ geschäftlich 66, 123
busy: I'm busy ich habe keine Zeit 125
but aber 19
butane gas Butangas nt 31
butcher shop Fleischerei f 130, Metzgerei f
130
butter Butter f 38, 160
button Knopf m
buy, to kaufen 67, 80
by *(time)* bis 13; vor 86
by car mit dem Auto 17, 94
by credit card mit Kreditkarte 17
bye! auf Wiedersehen!
bypass Umgehungsstraße f

C
cabaret Varieté nt 112
cabin Kabine f
cable car Seilbahn f
cable TV Kabelfernsehen nt 22
café Café nt 35, **40**
cake Kuchen m 40
calendar Kalender m 156
call, to rufen 92; *(phone)* anrufen 127, 128;
to ~ **collect** ein R-Gespräch führen 127;
to ~ **pick s.o. up** jemanden abholen 125;
call the police! rufen Sie die Polizei! 92;
I'll call back ich rufe zurück; **I'll come by**
ich komme vorbei
camcorder Camcorder m
camel hair Kamelhaar nt
camera Fotoapparat m 151; Kamera f 151,
153;
~ **case** Fototasche f 151; ~ **shop**
Fotogeschäft nt 130, 151
campbed Campingliege f 31
camping 30;
~ **equipment** Campingausrüstung f 31;

~ **stove** Campingkocher
m 31
campsite Campingplatz
m 30
can *(tin)* Dose f 159;
~ **opener** Büchsenöffner m
148
can I have …? kann ich … haben? 18
can I? kann ich? 18
can you help me? können Sie mir helfen?
18
Canada Kanada nt 119
Canadian *(n)* Kanadier(in) m/f
canal Kanal m
cancel, to stornieren 68
cancer *(disease)* Krebs m
candle Kerze f 148
candy Süßigkeiten fpl 150, 160
canoe Kanu nt
canoeing Kanufahren nt
cap Mütze f
capital city Hauptstadt f
captain *(boat)* Kapitän m
car Auto nt 81, 86, 87, 88, 89,
~ **alarm** Auto-Alarmanlage f;
~ **ferry** Autofähre f; ~ **rental**
Autovermietung f 70, 86;
~ **park** Parkplatz m 26, 87, 96;
~ **pound** Platz m für abgeschleppte
Fahrzeuge; ~ **repairs** Reparaturen 89;
~ **wash** Autowaschanlage f; **by** ~ mit
dem Auto 95; **rental** ~ Mietwagen m 153
carafe Karaffe f 37
caravan Wohnwagen m 30, 81
cardphone Kartentelefon nt
cards Karten fpl 121
careful: be careful! Vorsicht!
carousel Karussell nt
carpet *(fitted)* Teppichboden m; *(rug)*
Teppich m
carrier bag Tragetasche f 136
carton Tüte f 159
cartoon Cartoon m
carwash Autowaschanlage f
cash Bargeld nt;
~ **card** (Geld)automatenkarte f;
~ **desk** Kasse f 132; ~ **machine** *(dispenser)*
Geldautomat m 139; **to**
pay by ~ bar zahlen 136
cash, to einlösen 138
casino Spielkasino nt 112
cassette Kassette f 157
castle Schloss nt 99
cat Katze f

A-Z

catch, to (bus) nehmen
cathedral Dom m 99
cave Höhle f 107
CD CD f;
~-player CD-Spieler m
cemetery Friedhof m 99
central heating
Zentralheizung f
center of town Stadtzentrum nt 21
ceramics Keramik f
certificate Urkunde f 157; Zeugnis nt
certification Bescheinigung f 149
chair Stuhl m 14; **~ lift** Sessellift m 117
change (coins) Kleingeld nt 87
change (n) (money) Wechselgeld nt;
keep the change der Rest ist für Sie 84
change, to (buses) umsteigen 78, 79;
(trains) 75, 80; (clothes) sich umziehen;
(money) umtauschen; (reservation) ändern
68, 74; (baby) wickeln 39;
where can I change the baby? wo kann
ich das Baby wickeln?; **to ~ lanes** die
Spur wechseln
channel (sea) Kanal m
charcoal Holzkohle f 31
charge f 30;
what's the charge? wie viel kostet es? 115
charter flight Charterflug m
cheap billig 14; preiswert 134
cheaper billiger 21, 24, 109; preiswerter
134
check Rechnung f 32, 42
check in, to einchecken 68
check out, to (hotel) abreisen
check: please check ... bitte überprüfen
Sie ...
checkered (patterned) kariert
checkers (draughts) Damespiel nt
check-in desk Abfertigungsschalter m 69
checking in 69
checking out 32
checkout Kasse f 158
cheers! zum Wohl!
cheese Käse m 160
chemical toilet Chemietoilette f
check guarantee card Scheckkarte f
chess Schach f 121;
~ set Schachspiel nt 157
chest Brustkorb m 166
chewing gum Kaugummi m 150
child Kind nt 98, 152;
~ care provider Kinderbetreuung f 113;

~ seat (car) Kindersitz m; (high chair)
Kinderstuhl m 39
children Kinder ntpl 66, 81, 113, 120;
(reduction) 24, 74, 100; (meals) 39
children's entertainer Unterhalter m für
Kinder
children's meals Mahlzeiten fpl für
Kinder 39
China Geschirr nt
Chinese (adj) chinesisch 35
chips Chips pl 160
chocolate Schokolade f;
~ bar Schokoladenriegel m 150; (flavour)
40; **hot ~** (heiße) Schokolade f 40;
box of ~s Schachtel f Pralinen
chop (meat) Kotelett nt
Christian (adj) christlich
Christmas Weihnachten 219
church Kirche f 96, 99, 105
cigar Zigarre f 150
cigarette Zigarette f 150;
cigar store Tabakgeschäft nt 131;
~ machine Zigarettenautomat m;
packet of ~ Schachtel f Zigaretten 150
cinema Kino nt 96, 110
circle (balcony) Rang m
city wall Stadtmauer f 99
clamped, to be mit einer Parkkralle
festgesetzt werden 87
clean (adj) sauber 14, 41; **to ~** reinigen
137; **I'd like my shoes cleaned** ich hätte
gern meine Schuhe geputzt
cleaner Putzfrau f 28
cleaning Reinigung f 137
cleaning products Putzmittel ntpl 148
cleansing lotion Reinigungsmilch f
cleansing solution (for lenses)
Reinigungsflüssigkeit f
cliff Klippe f 107
close (near) nah 95
close, to schließen 100, 132; (shop) 140;
closed (shop) geschlossen 14
clothes Kleidungsstücke ntpl 144;
~ line Wäscheleine f; **~ pegs**
Wäscheklammern fpl 148;
~ store Bekleidungsgeschäft nt 130
cloudy, to be bewölkt sein 122
clubs (golf) Schläger mpl 115
coach Überlandbus m, Bus m 78; (train
compartment) Wagen m 75;
~ bay Bushaltestelle f 78;
~ station Busbahnhof m 78
coast Küste f

coat Mantel m 144
coatcheck Garderobe f 109
coat hanger Kleiderbügel m
cockroach Kakerlake f
code (area/dialling) Vorwahl f
coffee Kaffee m 40
coil (contraceptive) Spirale f
coin Münze f
cola Cola f
cold (adj) kalt 14, 24, 41, 122; (n)
Erkältung f 141, 163; ~ meats Aufschnitt
m
collapse: he's collapsed er ist
zusammengebrochen
collect, to abholen 151
college: to be at college studieren 121
color Farbe f 134, 143;
~film Farbfilm m 151
comb Kamm m 142
come back, to (return) wiederkommen 36,
165
comedy Komödie f
commission Gebühr f 138
communion Kommunion f
compact camera Kompaktkamera f 151
compact disc/disk CD f 157
company (business) Firma f;
(companionship) Gesellschaft f 126
compartment (train) Abteil nt
compass Kompaß m
complaint, to make a sich beschweren
137
complaints (restaurant) 41;(hotel) 25
computer Computer m
concert Konzert nt 108, 111;
~ hall Konzerthalle f 111
concession Ermäßigung f 100
concussion, to have eine
Gehirnerschütterung haben
conditioner Spülung f 142
condoms Kondome ntpl 141
conductor Dirigent(in) m/f 111
conference Konferenz f
confirm, to (reservation) bestätigen 22, 68
congratulations! herzlichen
Glückwunsch!
connection (transport) Anschluss m
conscious, to be bei Bewußtsein sein
constipated, to be Verstopfung haben
constipation Verstopfung f
Consulate Konsulat nt 152
consult: to consult a doctor zum Arzt
gehen 165

contact lens Kontaktlinse
f 167
contact, to erreichen 28
contact lens fluid
Kontaktlinsenflüssigkeit f
contagious, to be
ansteckend sein 165
contain, to enthalten 39, 69, 155
contemporary dance moderner Tanz m
111
contraceptive Verhütungsmittel nt
convenient günstig
conversion charts 85, 158
cook Koch m, Köchin f
cookbook Kochbuch nt
cook, to kochen
cooker Herd m 28, 29
cookie Keks m 160
cooking (cuisine) Küche f
copper Kupfer nt 149
copy Kopie f 155
corduroy Cord m
corkscrew Korkenzieher m 148
corner Ecke f 95
correct (also ➤ right) richtig
cosmetics Kosmetika pl
cot Kinderbett nt 22
cottage Ferienhaus nt 28
cotton Baumwolle f 145
cotton wool/absorbent cotton Watte f 141
cough Husten m 141;
~ syrup Hustensaft m; to ~ husten 164
could I have ...? könnte ich ... haben? 18
counter Theke f
country (nation) Land nt
country music Countrymusic f 111
countryside Landschaft f 119
couple (pair) Paar nt
courier (guide) Reiseleiter(in) m/f
course (meal) Gang m
cousin Cousin(e) m/f
cover (lid) Deckel m
cover charge Gedeck nt 112
craft shop Kunsthandwerksgeschäft nt
cramps Krämpfe mpl 163
crash: I've had a crash ich hatte einen
Unfall
creaks: the bed creaks das Bett knarrt
crèche Kinderkrippe f
credit card Kreditkarte
f 42, 136, 153;
~ number

A-Z

Kreditkartennummer f 109
credit status Kreditwürdigkeit f
credit, in im Haben
cross (crucifix) Kreuz nt
cross, to (road) gehen über 95
crossroad Kreuzung f
crowded überfüllt
crown (dental) Krone f 168
cruise Kreuzfahrt f
crutches Krücken fpl
crystal Kristall m 149
cuisine Küche f 119
cup Tasse f 39, 148
cupboard Schrank m
curlers Lockenwickler mpl
currency Währung f 67, 138;
  ~ exchange office Wechselstube f
  70, 73, 138
curtains Vorhänge mpl
cushion Kissen nt
customs Zoll m 67, 157;
  ~ declaration Zollerklärung f 155
cut (wound) Schnittwunde f 162
cut glass geschliffenes Kristallglas nt 149
cutlery Besteck nt 29, 148
cycling Rad fahren nt 114
cyclist Radfahrer(in) m/f
cystitis Blasenentzündung f 164
Czech Republic Tschechische Republik f

D **daily** täglich 13
damaged, to be beschädigt
  sein 28, 71
damp (n) Feuchtigkeit f; (adj) feucht
dance (performance) Tanz m 111
dancing, to go tanzen gehen 124
dangerous gefährlich
dark dunkel 14, 24, 134, 143
darts, to play Pfeilwerfen spielen
daughter Tochter f 120, 162
dawn Tagesanbruch m 221;
  Morgendämmerung f
day Tag m 97;
  ~ ticket Tageskarte f;
  ~ trip Tagesausflug m
dead tot; (battery) leer 88
deaf, to be taub sein 163
dear (greeting) lieber (liebe)
December Dezember m 218
deck (ship) Deck nt

deck chair Liegestuhl m 116
declare, to verzollen 67
deduct, to (money) abziehen
deep tief
defrost, to auftauen
degrees (temperature) Grad mpl
delay Verspätung f 70
delicate zart
delicatessen Feinkostgeschäft nt 130;
  Feinkostabteilung f
delicious köstlich 14
deliver, to liefern
denim Jeansstoff m 145
Denmark Dänemark nt
dental floss Zahnseide f
dentist Zahnarzt m, Zahnärztin f 131, 168
dentures Gebiss nt 168
deodorant Deodorant nt 142
depart, to (train, bus) abfahren
department (in store) Abteilung f;
  ~ store Kaufhaus nt 130
departure (train) Abfahrt f 76;
  ~ lounge Abflughalle f
depend: it depends on ...
  es hängt von ... ab
deposit Kaution f 24, 32, 83; **to pay a ~**
  eine Kaution hinterlegen
describe, to beschreiben 152
design (dress) Entwurf m
designer Designer(in) m/f
destination Reiseziel nt
details Einzelheiten fpl
detergent Waschmittel f
develop, to (photos) entwickeln 151
diabetes Zuckerkrankheit f
diabetic, to be Diabetiker sein 163
diagnosis Diagnose f 164
diamond Diamant m 149
diamonds (cards) Karo (nt sing)
diaper changing facilities Wickelraum m
  113
diapers Windeln fpl 142
diarrhea Durchfall m 141;
  to have ~ Durchfall haben 163
dice Würfel mpl
dictionary Wörterbuch nt 150
diesel Diesel m 87
diet: I'm on a diet ich mache eine Diät
different, something etwas anderes
difficult schwer 14
dine, to speisen
dinghy Dinghi nt
dining car Speisewagen m 75, 77

dining room Speisesaal m 26; Esszimmer nt 29
dinner jacket Smokingjacke f
dinner, to have zu Abend essen 124
direct durchgehend;
~-dial telephone Telefon nt mit Durchwahl
direct, to den Weg zeigen 18
direction Richtung f; **in the direction of ...** in Richtung ... 95
directions 94, 95
director *(movie)* Regisseur(in) m/f; *(of company)* Direktor(in) m/f
Directory Assistance Auskunft f 127
directory *(telephone)* Telefonbuch nt
dirty schmutzig 14
disabled *(n)* Behinderte pl 22, 100
discotheque Diskothek f 112
discount: can you offer me a discount? können Sie mir Rabatt geben?; **is there a discount for children?** gibt es eine Kinderermäßigung?
dish *(meal)* Gericht nt 37
dish cloth Spüllapen m 148
dishwashing detergent Spülmittel nt 148
disk film Disc-Film m
dislocated, to be verrenkt sein 164
disposable camera Einwegkamera f 151
distilled water destilliertes Wasser nt
district Gegend f
disturb: don't disturb nicht stören
dive, to tauchen 116
diversion Umleitung f
divorced, to be geschieden sein 120
DM DM f, Mark f 67, 138
do you accept ...? nehmen Sie ...? 136
do you have ...? haben Sie ...? 37
do, to unternehmen 123
dock Dock nt
doctor Arzt m, Ärztin f 131, 161, 167
doctor's office Arztpraxis f 161
dog Hund m
doll Puppe f 157
dollar Dollar m 67, 138
door Tür f 25, 29
dosage Dosierung f 140
double *(adj)* Doppel-;
~ bed Doppelbett nt 21;
~ cabin Doppelkabine f 81;
~ room Doppelzimmer nt 21
down hinunter
downstairs unten
downtown area Innenstadt f 99

dozen Dutzend nt 159, 217
drain Abflußrohr nt
drama Drama nt
dress Kleid nt 144
drink etwas zu trinken 70, 125, 126
drinking water Trinkwasser nt 30
drinks 49
drip: the tap drips der Hahn tropft
drive, to fahren 86
driver *(bus, etc)* Fahrer(in) m/f
driver's license Führerschein m
drop off, to absetzen 83; *(children)* abliefern 113
drowning: someone is drowning es ertrinkt jemand
drugstore Apotheke f 130, 140
drunk betrunken
dry-cleaner's Reinigung f 131
dry clothes, to Wäsche trocknen
dry-clean, to reinigen
dubbed, to be synchronisiert sein 110
due, to be *(payment)* fällig sein
during während 13
dusty staubig
duty-free goods zollfreie Waren fpl
duty-free shop Duty-Free m
duty-free shopping zollfreier Einkauf m 67
duty: to pay duty verzollen 67
duvet Federbett nt

E **each: how much are they each?** wie viel kosten sie pro Stück?
ear Ohr nt 166; **~ drops** Ohrentropfen mpl; **~ ache** Ohrenschmerzen pl 163
earlier früher 125
early früh 13, 14, 221
Easter Ostern nt 219
east of ... östlich von ... 95
easy einfach 14
eat, to essen 41, 123, 167
eaten: have you eaten? haben Sie schon gegessen?; **we've already eaten** wir haben schon gegessen
economical wirtschaftlich
economy class Touristenklasse f 68
egg Ei nt 160
eight acht 216
eighteen achtzehn 216

A-Z

eighty achtzig 217
either ... or entweder ... oder
elastic *(adj)* elastisch
electric blanket Heizdecke f
electric fire Elektroofen m
electric shaver elektrischer Rasierapparat m
electrical items Elektrogeräte ntpl
electrician Elektriker m
electricity Strom m;
~ **meter** Stromzähler m 28
electronic game Elektronikspiel m 157
elevator Aufzug m 26; Fahrstuhl m 132
eleven elf 216
else: something else etwas anderes
embark, to *(boat)* sich einschiffen
embassy Botschaft f
emerald Smaragd m
emergency Notfall m 127, 152;
~ **exit** Notausgang m; **it's an emergency** es ist ein Notfall ~ **room** Unfallstation f
empty leer 14
enamel Email nt 149
end, to aufhören 108
end: at the end am Ende 95
engine Motor m
engineer Ingenieur(in) m/f
England England nt 119
English *(adj)* englisch 110; *(language)* Englisch m 11, 150, 152, 161;
does anyone here speak English? spricht hier jemand Englisch? 67;
English-speaking englisch sprechend 98, 152;
enjoy: are you enjoying ...? gefällt Ihnen? 123; **are you enjoying your meal?** schmeckt Ihnen das Essen? 125;
do you enjoy ...? ... Sie gern? 124
enjoy: I enjoyed it es hat mir gefallen 110
enlarge, to *(photos)* vergrößern 151
enough *(adj)* genug 15, 42, 136
ensuite bathroom eigenes Bad nt
entertainment: ~ guide Veranstaltungskalender m
entirely ganz 17
entrance fee Eintritt m 100
entry visa Einreisevisum nt
envelope Briefumschlag m 150
epileptic, to be Epileptiker sein 140, 163
equally gleich 17
equipment *(sports)* Ausrüstung f 115

error Fehler m
escalator Rolltreppe f 132
essential wesentlich;
to make ~ repairs das Nötigste reparieren 89
Eurocheque Euroscheck m 138
evening dress Abendgarderobe f 112
evening, in the abends 221
events Veranstaltungen fpl 108
every day täglich 13
every week jede Woche 13
examination *(medical)* Untersuchung f
example, for zum Beispiel
except außer
excess baggage Übergepäck nt 69
exchange rate Wechselkurs m 138
exchange, to umtauschen
exclamations 19
excluding meals ohne Mahlzeiten 24
excursion Ausflug m 97
excuse me *(apology)* Entschuldigung, Verzeihung 10; *(getting attention)* entschuldigen Sie bitte 10, 37, 94
excuse me? wie bitte? 11
exhausted, to be erschöpft sein 106
exhibition Ausstellung f
exit Ausgang m 70;
at the ~ am Ausgang
expected, to be erwartet werden 111
expensive teuer 14, 134
expiration date Ablaufdatum nt
expire: when does it expire? wann läuft es ab?
express *(mail)* Express m 155
extension Apparat m 128
extension cord Verlängerungskabel nt
extra *(additional)* zusätzlich 27
extract, to *(tooth)* ziehen 168
extremely äußerst 17
eye Auge nt 166
eyeliner Lidstrich m
eyeshadow Lidschatten m

F
fabric *(material)* Stoff m
face Gesicht nt 166
facial Gesichtsbehandlung f 147
facilities Einrichtungen fpl 22, 30
factor *(sun-cream)* Lichtschutzfaktor m 142
faint: I feel faint mir ist schwindelig 163
fairground Festplatz m 113
fall Herbst m 219;
he's had a fall er ist gefallen

fall Herbst m 219
family Familie f 66 ,74, 120, 167
famous berühmt
fan *(air)* Ventilator m 25
fan: I'm a fan of …
  ich bin ein Fan von …
far weit 95;
  how far is it? wie weit ist es? 73
fare Fahrpreis m
farm Bauernhof m 107
fashionable, to be modern sein
fast schnell 93;
  ~ food Schnellgerichte ntpl 40;
  ~ food restaurant Schnellimbiss m 35;
  to be ~ *(clock)* vorgehen 221; **you were
  driving too fast** Sie sind zu schnell
  gefahren
fat Fett nt 39
father Vater m 120
faucet Wasserhahn m 25; Hahn m
fault: it's my/your fault es ist meine/Ihre
  Schuld
faulty nicht in Ordnung 137
favorite Lieblings-
fax Telefax nt 155;
  ~ facilities Telefaxdienst m 22;
  ~ machine Telefax m 155
February Februar m 218
feed, to füttern 39
feel ill, to sich nicht wohl fühlen 163
female weiblich 152
fence Zaun m
ferry Fähre f 81
festival Fest nt
feverish, to feel Fieber haben 163
few wenige 15
fiancé(e) Verlobte(r) (f/m)
field Feld nt 107
fifteen fünfzehn 216
fifth fünfte 217
fifty fünfzig 217
fight *(brawl)* Schlägerei f
fill in, to ausfüllen
filling *(dental)* Füllung f 168; *(in sandwich)*
  Belag m
film *(movie)* Film m, 108, 110; *(camera)*
  Film m 151
filter Filter m 151; **~ paper** *(for coffee)*
  Filterpapier nt
find out: could you find that out? können
  Sie das herausfinden?
fine *(penalty)* Bußgeld nt 93;
  (well) gut 118

finger Finger m 166
fire: there's a fire! es
  brennt!; **~ alarm**
  Feuermelder m; **~
  department** Feuerwehr f
  92; **~ escape** Feuerleiter f;
  ~ extinguisher Feuerlöscher
  m; **~lighters** Feueranzünder m 31;
  ~place Kamin m; **~wood** Brennholz nt
first erste 68, 75, 81, 217;
  ~ class erste Klasse f 68, 74;
  ~ floor Erdgeschoß nt
  I was first ich war zuerst da
first-aid kit Verbandskasten m
fish counter Fischtheke f 158
fish store Fischgeschäft nt 130
fishing rod Angelrute f
fishing, to go angeln gehen
fit, to *(clothes)* passen 146
fitting room Umkleidekabine f 146
five fünf 216
fix: can you fix it? können Sie es
  reparieren?
flag Fahne f
flannel Waschlappen m
(electronic) flash (Elektronen)blitz m 151
flat Platten m 88;
flavor: what flavors do you have? welche
  Geschmacksrichtungen haben Sie?
flea market Flohmarkt m
flight Flug m 70;
  ~ attendant Flugbegleiter(in)
  ~ number Flugnummer f 68
floats *(swimming)* Schwimmflügel mpl
flood Flut f
floor *(storey)* Etage f; Stock m 132;
  ~ mop Mop m; **~ show** Show f 112
florist's Blumengeschäft nt 130
flour Mehl nt 39
flower Blume f 106
flu Grippe f 165
**fluent: to speak fluent
  German** fließend Deutsch sprechen
flush: the toilet won't flush
  die Toilettenspülung funktioniert nicht
fly *(insect)* Fliege f
fly, to fliegen 68
foggy, to be neblig sein 122
folding table Klapptisch m 31
folk art Volkskunst f
folk music Volksmusik f 111
follow, to *(signs)* folgen 95; *(pursue)*
  verfolgen 152

food Essen nt 39, 41; ~ **poisoning** Lebensmittelvergiftung f 165
foot Fuß m 166
football (soccer) Fußball m 114
footpath Fußweg m 107
for a day für einen Tag 86
for a week für eine Woche 86
forecast Wetterbericht m 122
foreign ausländisch; ~ **currency** Devisen pl 138
forest Wald m 107
forget, to vergessen 41, 42
fork Gabel f 39, 41, 148; (in the road) Gabelung f
form Formular nt 23, 153, 168
formal dress Abendgarderobe f 111
forms Formulare ntpl
fortnight vierzehn Tage pl
fortunately glücklicherweise 19
forty vierzig 217
forward: please forward my mail bitte senden Sie meine Post nach
foundation (make-up) Grundierung f
fountain Brunnen m 99
four vier 216
four-door car viertüriges Auto 86
four-wheel drive Vierradantrieb m 86
fourteen vierzehn 216
fourth vierte 217
foyer (hotel/theater) Foyer nt
fracture Fraktur f 165
frame (glasses) Gestell nt
France Frankreich nt
free (of charge) kostenlos; (available/vacant) frei 36, 77, 124
freezer Gefrierschrank m 29
French (language) Französisch nt
French fries Pommes frites pl 38, 40, 160
frequent: how frequent? wie oft? 76
frequently oft
fresh frisch 41
Friday Freitag m 218
fridge Kühlschrank m 29
fried gebraten
friend Freund(in) m/f 162
friendly freundlich
fries Pommes frites pl 160;
frightened, to be Angst haben
from (place) von
from ... to (time) von ... bis 13

front door Vordereingang m 26
frosty, to be frostig sein 122
frozen tiefgefroren
fruit juice Fruchtsaft m
frying pan Bratpfanne f
fuel (gasoline) Treibstoff m 86
full voll 14
full board Vollpension f 24
full insurance Vollkaskoversicherung f 86
fun, to have Spaß haben
fun: it's great fun es macht Spaß 101
funny (amusing) lustig; (odd) merkwürdig
furniture Möbel pl
further: how much further to Berlin? wie weit ist es noch nach Berlin?
fuse Sicherung f 28;
~ **box** Sicherungskasten m 28;
~ **wire** Schmelzdraht m

G **gable** Giebel m
gallon Gallone f
gambling Glücksspiel nt
game (toy) Spiel nt 157
garage Garage f; Reparaturwerkstatt f 88
garbage bag Müllbeutel m
garbage cans Mülleimer mpl 30
garden Garten m
gardener Gärtner(in) m/f
gardening Gartenarbeit f
gas: I smell gas! es riecht nach Gas!;
~ **bottle** Gasflasche f 28;
~ **permeable lenses** gasdurchlässige Kontaktlinsen fpl
gas station Tankstelle f 87
gasoline Benzin nt 87, 88;
~ **can** Benzinkanister m
gastritis Magenschleimhautentzündung f 165
gate (airport) Flugsteig m 70
gay club Schwulenlokal nt 112
general delivery postlagernd 154
generous: that's very generous das ist sehr großzügig
genuine echt 134
geology Geologie f
German (language) Deutsch nt 11, 110, 126
German (person) Deutscher m, Deutsche f
Germany Deutschland nt 119
get, to (find) finden 84
get off, to (transport) aussteigen 79, 80

get to, to ankommen in 77;
how do I get to ...? wie komme ich
zu ...? 73; **wie komme ich nach ...?** 94
get help! holen Sie Hilfe!
gift Geschenk nt 67, 156;
~ shop Geschenkladen m 130
girl Mädchen nt 120, 157
girlfriend Freundin f 120
give, to geben
gland Drüse f 166
glass Glas nt 37, 39, 148
glasses Brille f sing 167
gliding Segelfliegen nt
glossy finish (photos) Hochglanz
glove Handschuh m
go, to gehen, fahren;
to ~ back (turn around) zurückfahren 95;
to ~ for a walk spazieren gehen 124
to ~ out (in evening) ausgehen;
to ~ shopping einkaufen gehen 124;
let's go! gehen wir!; **where does this
bus go?** wohin fährt dieser Bus?;
go away! gehen Sie weg!
goggles Schutzbrille f
gold Gold nt 149;
~plated vergoldet 149
golf Golf nt 114;
~ course Golfplatz m 115
good (adj) gut 14, 35, 42;
to be of ~ value preiswert sein 101
good afternoon guten Tag 10
good-bye auf Wiedersehen 10
good evening guten Abend 10
good morning guten Morgen 10
good night gute Nacht 10
got: have you got any ...? haben Sie ...?
gram Gramm nt 159
grandparents Großeltern pl
grapes Weintrauben fpl 160
grass Gras nt
gratuity Trinkgeld nt
gray grau 143
graze Schürfwunde f 162
greasy (hair) fettig
Greek (adj) griechisch 35
green grün 143
greetings 10
grilled gegrillt
grocery store Lebensmittelgeschäft
nt 130, 159
ground (camping) Boden m 31
group Gruppe f 66, 100

guide (tour) Führer(in)
m/f 98;
~book Reiseführer m
100, 150
guided tour Führung f
100
guitar Gitarre f
gum (mouth) Zahnfleisch nt
gym session Fitneßtraining nt
gynecologist Frauenarzt m, Frauenärztin
f 167

H **hair** Haar nt 147;
~ brush Haarbürste f;
~ dryer Haartrockner m;
~ gel Haargel nt; **~ mousse**
Schaumfestiger m 142;
~ slide Haarspange f;
~ spray Haarspray nt 142
haircare 142
haircut Haarschnitt m
hairdresser Friseur m,
Friseuse f 131, 147
half board Halbpension f 24
half fare halber Fahrpreis m
half past six halb sieben 220
half, a Hälfte f 217
hammer Hammer m 31
hand Hand f 166;
~ cream Handcreme f;
~ luggage Handgepäck 69;
~ towel Handtuch nt
handbag Handtasche f 144, 153
handicap (golf) Vorgabe f
handicapped, to be behindert sein 163
handicrafts Kunsthandwerk nt
handkerchief Taschentuch nt
handle Griff m
hang-gliding
Drachenfliegen nt
hanger Kleiderbügel m 27
hangover (n) Kater m 141
happen: what happened?
was ist passiert?
happy: I'm not happy with the service
ich bin mit dem Service nicht zufrieden
hard shoulder (road) Seitenstreifen m
hardware store Eisenwarenhandlung f
130
hat Hut m 144
hatchback Hecktürmodell nt
have, to (➤ 187) haben 18;

A-Z

have to, to *(must)*
müssen 79
hayfever Heuschnupfen
m 141
head Kopf m 166;
~ache Kopfschmerzen pl
163; ~band Stirnband nt
head for, to fahren nach 83
heading: where are you heading?
wohin fahren Sie? 83
head waiter Oberkellner m 41
health food store Naturkostladen m 130
health insurance Krankenversicherung f
hear, to hören
hearing aid Hörgerät nt
heart Herz nt 166;
~ attack Herzanfall m 163;
~ condition Herzleiden nt 163
hearts *(cards)* Herz nt sing
heater Ofen m
heating Heizung f 25
heavy schwer 14, 134
height Größe f 152; Höhe f
helicopter Hubschrauber m
hello Guten Tag 10, 118; hallo 10
help Hilfe f 94;
to help helfen 18; could you help me?
können Sie mir helfen? 92
helper Helfer(in) m/f 113
hemorrhoids Hämorrhoiden pl
her sie; *(possessive)* ihr 16
here hier 12, 17; *(to here)* hierher 12
hernia Bruch m 165
hers ihre(-r, -s) 16;
it's hers es gehört ihr
hi! hallo! 10
high hoch 106;
~ tide Flut f
highlight, to *(hair)* Strähnchen
machen 147
hike *(walk)* Wanderung f 106
hiking Wandern nt;
~ gear Wanderausrüstung f 145
hill Hügel m 107
him ihn
Hindu *(n)* Hindu m; *(adj)* hinduistisch
his seine(-r, -s) 16;
it's his es gehört ihm
history Geschichte f
hitchhike, to trampen, per Anhalter
fahren
hitchhiking Trampen nt 83
HIV-positive HIV-positiv

hobby *(pastime)* Hobby nt 121
hockey *(field)* Hockey nt
hold on! *(telephone)* bleiben Sie am
Apparat! 128
hold, to *(contain)* enthalten
hole *(in clothes)* Loch nt
holiday resort Ferienort m
Holland Holland nt
home: to go home nach Hause fahren;
we're going home on ... wir fahren am
... nach Hause
homeopathic remedy homöopathisches
Mittel nt
homosexual *(adj)* homosexuell
honeymoon, to be on auf der
Hochzeitsreise sein
hopefully hoffentlich 19
horse Pferd nt
horseback trip Reiterausflug m
horseracing Pferderennen nt 114
hospital Krankenhaus nt 131, 164, 167
hot heiß 14; warm 24, 122;
~ dog heißes Würstchen nt 110;
~ spring Thermalquelle f;
~ water heißes Wasser nt 25;
~ water bottle Wärmflasche f
hotel Hotel nt 21;
~ booking 21
hour Stunde f 97;
in an ~ in einer Stunde 84
hours *(doctor's office)* Sprechstunden fpl
161
house Haus nt
household articles Haushaltsartikel
mpl 148
housewife Hausfrau f 121
hovercraft Luftkissenboot nt
how are you? wie geht es Ihnen? 118
how far? wie weit? 94, 106
how long? wie lange? *(hotel)* 23, *(journey)*
75, *(ticket valid)* 76, *(breakdown)* 88
how many? wie viele? 15, 69, 80
how much? wie viel? 15, 84, 109
how often? wie oft? 140
how old? wie alt? 120
how? wie? 17
hundred hundert, einhundert 217
Hungary Ungarn nt
hungry, to be Hunger haben
hurt: it hurts es tut weh 163;
to be ~ verletzt sein 162
husband Mann m 120 ,162

I **I'd like ...** ich hätte gern ... 18, 37, 40

I'd like to ... ich möchte ... 36

I'll have ... ich nehme ... 37

ice Eis nt 38;
~ dispenser Eisspender m;
~ hockey Eishockey nt; **~ rink** Eisbahn f

ice cream Eis nt 40, 160; **~ parlour** Eisdiele nt 35; **~ cone** Eistüte f

icy, to be eisig sein 122

identification Ausweis m 136

ill, to be krank sein

illegal, to be nicht erlaubt sein

illness Krankheit f

imitation imitiert 134

immediately sofort 13

in *(place/time)* in 12, 13

in-law: father~ Schwiegervater m; **mother~** Schwiegermutter f

included: is ... included? ist ... inbegriffen? 86, 98

inconvenient: it's inconvenient es ist ungünstig

Indian *(adj)* indisch

indicate, to *(in car)* blinken

indigestion Verdauungsstörungen fpl

indoor Hallen-;
~ pool Hallenbad nt 116

inexpensive preiswert 35

infected, to be entzündet sein 165

infection Entzündung f 165

inflammation Entzündung f 165

informal *(dress)* zwanglos

information Informationen fpl 97;
~ desk Auskunft f 73;
~ office Verkehrsbüro nt 96

injection Spritze f 168

injured, to be verletzt sein 92, 162

innocent unschuldig

insect Insekt nt 25;
~ bite Insektenstich m 141, 162;
~ repellent Insektenschutzmittel m 141;
~ spray Insektenspray nt 141

inside drinnen 12

inside lane Innenspur f

insist: I insist ich bestehe darauf

insomnia Schlaflosigkeit f

instant coffee Pulverkaffee m 160

instead of statt

instructions Gebrauchsanweisung f 135

instructor Lehrer(in) m/f

insulin Insulin nt

insurance Versicherung f 86, 89, 93, 168;
~ certificate Versicherungsschein m 93;
~ claim Versicherungsanspruch m 153;
~ company Versicherungsgesellschaft f 93

interest rate Zinssatz m

interest: what are your interests? wofür interessieren Sie sich?

interesting interessant 101

international international

International Student Card Internationaler Studentenausweis m 29

interpreter Dolmetscher m 93, 153

intersection Kreuzung f 95

interval Pause f

into in (... hinein)

introductions 118

invitation Einladung f 124

invite, to einladen 124

involved, to be beteiligt sein 93

iodine Jod nt

Ireland Irland nt 119

Irish *(adj)* irisch

Irish *(n)* Ire m, Irin f

iron *(for clothing)* Bügeleisen nt; **travel ~** Reisebügeleisen nt; **to iron** bügeln

is there ...? gibt es ...? 17

island Insel f

it is ... es ist ... 17

Italian *(adj)* italienisch 35

Italy Italien nt

itch: it itches es juckt

itemized bill spezifizierte Rechnung f 42

J **jack/knave** *(cards)* Bube m
jacket Jacke f 144;
(of suit) Jackett nt 144

jam Marmelade f 160

jammed, to be klemmen 25

January Januar m 218

jar Glas nt 159

jaw Kiefer m 166

jeans Jeans pl 144

jellyfish Qualle f

jet lag: I have jet lag

A-Z

der Zeitunterschied macht mir zu schaffen
jet ski Jet-Ski m 116
Jew *(n)* Jude m, Jüdin f
jewelry store Juwelier m 130, 149
Jewish *(adj)* jüdisch
job: what's your job? was machen Sie beruflich?
jogging pants Jogging-Hose f
jogging, to go einen Dauerlauf machen
join: may we join you? dürfen wir uns zu Ihnen setzen? 124
joint *(body)* Gelenk nt 166
joint passport gemeinsamer Paß m 66
joke Witz m
joker *(cards)* Joker m
journalist Journalist(in) m/f
journey Fahrt f 76
judo Judo nt
jug *(of water)* Krug m
July Juli m 218
jumper cables Starthilfekabel nt sing
junction *(exit)* Ausfahrt f; *(intersection)* Kreuzung f
June Juni m 218

K

kaolin Kaolin nt
keep: keep the change der Rest ist für Sie
kettle Kessel m 29
key Schlüssel m 27, 28, 88;
  ~ ring Schlüsselanhänger m 156
kidney Niere f 166
kilo(gram) Kilo nt 69, 159
kilometer Kilometer m 86
kind *(pleasant)* nett
kind: what kind of ... welche Art von ...
king *(cards/chess)* König m
kiss, to küssen 126
kitchen Küche f 29;
  ~ paper Küchenpapier nt
kitchenette Kochnische f
knee Knie nt 166
knife Messer nt 39, 41, 148
knight *(chess)* Springer m
knocked down, to be angefahren werden
know: I don't know ich weiß nicht
kosher koscher

L

label Etikett nt
lace Spitze f 145
ladder Leiter f

ladies' toilet Damentoilette f
lake See m 107
lamp Lampe f 25
land, to landen 70
landfill *(dump)* Müllabladeplatz m
landing *(house)* Gang m
landlord/landlady Vermieter(in) m/f
lane Spur f
language course Sprachkurs m
large *(adj)* groß 40; *(drink)* 110
last *(final/previous)* letzte 14, 68, 75, 81
late spät 14, 221; *(delayed)* verspätet;
  to be late Verspätung haben 70
later später 125
laugh, to lachen 126
laundromat Waschsalon m 131
laundry service Wäschedienst m 22
lawn Rasen m
lawyer Anwalt m, Anwältin f 152
laxative Abführmittel nt
lead, to *(road)* führen nach 94
leader *(of group)* Leiter(in) m/f
leaflet Broschüre f
leak, to *(roof, pipe)* undicht sein
learn, to *(language, sport)* lernen
learner Anfänger(in) m/f
least expensive preiswerteste
leather Leder nt 145
leave me alone! lassen Sie mich in Ruhe! 126
leave, to *(depart)* abfahren 76, 78, 81, 98;
  abreisen 32; gehen; *(plane)* abfliegen 68;
  (leave behind car) stehen lassen 73; *(hand in luggage)* einstellen; **I've left my bag in ...**
  ich habe meine Tasche in ... gelassen
lecturer Dozent(in) m/f
left-hand side linke Seite
left, on the auf der linken Seite 76, 95
left-handed linkshändig
left-luggage office Gepäckaufbewahrung f 71, 73
left: are there any seats left? sind noch Plätze frei?
leg Bein nt 166
legal matters *(car accident)* 93
legal, to be erlaubt sein
leggings Leggings pl 144
lemon Zitrone f 38
lemonade Limonade f
lend: could you lend me ...? könnten Sie mir ... leihen?
length *(of)* Länge f

184

lens *(camera)* Objektiv nt 151; *(optical)*
Brillenglas nt 167;
~ **cap** Objektivdeckel m 151
lesbian club Lesbenlokal nt
less weniger 15
lessons Unterricht m sing 117
let: please let me know bitte sagen Sie mir
Bescheid
letter Brief m 154;
~ **box** Briefkasten m;
by letter schriftlich 22 ;
~ **carrier** Postbote m
level *(ground)* eben
library Bibliothek f; Bücherei f 131
lie down, to sich hinlegen
lifebelt Rettungsring m
lifeboat Rettungsboot nt
lifeguard Rettungsschwimmer m 116
lifejacket Schwimmweste f
lift pass Liftkarte f 117
lift: to give someone a lift
jemanden mitnehmen 83
light *(adj)* *(color)* hell 14, 134, 143; *(weight)*
leicht 14, 134; *(n)* *(cigarette)* Feuer nt;
(electric) Licht nt 25;
~**bulb** Glühbirne f 148
lighter Feuerzeug nt 150
lighthouse Leuchtturm m
lightning Blitz m
lights *(bicycle)* Beleuchtung f 83
like: I'd like ich hätte gern;
I'd like to buy ... ich möchte ... kaufen
133;
like this *(similar to)* ähnlich wie dies, so
limousine Limousine f
line *(metro)* Linie f 80;
(profession) Beruf m 121; Schlange f;
an outside line, please
einen Amtsanschluß, bitte
linen Leinen nt 145
lip Lippe f 166;
~**salve** Fettstift m 142;
~**stick** Lippenstift m
liqueur Likör m
liquor store Wein und
Spirituosenhandlung f 131
liter Liter m 87, 159
little klein;
a ~ ein wenig
live, to wohnen;
to ~ **together** zusammenleben 120
liver Leber f 166
living room Wohnzimmer nt 29
loaf of bread Brot nt 160

lobby *(theater, hotel)*
Foyer nt
local hiesig 37;
~ **anesthetic** örtliche
Betäubung f 168
lock Schloss nt 25; *(canal)*
Schleuse f
lock, to abschließen;
to ~ **oneself out** sich aussperren 27
locked, to be abgeschlossen sein 26;
it's locked es ist abgeschlossen
locker Schließfach nt
lollipop Lutscher m
long *(clothing)* lang 146; *(time)* lange;
how long? wie lange? 164
long-distance call Ferngespräch nt
long-distance bus Überlandbus m 78
longer: how much longer?
wie lange noch? 41
long-sighted weitsichtig 167
**look after: please look after my case
for a minute** bitte achten Sie einen
Moment auf meinen Koffer
look for, to suchen 18
look forward: I'm looking forward to it
ich freue mich darauf
look like, to aussehen wie 71
look, to have a *(check)* sich ... ansehen 89
I'm just looking ich sehe mich nur um
loose weit 146; *(clothing)* locker 117
lose, to verlieren 28, 153;
I've lost ... ich habe ... verloren 71, 153
lost, to be verlorengehen 71; sich verirrt
haben
lost property Fundbüro nt 73
lotion Lotion f
lots viel
loud, it's too es ist zu laut
louder lauter 128
love: I love German food
ich mag das deutsche
Essen sehr gern;
I love you ich liebe dich
low-fat fettarm
lower: I'd like a lower berth
ich möchte unten schlafen 74
lubricant Schmiermittel nt
luck: good luck! viel Glück! 219
luggage Gepäck nt 32, 67, 69, 71;
~ **allowance** Freigepäck nt;
~ **carts** Kofferkulis mpl 71
~ **locker** Schließfach nt 71, 73;
~ **tag** Gepäckanhänger m;
~ **ticket** Gepäckaufbewahrungsschein
m 71;

A-Z

lump Knoten m 162
lumpy *(mattress)* klumpig
lunch Mittagessen nt 98
Luxemburg Luxemburg nt
luxury Luxus m

M *(dear)* **madam** sehr
geehrte Frau
made of: what is it made of? woraus
besteht es?
magazine Zeitschrift f 150
magnetic north nördlicher Magnetpol m
magnificent großartig 101
maid Zimmermädchen nt 27
maiden name Mädchenname m
mail *(post)* Post f 27, 154;
~ **box** Briefkasten m 154;
~ **office** Postamt 96, 131, 154
main Haupt 130;
~ **course** Hauptgericht nt;
~ **rail station** Hauptbahnhof m 73;
~ **street** Hauptstraße f 95, 96
mains Stromnetz nt
make *(brand)* Marke f
make an appointment, to einen Termin
bekommen 161
makeup Make-up nt
make, to machen;
~ **tea/coffee** Tee/Kaffee kochen
male männlich 152
mallet Holzhammer m 31
man Mann m
manager Geschäftsführer(in) m/f 25, 41;
(of shop) 137
manicure Maniküre f 147
manual *(handbook)* Handbuch nt
many viele 15
map Karte f, 106; Landkarte f
March März m 218
margarine Margarine f 160
mark D-Mark f 67
market Markt m 99, 131;
~ **day** Markttag m
married, to be verheiratet sein 120
mascara Wimperntusche f
mask *(diving)* Maske f
mass Messe f 105
massage Massage f 147
mat/matt *(photos)* matt
match *(game)* Spiel nt 114
matches *(game)* Streichhölzer ntpl 31, 148, 150
material Material nt, Stoff m

matinée Nachmittagsvorstellung f 109
matter: it doesn't matter es macht nichts;
what's the matter? was ist los?
mattress Matratze f 31
May Mai m 218
may I? kann ich? 18
maybe vielleicht
me mich
meal Essen nt 38, 42, 125
mean, to bedeuten 11
measles Masern pl 165
measure, to Maß nehmen 146
measurement Maß nt
meat Fleisch nt 41
medical certificate ärztliches Zeugnis nt
medication Medikament nt 164, 165
medium *(adj)* mittel/normal 40; *(steak)*
mittel
meet, to treffen 125;
pleased to meet you sehr angenehm 118
meeting place Treffpunkt m
member *(of club)* Mitglied nt 112, 115
men's room Herrentoilette f
mend, to reparieren 137
mention: don't mention it gern geschehen
10; es ist nicht der Rede wert
menu Speisekarte f
message Nachricht f 27
metal Metall nt
methylated spirits Brennspiritus m 31
microwave oven Mikrowellenherd m
midday Mittag m
midnight Mitternacht f 220
might: I might not vielleicht nicht
migraine Migräne f
mileage Kilometergeld nt 86
milk Milch f 160;
with ~ mit Milch 40;
~ **of magnesia** Magnesiamilch f
million Million f 217
mince Hackfleisch nt 160
mind: do you mind? stört es Sie? 77, 126;
I've changed my mind ich habe es mir
anders überlegt
mine meine(-r, -s) 16;
it's mine es gehört mir
mineral water Mineralwasser nt
minibar Minibar f 32
minibus Kleinbus m
minimum *(n)* Minimum nt
minister Pfarrer m
minor road Nebenstraße f
minute Minute f 76

rror Spiegel m
ss, to verpassen; **have I missed the bus ...?** habe ich den Bus nach ... verpaßt?
ssing, to be *(lacking)* fehlen; *(person)* verschwunden sein 152
stake Fehler m 41, 136; Irrtum m 41
sunderstanding, there's been a s hat ein Mißverständnis gegeben
ttens Fausthandschuhe mpl
dern modern 14;
art moderne Kunst f
oisturizing cream Feuchtigkeitscreme f 142
nastery Kloster nt 99
nday Montag m 218
ney Geld nt 42, 139, 153
nth Monat m 218
nthly ticket Monatskarte f
nument Denkmal nt
or, to anlegen
oring Anlegeplatz m
ped Moped nt 83
re mehr 15, 67;
d like some more ... ich hätte gern noch was ... 39
rning, in the morgens 221
rning-after pill Pille f danach
slem *(adj)* moslemisch; *(n)* Moslem m
squito Stechmücke f;
bite Mückenstich m
ther Mutter f 120
torbike Motorrad nt 83
torboat Motorboot nt 116
torcycle Motorrad nt;
parts 82
torway Autobahn f 94
ountain Berg m 107;
bike Mountain-Bike nt;
range Gebirge nt 107
ountaineering Bergsteigen nt
ousetrap Mausefalle f
ustache Schnurrbart m
outh Mund m 166;
ulcer Aphthe f
ove, to *(rooms)* umziehen 25; *(car)* woanders hinstellen; **don't move him!** bewegen Sie ihn nicht! 92; **to ~ house** umziehen
ovie Film m 108, 110;
theater Kino nt 110
. Herr
s./Ms. Frau
ch viel 15

mug Becher m 148
mugged, to be auf der Straße überfallen werden 153
mugging Straßenraub m 152
multiple journey ticket Mehrfachkarte f
multiplex cinema Multiplexkino nt 110
multipurpose vehicle Geländewagen m
mumps Mumps m
muscle Muskel m 166
museum Museum nt 99
music Musik f 111;
~ **box** Musikbox f
musician Musiker(in) m/f
Muslim *(adj)* moslemisch; *(n)* Muslim m
must: I must ich muss
mustard Senf m 38, 160
my mein 16
myself: I'll do it myself
ich mache es selbst

N

nail polish Nagellack m
nail scissors Nagelschere f sing
name Name m 22, 36, 93, 118
my name is ich heiße 118;
what's your name? wie heißen Sie? 118
napkin *(serviette)* Serviette f 139
narrow eng 14
national national
nationality Nationalität f
natural history Naturkunde f
nature reserve Naturschutzgebiet nt 107
nausea Übelkeit f
navigation channel Fahrrinne f
navy blue marineblau
near nah; **near here** hier in der Nähe 84
nearby in der Nähe 21, 87
nearest nächste 80, 88, 92, 130, 140
necessary nötig 89
neck Hals m 166; *(clothes)* Ausschnitt m
need: I need to ... ich möchte ...
needle Nadel f
negative *(photo)* Negativ nt
neighbor Nachbar(in) m/f
nephew Neffe m
nerve Nerv m 166
nervous system Nervensystem nt 166
Netherlands Niederlande pl
never nie 13
never mind das macht nichts 10

A-Z

A-Z

new neu 14
new year Neujahr nt 219
New Zealand Neuseeland nt 119
newspaper Zeitung f 150
newsstand Zeitungskiosk m 150

next nächste 14, 68, 75, 78, 80, 81, 87; **next stop!** die nächste Haltestelle! 79
next to neben 95
nice nett 14
niece Nichte f
night porter Nachtportier m
night: per night pro Nacht; **at night** nachts 221
nightclub Nachtklub m 112
nightdress Nachthemd nt
nine neun 216
nineteen neunzehn 216
ninety neunzig 217
no nein 10
no one niemand 16, 92
noisy laut 14, 24
non-alcoholic alkoholfrei
none keine(-r, -s) 15, 16
non-smoking (adj) Nichtraucher pl 36
non-smoking (area) Nichtraucher pl 69
noon Mittag m 220
normal normal 67
Northern Ireland Nordirland nt
north of nördlich von 95
nose Nase f 166
not that one nicht das da 16
not yet noch nicht 13
note (money) Schein m
nothing else sonst nichts 15
nothing for me nichts für mich
nothing to declare nichts zu verzollen 15
notice board Anschlagbrett nt 26
notify, to benachrichtigen 167
November November m 218
now jetzt 13; (immediately) sofort 84
nudist beach Nacktbadestrand m
number (telephone) Nummer f 84; **sorry, wrong number** falsch verbunden
number plate (registration plate) Nummernschild nt
nurse Krankenschwester f
nut (for bolt) Schraubenmutter f
nylon Nylon nt

O **o'clock, it's ...** es ist ... Uhr 220
observatory Observatorium nt
occasionally gelegentlich
occupations 121
occupied besetzt 14
October Oktober m 218
odds (betting) Chancen fpl 114
of von
of course natürlich 19
off-road (multipurpose) vehicle Geländewagen m
off-season Nebensaison f
office Büro nt
often oft
oil Öl nt
okay in Ordnung 10
old alt 14
old town Altstadt f 96, 99
old-fashioned altmodisch 14
olive oil Olivenöl nt
omelet Omelett nt
on (day, date) am 13; (place) auf 12; **this round's on me** diese Runde gebe ich aus
on/off switch Ein- und Ausschalter m
on board (ship) an Bord; (train) im Zug 74
on foot zu Fuß 17, 95
on the left links 12
on the other side auf der anderen Seite
on the right rechts 12
on the spot (immediately) sofort 93
once einmal 217; **once a week** einmal in der Woche 13
one eins 216; **~way ticket** einfaches Flugticket nt 68; **one like that** so eins 16
open (door) auf; (shop) geöffnet 14; **open to the public** der Öffentlichkeit zugänglich 100
open, to öffnen 132; (shop) 140
opening hours Öffnungszeiten fpl
opera Oper f 108, 111; **~ house** Opernhaus nt 99, 111
operation Operation f
operator Vermittlung f
opposite gegenüber
optician Optiker(in) m/f 131, 167
or oder 19
orange (adj) orange 143; (fruit) Orange f 160

orchestra Orchester nt 111
order, to bestellen 37, 41, 89, 135;
    (taxi) 32
ordering Bestellen nt 37
organized walk/hike geführte
    Wanderung f 106
ornithology Ornithologie f
others anderes
our unser 16;
    ours unsere(-r, -s) 16
out: he's out er ist nicht da
outdoor Frei- ~ pool Freibad nt 116
outside draußen 12; im Freien 36
oval oval 134
oven Backofen m
over über;
    over there dort drüben 76
overcharged: I've been overcharged man
    hat mir zuviel berechnet
overdone *(food)* zu stark gebraten 41
overdraft Überziehungskredit m;
    I am overdrawn mein Konto ist
    überzogen
overnight über Nacht
owe: how much do I owe you? wie viel
    bin ich Ihnen schuldig?
own: on my own allein 65
owner Besitzer(in) m/f

P **p.m.** nachmittags
    pacifier Schnuller m
pack of cards Kartenspiel nt
pack, to packen 69
package Paket nt
packed lunch Lunchpaket nt
packet Packung f 159;
    ~ of cigarettes Schachtel f
    Zigaretten nt
paddling pool Planschbecken nt 113
padlock Vorhängeschloss nt
pain, to be in Schmerzen haben 167
pain killer Schmerzmittel nt 141, 165
paint, to malen 104
painted gemalt 104
painter Maler(in) m/f
painting Gemälde nt
pair of, a Paar nt 217
pajamas Schlafanzug m
palace Palast m 99
panorama Panorama nt 107
pants Hose f 144
panty hose Strumpfhose f 144

paper Papier nt;
    ~ napkins
    Papierservietten fpl 148
paraffin Paraffin nt 31
paralysis Lähmung f
parcel *(package)* Paket nt
    155
parents Eltern pl 120
park Park m 96, 99, 107;
    ~ ranger Parkaufseher m
park, to parken 30
parka Anorak m 145
parking Parken nt 87;
    ~ disk Parkscheibe f;
    ~ lot Parkplatz m 87, 96;
    ~ meter Parkuhr f 87
partner *(boyfriend/girlfriend)*
    Partner(in) m/f
parts *(components)* Ersatzteile pl 89
party *(social)* Party f 124;
    (group) Gruppe f
pass Pass m 107
pass, to vorbeikommen an 77;
    to ~ through auf der Durchreise sein 66
passenger Passagier m
passing lane Überholspur f
passport Paß m 32, 66, 69;
    Reisepass m 153;
    passport control 66
pastry shop Konditorei f 131
path Weg m 107
patient Patient(in) m/f 161
pay phone Münzfernsprecher m
pay, to bezahlen 136; zahlen 42, 87, 136;
    ~ a fine ein Bußgeld bezahlen 93;
    ~ by credit card mit Kreditkarte
    bezahlen
paying *(hotel)* 32; *(resataurant)* 42;
    (shopping) 136
payment Zahlung f
peak Gipfel m 107
pearl Perle f 149
peddle boat Tretboot nt·
pedestrian crossing Fußgängerüberweg
    m 96
pedestrian zone Fußgängerzone f 96
pedicure Pediküre f
pen *(ballpoint)* Kugelschreiber m 150
pencil Bleistift m
penfriend Brieffreund(in) m/f
penicillin Penizillin nt
penknife Taschenmesser nt 31
people Leute pl

pepper Pfeffer m 38

per: per day pro Tag 30, 83, 86, 87, 115;
~ per hour pro Stunde f 87, 115;
~ per night pro Nacht f 21;
~ per week pro Woche f 83, 86

performance Vorstellung f

perhaps vielleicht 19

period Zeit f 105; (menstrual) Periode f 167; ~ pains Menstruationsbeschwerden pl 167

perm Dauerwelle f 147;
to ~ eine Dauerwelle machen 147

permit Genehmigung f

pet (n) Haustier nt

pewter Zinn nt 149

pharmacy Apotheke f 130, 140, 158

phone Telefon nt;
~ call Anruf m; to make a ~ call telefonieren 127;
~ card Telefonkarte f 127, 155

photo: passport-size photo Passbild nt 115; to take a ~ ein Foto machen

photocopier Fotokopiergerät nt 155

photographer Fotograf m

photography Fotografie f 151

phrase Ausdruck m 11;
~ book Sprachführer m

piano Klavier nt

pick someone up, to jemanden abholen 125; (children) 113; (ticket) 109

pick-up truck Kleintransporter m

picnic Picknick nt;
~ area Picknickplatz m 107

piece Stück nt 159;
a ~ of ... ein Stück ... 40;
~ of luggage Gepäckstück nt 69

pill (contraceptive): to be on the pill die Pille nehmen 140, 167

pillow Kopfkissen nt 27;
~ case Kopfkissenbezug m

pilot light Zündflamme f

pink rosa 143

pint Pint nt

pipe Pfeife f;
~ cleaners Pfeifenreiniger mpl;
~ tobacco Pfeifentabak m

pitch (for camping) Platz m;
~ charge Platzgebühr f

pity: it's a pity es ist schade

place Ort m; (space) Platz m 29

place a bet, to eine Pferdewette abschließen 114

plain (not patterned) einfarbig

plane Flugzeug nt, Maschine f 68

plans Pläne mpl

plant Pflanze f

plastic bag Plastiktüte f

plastic wrap Klarsichtfolie f 148

plate Teller m 39, 148

platform Bahnsteig m 73, 76

platinum Platin nt 149

play, to (sport/games) spielen 121; (drama) gegeben werden 110; (music) spielen 111

playground Spielplatz m 113

playgroup Spielgruppe f 113

playing cards Spielkarten fpl

playing field Sportplatz m

playwright Autor m 110

pleasant freundlich 14

please bitte 10

pliers Zange f sing

plug Stecker m 148

plumber Klempner m

pneumonia Lungenentzündung f 165

point of interest Sehenswürdigkeiten fpl 97

point to, to zeigen auf 11

poison Gift nt 141

poisonous giftig

poker (cards) Poker nt

Poland Polen nt

police Polizei f 92, 152;
~ certificate polizeiliche Bescheinigung f 153

police station Polizeiwache f 96, 152; Polizei f 131

pollen count Pollenflug m 122

polyester Polyester nt

pond Teich m 107

popcorn Popcorn nt 110

popular beliebt 157

port (harbor) Hafen m

porter (hotel) Portier m 27; (station) Gepäckträger m 71

portion Portion f 40

possible: as soon as possible so bald wie möglich

possibly möglicherweise

post (mail) Post f;
~card Postkarte f 150, 154, 156;
~ office Postamt nt 96, 131, 154;
to ~ aufgeben

poster Poster nt

otatoes Kartoffeln fpl 38
ottery Töpferei f
ound *(sterling)* Pfund nt 67
owder puff Puderquaste f
ower cut Stromausfall m
ower point Steckdose f
ractice: to practice speaking German
 Deutsch sprechen üben
regnant, to be schwanger sein 163
remium *(gas)* Super nt 87
rescribe, to verschreiben 165
rescription Medizin f 140; Rezept nt 141
resent *(gift)* Geschenk nt
ress, to bügeln 137
retty hübsch 101
riest Priester m
rison Gefängnis nt
rivate bathroom eigenes Bad nt
robably wahrscheinlich
roduce store Gemüsehandlung f 130
rogram Programm nt;
 ~ of events Veranstaltungskalender m
 108
rohibited: is it prohibited? ist es
 verboten?
romenade deck Promenadendeck nt
ronounce, to aussprechen 11
ropelling pencil Drehbleistift m
roperly richtig
rotestant Protestant(in) m/f
ublic building öffentliches Gebäude
 nt 96
ublic holiday Feiertag m 219
ullover Pullover m 144
ump Pumpe f
uncture Platten m 83, 88
uppet show Puppentheater nt 113
ure *(material)* rein 145
urple violett 143
urpose Zweck m 66
urse Geldbeutel m 153; Handtasche
 f 153
ut: where can I put …? wo kann ich …
 hintun?; **can you put me up for the night?**
 können Sie mich heute nacht
 unterbringen?

quality Qualität f 134
quantity Menge f 134
quarantine Quarantäne f
quarter past/after Viertel nach 220
quarter to/before Viertel vor 220

quarter, a Viertel nt 217
quarter-deck *(ship)*
 Achterdeck nt
quay Kai m
queen *(cards/chess)* Dame f
question Frage f
quick schnell 14
quickest: what's the quickest way to …?
 was ist der schnellste Weg nach …?
quickly schnell 17
quiet leise 14
quieter ruhiger 24, 126

R rabbi Rabbiner
 m
race *(cars/horses)* Rennen nt;
 ~ course *(track)* Pferderennbahn f 114
racing bike Rennrad nt
racket *(tennis, squash)* Schläger m 115
radio Radio nt
rail station Bahnhof m 73
railroad Bahn f, Eisenbahn f
railway Bahn f, Eisenbahn f
rain, to regnen 122
raincoat Regenmantel m 144
rape Vergewaltigung f 152
rapids Stromschnellen fpl 107
rare *(steak)* blutig; *(unusual)* selten
rarely selten
rash Ausschlag m 162
rather ziemlich
razor Rasierapparat m;
 ~ blades Rasierklingen fpl 142;
 ~ socket Steckdose f für Rasierapparate
 26
reading *(interest)* Lesen nt;
 ~ glasses Lesebrille f
ready fertig 89;
 to be ~ fertig sein 137, 151; **are you
 ready?** sind Sie fertig?
real *(genuine)* echt 149
real estate agent Immobilienmahler m
receipt Quittung f 32, 42, 89, 136, 137;
 Schein m 151
reception (desk) Empfang m
receptionist Empfangschef(in) m/f
reclaim, to zurückfordern ·
recommend, to empfehlen 21, 35, 141;
 can you recommend …? können Sie …
 empfehlen? 97, 112; **what do you
 recommend?** was empfehlen Sie?
record *(lp)* Schallplatte f 157;

~ store Plattengeschäft nt 131

red rot 143;

~ wine Rotwein m 40

reduction *(in price)* Ermäßigung f 24, 74, 100

re-enter, to wieder hereinkommen

refund: I'd like a refund ich hätte gern mein Geld zurück 137

regards: give my regards to … grüßen Sie … von mir 219

region Gegend f 106

registered mail Einschreiben nt

registration form Anmeldeformular nt

registration number Mitgliedsnummer f 88; Kraftfahrzeugkennzeichen nt 93

regular *(gas)* Normal nt 87; *(size of drink)* mittel 110

regulations: I didn't know the regulations ich kannte die Vorschriften nicht

religion Religion f

remember: I don't remember ich weiß es nicht mehr

rent, to mieten 86;

to ~ out vermieten; *(bedding)* verleihen 29; **for rent** zu vermieten

repair, to reparieren 89, 137, 168

repairs Reparaturen fpl 89, 137

repeat, to wiederholen 94, 128;

please repeat that bitte wiederholen Sie das 11

replacement *(n)* Ersatz m;

~ part Ersatzteil nt 137

report, to melden 152

representative Reiseleiter(in) m/f

required, to be verlangt werden 112

reservation *(hotel)* Reservierung f 22; *(plane)* 68; *(train ticket)* Platzkarte f 77;

to have a ~ reserviert haben

reservations desk *(plane)* Vorverkaufskasse f

reserve, to *(table)* bestellen 36; *(tickets)* vorbestellen 109

rest, to Pause machen

restaurant Restaurant nt 35

restrooms Toilette f

retired, to be pensioniert sein 121 68; *(train)* Rückfahrkarte f 74

return, to *(give back)* zurückbringen; *(come back)* zurückfahren 75; wiederkommen 81; zurückkommen

reverse the charges, to ein R-Gespräch führen 127

revolting scheußlich 14

rheumatism Rheumatismus m

rib Rippe f 166

right *(correct)* richtig 14, 77, 79, 80, 94;

that's right das ist richtig, das stimmt

right of way Vorfahrt f 93;

is there a right of way? darf man dort hergehen? 106

right, on the auf der rechten Seite 76, 95

right-hand drive rechtsgesteuert

right-handed rechtshändig

rip-off *(n)* Wucher m 101

river Fluss m 107;

~ cruise Flußfahrt f 81

road Straße f 94, 95;

~ accident Verkehrsunfall m;

~ assistance Pannendienst m 88;

~ map Straßenkarte f 150;

~ signs Verkehrszeichen ntpl 96;

is this the road for …? ist dies die Straße nach …?

roast chicken Brathähnchen nt

roasted im Backofen gebraten

robbed, to be bestohlen werden 153

robbery Raub m

rock climbing Felsklettern nt

rocks Felsen mpl

roller blades Roller-Blades pl

rolls Brötchen nt 160

romantic romantisch 101

roof *(house/car)* Dach nt;

~rack Dachgepäckträger m

rook *(chess)* Turm m

room Zimmer nt 21;

~ service Zimmerservice m 26

rope Seil nt

rouge Rouge nt

round *(adj)* rund 134; *(of golf)* Runde f 115;

it's my round diese Runde gebe ich aus

round-trip ticket *(plane)* Rückflugticket nt 68; *(train)* Rückfahrkarte f 74

route Weg m 106

rowboat Ruderboot nt 116

rowing Rudern m;

rucksack Rucksack m 31, 145

rude, to be unhöflich sein

rugby Rugby nt

ruins Ruine f

run out: to run out of gas kein Benzin mehr haben 88

rush hour Hauptverkehrszeit f

safe Safe m 27; *(not dangerous)* ungefährlich 116;
to feel ~ sich sicher fühlen 65
safety Sicherheit f 65
safety pins Sicherheitsnadeln fpl
sag: the bed sags das Bett hängt durch
sailboard Windsurfbrett nt
sailboarding Windsurfen nt
sailboat Segelboot nt 116
salad Salat m
sales rep Vertreter(in) m/f
sales tax Mehrwertsteuer f 24, 136
salt Salz nt 38, 39
same: the same again please
bitte nochmal das Gleiche;
the same der/die/dasselbe 75
sand Sand m
sandals Sandalen fpl 145
sandwich belegtes Brot nt 40
sandy sandig;
~ beach Sandstrand m 116
sanitary napkins Damenbinden fpl 142
satellite TV Satellitenfernsehen nt 22
satin Satin m
satisfied: I'm not satisfied with this ich bin damit nicht zufrieden
Saturday Samstag m 218
sauce Soße f 38
saucepan Kochtopf m 29
sauna Sauna f 22
sausage Wurst f 40; Würstchen nt 160;
~ stand Würstchenstand m 35
saw *(tool)* Säge f
say: how do you say ...?
wie sagt man ...?
what did he say? was hat er gesagt?
scarf Halstuch nt 144
scheduled flight Linienflug m
school Schule f
sciatica Ischias f 165
scissors Schere f 148
Scotland Schottland nt 119
Scottish *(adj)* schottisch
Scottish *(person)* der Schotte m/ die Schottin f
scouring pad Topfkratzer m
screw Schraube f
screwdriver Schraubenzieher m 148
scrubbing brush Scheuerbürste f
scuba-diving equipment
Taucherausrüstung f 116

sea Meer nt 107
seafront
Strandpromenade f
seasick: I feel seasick ich bin seekrank
season ticket Zeitkarte f
seasoning Würze f 38
seat Platz m 74, 77;
(place) 109
second zweite 217;
~ class zweiter Klasse 74;
~ floor erster Stock
secondhand gebraucht;
~ shop
Gebrauchtwarenladen m
secretary Sekretär(in) m/f
security guard Wächter(in) m/f
sedative Beruhigungsmittel nt
see, to sehen; *(inspect)* 24; *(witness)* 93;
to ~ s.o. again jemanden wiedersehen 126
self-catering Selbstversorgung f 28
self-employed, to be selbständig sein 121
self-service Selbstbedienung f 87
sell, to verkaufen
send, to schicken 155; *(help)* 88
senior citizen Senior(in) m/f 74
seniors Rentner(in) m/f 100
separated, to be getrennt leben 120
separately getrennt 42
September September m 218
septic tank Faulbehälter m
serious ernst
served, to be *(meal)* serviert werden 26
service *(religious)* Gottesdienst m 105
service charge Bedienung f;
is service included? ist die Bedienung inbegriffen? 42
service station *(gas/petrol)* Tankstelle f 87
services 131
set menu Menü nt 37
seven sieben 216
seventeen siebzehn 216
seventy siebzig 217
sex *(gender)* Geschlecht nt; *(act)* Geschlechtsverkehr m
shade Farbton m 143
shady schattig
shallow flach
shampoo Haarwaschmittel nt 142;
~ for dry/oily hair Shampoo nt für trockenes/fettiges Haar;
~ and set waschen und legen 147

A-Z

shape Form f 134
share, to (room) teilen
sharp scharf
shavingbrush Rasierpinsel m;
~ cream Rasiercreme f
she sie
sheet (bed) Bettlaken nt 28
shelf Regal nt
ship Schiff nt 81
shirt Hemd nt 144
shock (electric) Schlag m
shoe laces Schnürsenkel mpl
shoe polish Schuhcreme f
shoe repair Schuhreparatur f
shoe store Schuhgeschäft nt 131
shoe-cleaning service Schuhputzdienst m
shoes Schuhe mpl 145
shop Geschäft nt 130
shop assistant Verkäufer(in) m/f
shopping: ~ area Geschäftsviertel nt 99;
~ basket Einkaufskorb m;
~ cart Einkaufswagen m;
~ list Einkaufsliste f;
~ mall Einkaufszentrum nt 131;
to go ~ einkaufen gehen
shore (sea/lake) Ufer nt
short kurz 146
shorts Shorts pl 144
shortsighted kurzsichtig 167
shoulder Schulter f 166
shovel Schaufel f 157
show, to zeigen 18, 133;
can you show me? können Sie es mir zeigen? 94, 106; gegeben werden 108; laufen 110
shower Dusche f 30;
~ gel Duschgel nt; ~ room Dusche f 26
shrunk: they've shrunk sie sind eingelaufen
shut (door) zu
shutter Fensterladen m
shy schüchtern
sick: he feels sick ihm ist schlecht;
I feel sick mir ist schlecht; I'm going to be sick ich muß mich übergeben
sickbay (ship) Krankenrevier nt
side (of road) Seite f 95
side order Beilage f 38
side street Seitenstraße f 95
sidewalk, on the auf dem Gehsteig
sights Sehenswürdigkeiten fpl

sightseeing tour Stadtrundfahrt f 97
sightseeing, to go auf Besichtigungstour gehen
sign (road) Schild nt
signal: he didn't give a signal er hat nicht geblinkt
signpost Wegweiser m
silk Seide f
silver Silber nt 149;
~plated versilbert 149
similar, to be ähnlich sein
since (time) seit
singer Sänger(in) m/f 157
single einfach 74;
~ ticket einfaches Flugticket nt 68;
einfache Fahrt f 79;
~ cabin Einzelkabine f 81;
~ room Einzelzimmer nt 21;
to be ~ unverheiratet sein 120
sink sinken
sister Schwester f 120
sit, to sitzen 36, 77, 126;
sit down, please bitte, setzen Sie sich
six sechs 216
six-pack of beer Sechserpack m Bier 160
sixteen sechzehn 216
sixty sechzig 217
size Größe f 115, 146
skates Schlittschuhe mpl 117
skating rink Eisbahn f
ski:
~ bindings Skibindungen fpl;
~ boots Skischuhe mpl 117;
~ instructor Skilehrer(in) m/f;
~ lift Skilift m;
~ poles Skistöcke mpl 117;
~ school Skischule f;
~ suit Skianzug m;
~ trousers Skihose f
skid: we skidded wir sind geschleudert
skiing Skifahren nt 117
skin Haut f 166
skirt Rock m 144
skis Skier mpl 117
slalom Slalom m
sledge Schlitten m;
~ run Schlittenbahn f
sleep, to schlafen 167
sleeping bag Schlafsack m 31
sleeping car Schlafwagen m 77
sleeping pill Schlaftablette f 167
sleeve Ärmel m
slice Scheibe f

slide film Diafilm m

slip *(undergarment)* Unterrock m

slippers Hausschuhe mpl 145

slope *(ski)* Piste f

slot machine Spielautomat m

Slovakia Slowakei f

Slovenia Slowenien nt

slow langsam 14;
slow down! langsamer, bitte!

slow, to be *(clock)* nachgehen 221

slowly langsam 11, 94, 128; *(speak)* 11

SLR camera Spiegelreflexkamera f

small klein 14, 24, 40, 117, 134; *(drink)* 110;
~ change Kleingeld nt 138

smell: there's a bad smell es riecht unangenehm

smoke, to rauchen 126;
I don't smoke ich rauche nicht

smoking *(adj)* Raucher pl 36, 69

snack bar Schnellimbiss m 73

snacks kleine Gerichte ntpl

sneakers Turnschuhe mpl

snooker Taschenbillard nt

snorkel Schnorchel m

snow Schnee m 117

snow, to schneien 122

snowed in, to be eingeschneit sein

snowplow Schneepflug m

soaking solution *(contact lenses)* Aufbewahrungsflüssigkeit f

soap Seife f 142;
~ powder Seifenpulver nt

socket Steckdose f

socks Socken fpl 144

soda Erfrischungsgetränk nt 110, 160

sofa Sofa nt;
~bed Sofabett nt

soft drink *(soda)* Erfrischungsgetränk nt 110, 160

sold out ausverkauft

sole *(shoes)* Sohle f

some einige

someone jemand 16

something etwas 16;
~ cheaper etwas Billigeres

sometimes manchmal 13

son Sohn m 120, 162

soon bald 13;
as soon as possible so bald wie möglich 161

sore: it's sore es ist wund;
~ throat Halsschmerzen pl 141, 163

sorry! Entschuldigung, Verzeihung 10

sort Art f 134;
a ~ of eine Art

sour sauer 41

south of ... südlich von ... 95

South Africa Südafrika nt

South African *(n)* Südafrikaner(in) m/f

souvenir Reiseandenken nt 98; Andenken nt 156;
~ guide Andenkenbildband m 156
~ store Andenkenladen m 131

spa Kurort f

space Platz m 30

spade Schaufel f 157

spades *(cards)* Pik nt sing

spare *(extra)* überzählig

speak, to sprechen 11, 41, 67, 128;
to ~ to s.o. mit jemandem sprechen 128;
do you speak English? sprechen Sie Englisch? 11

special rate Sonderpreis m

specialist Facharzt m, Fachärztin f 164

speed limit Geschwindigkeitsbegrenzung f 93

speed, to zu schnell fahren 93

spell, to buchstabieren 11

spend, to *(money)* ausgeben; *(time)* verbringen

spicy würzig

spin-dryer Wäscheschleuder f

spine Wirbelsäule f

sponge Schwamm m 148

spoon Löffel m 39, 41, 148

sport Sport m 114

sports club Sportverein m 115

sports ground Sportplatz m 96

sports store Sportgeschäft nt 131

sprained, to be verstaucht sein 164

spring *(season)* Frühling m 219; *(water)* Quelle f

square quadratisch 134

squash Squash nt

stadium Stadion nt 96

stain Fleck m

stainless steel Edelstahl m 149

stairs Treppe (f sing)

stall: the engine stalls der Motor stirbt ab

stamp Briefmarke f;
~ machine Briefmarkenautomat m

stamps Briefmarken fpl 150

stand in line, to Schlange stehen 112

start (n) Beginn m

start, to beginnen 98, 108, 112; (car) anspringen 88

starter Vorspeise f

statement Aussage f; (police) Aussage f 93

station Bahnhof m 73, 96

station wagon Kombiwagen m

stationer's Schreibwarenhandlung f

statue Statue f 99

stay Aufenthalt m 32

stay, to (lodge) bleiben 23; wohnen 123; (remain) bleiben 65

steak house Steakhaus nt 35

stereo Stereoanlage f

sterilizing solution Sterilisierlösung f 142

stern (ship) Heck nt

stiff neck steifer Nacken m 163

still: I'm still waiting ich warte immer noch

sting Stich m 162

stockings Strümpfe mpl 144

stolen, to be gestohlen werden 71

stomach Magen m 166;
~ **ache** Magenschmerzen pl 163;
~ **cramps** Magenkrämpfe mpl

stool (feces) Stuhl m 164

stop (bus, tram) Haltestelle f 79; (metro) 80

stop, to halten 77, 81, 84; anhalten 98;
to ~ at halten in 76;
please stop here bitte halten Sie hier 84; **which stop?** welche Haltestelle? 80

stopover Zwischenlandung f

store Geschäft nt 130;
~ **detective** Kaufhausdetektiv m;
~ **guide** Kaufhaus-Wegweiser m 132; ~ **keeper** Ladenbesitzer(in) m/f;
~ **owner** Ladenbesitzer(in) m/f

straight ahead geradeaus 95

strained muscle Muskelzerrung f 162

strange seltsam 101

straw (drinking) Strohhalm m

strawberry (flavour) Erdbeere f 40

stream Bach m 107

string Schnur f

striped (patterned) gestreift

strong stark

student Student(in) m/f 74, 100

study, to studieren 121

stunning hinreißend 101

stupid: that was stupid! das war dumm!

sturdy robust

style Stil m 104

styling mousse Schaumfestiger m

subtitled, to be Untertitel haben 110

subway U-Bahn f 80;
~ **station** U-Bahnstation f 80, 96

suede Wildleder nt

sugar Zucker m 38, 39, 160

suggest, to vorschlagen 123

suit Anzug m 144

suitable for ..., to be für ... geeignet sein 140

summer Sommer m 219

sun Sonne f;
~ **burn** Sonnenbrand m 141;
~ **block** Sonnenschutzcreme f 142;
~ **deck** (ship) Sonnendeck nt;
~ **deck chair** Sonnenliege f;
~ **glasses** Sonnenbrille f sing 144;
~ **shade** (umbrella) Sonnenschirm m 116; ~ **stroke** Sonnenstich m 163

sunbathe, to sonnenbaden

Sunday Sonntag m 218

suntan cream Sonnencreme f 142

suntan lotion Sonnenmilch f 142

super (gas) Super nt 87

superb phantastisch 101

supermarket Supermarkt m 131, 158

supervision Aufsicht f

supplement Zuschlag m 68, 69, 74

suppositories Zäpfchen ntpl 165

sure: are you sure? sind Sie sicher?

surfboard Surfbrett m 116

surname Nachname m

suspicious verdächtig

swallow, to herunterschlucken

sweater Pullover m

sweatshirt Sweatshirt nt 144

sweet (taste) süß

sweets Süßigkeiten fpl 150, 160

swelling Schwellung f 162

swim, to schwimmen, baden 116

swimming Schwimmen nt 114;
~ pool Schwimmbad nt 22, 26, 116;
~ trunks Badehose f 144
swimsuit Badeanzug m 144
Swiss (person) Schweizer(in) m/f
switch Schalter m
switch on, to einschalten
switch off, to ausschalten
Switzerland die Schweiz f 119
swollen, to be geschwollen sein
symptoms Symptome ntpl 163
synagogue Synagoge f
synthetic fabric Synthetik nt 145

T

T-shirt T-Shirt nt 156
table (restaurant) Tisch m 36; 112;
~ cloth Tischdecke f;
~ tennis Tischtennis nt
tablet Tablette f 140
traffic jam Stau m
take, to (bus) nehmen; (carry) tragen 71;
(medicine) nehmen 140, 165; (time)
dauern;
I'll take it ich nehme es 135; (room) 24;
to ~ away zum Mitnehmen 40;
to ~ photographs Fotos machen 98;
to ~ pictures Fotos machen 100
taken (occupied) besetzt;
is this seat taken? ist dieser Platz besetzt?
take out (restaurant) Imbissstube f 35
talcum powder Körperpuder m
talk, to sprechen
tall groß 14
tampons Tampons mpl 142
tan Bräune f
tap Wasserhahn m 25
tape measure Maßband nt
taste Geschmack m
taxi Taxi nt 70, 71, 84;
~ driver Taxifahrer m;
~ rank Taxistand m 96
tea Tee m 40;
~ bags Teebeutel mpl 160;
~ towel Geschirrtuch nt 156
teacher Lehrer(in) m/f
team Mannschaft f 114
teaspoon Teelöffel m 140, 148
teat (for baby) Sauger m
teddy bear Teddybär m 157
teenager Teenager m
telephone Telefon nt 22, 70, 92, 127;
telephone bill Telefonrechnung f 32

~ booth Telefonzelle f
127;
~ calls Anrufe mpl 32;
~ directory Telefonbuch
nt;
~ number Telefonnummer
f 127;
to ~ anrufen 128
television Fernseher m 25
tell, to sagen 18, 79;
tell me können Sie mir sagen 79
temperature (water) Temperatur f
temporarily provisorisch 89
temporary vorübergehend
ten zehn 216
tennis Tennis nt 114;
~ ball Tennisball m;
~ court Tennisplatz m 115
tent Zelt nt 30, 31;
~ floor boden m 31;
~ pegs Heringe mpl 31;
~ pole Zeltstange f 31
terminus (for streetcar) Straßenbahndepot
nt 78
terrible schrecklich 101
tetanus Wundstarrkrampf m 164
thank you danke 10
thanks for your help vielen Dank für Ihre
Hilfe 94
that das; ~ one jenes 16; das da 134
that's all das ist alles 133
thawing snow tauender Schnee m
theater Theater nt 96, 99, 110
theft Diebstahl m 153
their ihr 16; theirs ihre(-r, -s) 16
them sie;
for them für sie;
to them zu ihnen
then (time) dann 13
there dort 12; (to there) dorthin 12
there is ... es gibt ... 17
there you go bitte schön 11
thermometer Thermometer nt
thermos flask Thermosflasche f
these diese 134
they sie
thick dick 14
thief Dieb m
thigh Oberschenkel m 166
thin dünn 14
think: I think ich glaube 42, 77;
to ~ about it es sich überlegen 135

third dritte 217;
 ~-party insurance Haftpflichtversicherung f
.third, a Drittel nt 217
thirsty durstig
 thirteen dreizehn 216
thirty dreißig 217
this one dieses 16; dieses hier 134
those diese 134
thousand tausend, eintausend 217
three drei 216
throat Hals m 166
thrombosis Thrombose f
through durch 12
ticket Fahrschein m 79; (sights) Eintrittskarte f; (sport) Karte f 114;
 ~ agency Kartenvorverkaufsstelle f 131;
 ~ office Fahrkartenschalter m 73
tickets (plane) Flugtickets ntpl 68; (train) Fahrkarten fpl 74
tie Krawatte f 144;
 ~ pin Krawattennadel f
tight (clothing) eng 117, 146
tights Strumpfhose f 144
time Uhrzeit f 220; **free time** Zeit f zur freien Verfügung 98; **on time** pünktlich 76; **what time?** wann? 76, 78; **time of day** Tageszeit f; **5 times** fünfmal 76
timetable Flugplan m
tinfoil Stanniolpapier nt
tint, to tönen 147
tip Trinkgeld nt
tipping 42
tire Reifen m
tired, to be müde sein
tissues Papiertaschentücher ntpl 142
to (place) nach
toaster Toaster m 29
tobacco Tabak m 150
tobacco store/cigar shop Tabakgeschäft nt 131
today heute 124, 218
toe Zehe f 166
together (pay) zusammen 42
toilet Toilette f 25, 26, 29;
 toilets Toiletten fpl 96, 98
toilet paper Toilettenpapier nt 25, 29, 142
toiletries 142
tomorrow morgen 84, 124, 218
tongue Zunge f 166
tonic water Tonicwater nt

tonight heute abend 110, 124;
 for tonight für heute abend 108
tonsillitis Mandelentzündung f
tonsils Mandeln fpl 166
too (also) auch; (extreme) zu 17, 93;
 too much zu viel 15
tooth Zahn m 168;
 ~ache zahnschmerzen pl;
 ~brush Zahnbürste f;
 ~paste Zahnpasta f 142
top (adj) oberste(-r, -s);
 ~ floor oberster Stock m
torn, to be (muscle) gerissen sein 164
totaled (car) Totalschaden m 89
totally völlig 17
tough (food) zäh 41
tour Rundfahrt f 97;
 ~ guide Reiseleiter(in) m/f;
 ~ operator Reiseveranstalter m 26
tourist Tourist(in) m/f;
 ~ office Fremdenverkehrsbüro nt 97
tow rope Abschleppseil nt
tow, to abschleppen
toward in Richtung ... 12
towel Handtuch n
toweling Frottee m
tower Turm m
town Stadt f 70, 94;
 ~ hall Rathaus nt 99;
 ~ plans 96
toy Spielzeug nt 157;
 toy store Spielwarengeschäft nt 131
track Weg m
tracksuit Trainingsanzug m
traffic Verkehr m;
 ~ jam Stau m 94;
 ~ violation Verkehrsdelikt nt
trail Wanderweg m 106
trailer Wohnwagen m 30, 81;
 ~ park Campingplatz m für Wohnwagen
train Zug m 75, 76, 77; (subway) U-Bahn f 80; **~ times** Abfahrtszeiten fpl der Züge 75
transfer, to übertragen; (money) überweisen; (transport) befördern
transit, in beim Transport 71
translate, to übersetzen 11
translation Übersetzung f
translator Übersetzer(in) m/f

travel, to fahren
~ **agency** Reisebüro nt 131;
~ **sickness** Reisekrankheit f 141
traveler's check Reisescheck m 136, 138
tray Tablett nt
tree Baum m 106
trim nachschneiden 147
trip Ausflug m 97
trouble: I'm having trouble with ich habe
Schwierigkeiten mit
truck Lastwagen m
true: that's not true das ist nicht wahr;
true north geographischer Nordpol m
try on, to anprobieren 146
Tuesday Dienstag m 218
tumor Tumor m 165
tunnel Tunnel m
Turkish *(adj)* türkisch 35
turn down, to *(heat)* herunterdrehen;
(volume) leiser stellen
turn off, to ausmachen 25
turn on, to anmachen 25
turn up, to *(volume, heat)* aufdrehen
turn, to abbiegen 95
turning Straße f 95
TV Fernseher m 22
tweezers Pinzette f
twelve zwölf 216
twenty zwanzig 216
twice zweimal 217
twin bed Einzelbett nt 21
twist: I've twisted my ankle ich habe mir
den Knöchel verstaucht
two zwei 216;
~ **door car** zweitüriges Auto 86
type: what type of? welche Art? 112
typical typisch 37

U

ugly hässlich 14, 101
UK Vereinigtes Königreich nt
ulcer Geschwür nt
umbrella Regenschirm m
uncle Onkel m 120
unconscious, to be bewusstlos sein
92, 162
under *(place)* unter
underdone *(adj)* zu roh 41
underpants Unterhose f 144
underpass Unterführung f 76, 96
undershirt Unterhemd nt

understand, to verstehen
11;
do you understand?
verstehen Sie? 11;
I don't understand ich
verstehe nicht 11
understanding 11
undress, to *(at doctor's)* freimachen 164
unfortunately leider 19
uniform Uniform f
United States Vereinigte Staaten pl
university Universität f 99
unleaded gas bleifreies Benzin nt 87
unlimited mileage unbegrenzte
Kilometerzahl f
unlock, to aufschließen
unpleasant *(person)* unfreundlich;
unangenehm
unscrew, to aufschrauben
until bis 221
up to bis zu 12
upmarket anspruchsvoll
upset stomach Magenverstimmung f 141
upstairs oben
urgent dringend
urine Urin m 164
us: for/with us für/mit uns
U.S. USA pl 119
use, to benutzen
useful nützlich

V

vacancy freies Zimmer nt
vacant frei 14
vacate, to räumen 32
vacation Ferien pl,
Urlaub m;
on vacation im Urlaub
66, 123
vaccinated against, to be
geimpft sein gegen 164
vaccination Impfung f
vaginal infection Scheidenentzündung
f 167
valid gültig 75
validate, to *(ticket)* entwerten 79
valley Tal nt 107
valuable wertvoll
value Wert m 155
vanilla *(flavor)* Vanille f 40
VAT *(sales tax)* Mehrwertsteuer f 24, 136
vegan, to be Veganer(in) m/f sein

vegan: suitable for vegans für Veganer geeignet;
~ **dishes** veganische Gerichte ntpl
vegetable store Gemüsehändler m 131
vegetables Gemüse nt sing 38
vegetarian (adj) vegetarisch 35; (n) Vegetarier(in) m/f;
to be ~ Vegetarier(in) m/f sein
vehicle Fahrzeug nt;
~ **registration document** Kraftfahrzeugbrief m 93
vein Vene f
velvet Samt m
vending machine Automat m
venereal disease Geschlechtskrankheit f 165
ventilator Ventilator m
very sehr 17
vet(erinarian) Tierarzt m, Tierärztin f
video Video nt;
~ **game** Videospiel nt;
~ **recorder** Videorekorder m
view: with a view of the sea mit Meerblick
village Dorf nt 107
vineyard/winery Weinberg m 107
visa Visum nt
visit Aufenthalt m 66
visit, to (sights) besichtigen 123; (person in hospital) besuchen 167
visiting hours Besuchszeit f sing 167
vitamins/vitamin tablets Vitamintabletten fpl 141
voice Stimme f
volleyball Volleyball m 114
voltage Spannung f
vomit, to sich übergeben 163

W **waist** Taille f
waist pouch Gürteltaschl f
wait, to warten 41, 140;
to ~ for warten auf 76, 89, 126
wait! warten Sie! 98
waiting room Wartesaal m 73
wake, to (self) aufwachen; (s.o. else) jemanden wecken 27;
wake-up call Weckruf m
Wales Wales nt 119

walk: to go for a walk spazieren gehen;
to ~ home zu Fuß nach Hause gehen 65
walking Wandern nt;
~ **boots** Wanderschuhe mpl 145;
~ **gear** Wanderausrüstung f 145;
~ **route** Wanderweg m 106;
wall Wand f
wallet Brieftasche f 42, 153
want, to wünschen
ward (hospital) Station f 167
warm warm 14; (weather) 122
warm, to wärmen 39
warranty Garantie f 135;
is there a warranty on it? ist darauf Garantie?
wash, to waschen
washable:
is it hand ~? kann man es mit der Hand waschen?; **is it machine ~?** kann man es in der Maschine waschen?
wash basin Waschbecken nt 25
washer (for faucet) Dichtung f
washing: ~ instructions Waschanleitung f sing; ~ **machine** Waschmaschine f;
~ **powder** Waschpulver nt 148
washing, to do Wäsche waschen
wasp Wespe f
watch Uhr f 153;
~ **strap** Uhrarmband nt
watch TV, to fernsehen
watch repairs/watchmender's Uhrmacher m
water Wassser nt;
~ **bottle** Wasserflasche f;
~ **heater** Heißwassergerät nt 28;
~**fall** Wasserfall m 107
waterskiing Wasserskilaufen nt
waterskis Wasserskier mpl 116
wave Welle f
waxing Wachsbehandlung f 147
way: I've lost my way (on foot) ich habe mich verlaufen 94;
on the way auf dem Weg 83
we wir
weak schwach;
I feel weak mir ist schwach
wear, to tragen 152
weather Wetter nt 122;
~ **forecast** Wetterbericht m 122
wedding Hochzeit f;
~ **ring** Ehering m
Wednesday Mittwoch m 218

week Woche f 23, 97, 218
weekend Wochenende nt;
~ **rate** Wochenendpauschale f 86;
at the ~ am Wochenende 218
weekly ticket Wochenkarte f
weight: my weight is ... ich wiege ...
welcome to ... herzlich willkommen in ...
well-done (steak) durchgebraten
Welsh (adj) walisisch
Welsh (person) der Waliser m/
die Waliserin f
west of ... westlich von ... 95
wetsuit Taucheranzug m
what kind of? welche Art von ...? 37
was für ein(e) ...? 106
what time...? wann ...? 68, 81
what's the time? wie spät ist es? 220
what? was?
wheelchair Rollstuhl m
when? wann? 13
where? wo? 12
where are you from? woher kommen
Sie? 13
where can we ...? wo können wir ...?
where else? wo sonst? 135
where is ...? wo ist ...? 99
which? welcher/welche/welches? 16
while während
whist (cards) Whist nt
white weiß 143;
~ **wine** Weißwein m 40
who? wer? 16
whole: the whole day den ganzen Tag
whose wessen 16
why? warum?
wide weit 14
wife Frau f 120, 162
wildlife Tierwelt f
window Fenster nt 25, 69, 77; (shop)
Schaufenster nt 149
window seat Fensterplatz m 74
windshield/windscreen
Windschutzscheibe f 90
windsurfer Windsurfer m 116
windy, to be windig sein 122
wine Wein m 49;
~ **list** Weinkarte f 37;
~**box** Zapfpack m
winery Weinberg m 107
winter Winter m 219
wishes: best wishes! alles Gute! 219

with mit 17
without ohne 17
witness Zeuge m, Zeugin
f 93
women's underpants
Schlüpfer m
wood (forest) Wald m 107;
(material) Holz nt
wool Wolle f 145
work, to (job) arbeiten 121; (function)
funktionieren 28, 83, 88, 89;
it doesn't work es funktioniert nicht 25
worry: I'm worried ich mache mir Sorgen
worse schlechter 14;
it's gotten worse es ist schlimmer
geworden
worst, the das Schlimmste
worth: is it worth seeing?
lohnt es einen Besuch?
wound Wunde f 162
write down, to aufschreiben 136
write: write soon! schreiben Sie bald!
wrong (incorrect) falsch 14, 136;
~ **number!** falsch verbunden! 128
wrong: what's wrong? (car) wo liegt
der Fehler? 88;
there is something ~ with ...
mit ... stimmt etwas nicht

X Y Z X-ray, to have an geröntgt
werden 164
yacht Jacht f
year Jahr nt 218
yellow gelb 143
yes ja 10
yesterday gestern 218
yogurt Jogurt m 160
you (sing/plur) Sie [du]; Sie [ihr]
you are here Standort m 96
young jung 14
your (sing/plur) Ihr [dein]; Ihr [ihr] 16
yours Ihre(-r, -s); deine(-r, -s) 16;
it's yours es gehört Ihnen/dir
youth hostel Jugendherberge f 29
zebra crossing Zebrastreifen m
zero null
zip(per) Reißverschluß m
zoo Zoo m 113
zoology Zoologie f

A-Z Dictionary
German-English

This German–English dictionary concentrates on all the areas where you may need to decode written German: hotels, public buildings, restaurants, shops, ticket offices and on transport. It will also help with understanding forms, maps, product labels, road signs and operating instructions (for telephones, parking meters, etc.).

If you can't locate the exact sign, you may find words or terms listed separately.

A ab 18 Jahre under 18 not allowed
Abendgarderobe formal wear
Abendgebet evensong
Abendkasse evening box office
Abendvorstellung evening performance
Abfahrt departure
Abfertigung check-in counter
Abflüge departures
Abgeordnetenhaus parliament building
Abo subscription *(to concert)*
Abseilen abseiling
Absender sender
(bitte) Abstand halten (please) keep your distance/stand behind this point
Abtei abbey
...-abteilung ...department
Abteilungsleiter manager
Adresse address
Aduädukt aqueduct
Aerobic aerobics
alkoholfreies Bier non-alcoholic beer
alle ... Stunden every ... hours
Allee avenue, boulevard
Altglas recycled glass
Altglascontainer recycling container for glass bottles
Altpapier recycled paper
Altstadt old town
Aluminium aluminum
ambulante Patienten outpatients
amerikanischer Fußball American football
5 Ampere 5 amp
Amtszeichen abwarten wait for tone
an Bord gehen embark

an der Kasse bezahlen please pay at counter
an Sonn- und Feiertagen on Sundays and holidays
Andacht prayer service
Andachtsraum chapel
andere Orte other destinations
Anfängerpiste for beginners *(ski run)*
Angebot special offer
Angeln fishing, angling
Ankauf currency bought at
Ankunft arrivals
Anlegehafen port, harbor
Anlegeplatz dock
Anlieger frei residents only
annulliert cancelled
Anprobe fitting rooms
Anschlussflug connecting flight
Anschlussstelle junction/interchange
(bitte) anschnallen fasten your seatbelt
Ansichtskarten picture postcards
Antik/Antiquitäten antiques
Antiquitätenladen antique store
Anwohner frei access (to residents) only
Apartment Class self-catering
Apotheke drugstore, pharmacy
April April
Art ... style
Ärztlicher Notfalldienst emergency medical service
Arztpraxis doctor's surgery
auf Tournee on tour
Aufführung performance, recital
Aufnahme admissions
(bitte) aufräumen this room needs making up
Aufzug elevator/lift
Augenarzt eye doctor
Augenoptik optician's

August August
Ausfahrt freihalten keep exit clear
Ausgang exit
ausgebucht full up
Auskunft information
Auskunft, international international directory enquiries
Auskunft, national national directory enquiries
Ausreisedatum date of departure
Außenschwimmbad outdoor swimming pool
außer Betrieb out of order
Aussichtspunkt viewpoint
Ausstellungsgebäude pavilion
Ausstellungsort place of issue
Ausverkauft sold out
Ausweich-Parkplätze extra parking places
Ausweis vorzeigen proof of identity required
Autobahn expressway/motorway
autobahnähnliche Straße main road/principal highway
Autobahnpolizei expressway police
Autofähre car ferry
Autokino drive-in
Autoreparaturwerkstatt car repairs
Autovermietung car rental
Autowaschanlage car wash
Autozubehör car accessories

B **Babybekleidung** baby's wear
Babyraum nursery
Babywickelraum baby diaper changing room
Backartikel baking supplies
Bäckerei bakery
Backwaren bread, cakes and pastries
Bademoden swimwear
Bademöglichkeit swimming facilities
Bademützen bathing caps must be worn
Baden verboten bathing prohibited
Bahn railroad/railway
Bahnhof rail station
Bahnübergang train-crossing
Balkon balcony
Ballett ballet
Ballspielen verboten no ball games
Bankautomat cash dispenser/ATM
Bankgebühren bank charges
Barauszahlung withdrawal
Basel Basle
Basteln craft books

Batterien batteries
Bauernhof farm
Baumwolle cotton
beginnt um ... commencing ...
Behandlungsraum treatment room
belegt full up
Benzin gas
Benzin Bleifrei unleaded gas/petrol
Benzinpumpe fuel pump
Berg mountain
Bergspitze peak
Bergsteigen mountaineering
Bergwerk mine
besetzt occupied, engaged
beste Qualität excellent quality
Bestimmungsort destination
Besucher-Terrasse visitors' terrace
Betreten verboten keep out
Betriebszeiten von ... bis ... opening hours from ... to ...
bezahlt paid
Bibliothek library
Bier beer
Bildsäule statue
Billard billiards
Binnensee lake
Biographie biography
Biokost health foods
Bischof bishop
Bistro buffet car
Bleiben Sie auf der Piste no off-piste skiing
bleifrei unleaded
Bleistift pencil
Blick aufs Meer with sea view
Blumen(laden) florist's
Bodensee Lake Constance
Bordkarte boarding card
Börse stock exchange
botanischer Garten botanical garden
Botschaft embassy
brandneu brand new
Bremse brake
Briefe letters
Briefkasten mailbox
Briefmarken stamps
Briefumschläge envelopes
Brot bread
Brot und Kuchen bread and cakes
Brücke bridge
Brunnen well, fountain
Bücherei library
Buchhandlung bookstore

Buchungen (ticket) reservations
Bühne stage
Bühnenbild scenery
Bundesgrenzschutz border police
Bundesstraße secondary road
Burg castle
Bürgersteig sidewalk
Burgruine ruins of a castle
Bus bus
Bushaltestelle bus stop

Camping verboten no camping/tenting
Campingausweis camping permit
Campingplatz campsite
Caravan trailer/caravan
CD-Hitparade und Neuheiten chart CDs and new releases
Chemische Reinigung dry cleaner's
Chlorbleiche nicht möglich do not bleach
cholesterinfrei no cholesterol
Chor choir

Damenmode ladies wear
Damentoiletten ladies (restrooms)
Damenwäsche lingerie
Damm dam
Dampfer/Dampfschiff steamboat/steamer
Dauerkarte season ticket
Deckspassage deck passage
Denkmal (ancient) monument, memorial
Dezember December
Diät diet foods
Diätküche diet meals
Dichterlesung poetry reading
Dienstag Tuesday
Diesel diesel
Diözese diocese
Dirigent conductor
Dom cathedral
Domherr canon
Donnerstag Thursday
Dorf village
Dosen cans
Drogerie drugstore
drücken push
Düne dune
Durchfahrt verboten no throughway
durchschnittliche Nährwerte nutritional information
Duschen showers

Duty-Free duty-free shop
DZ (Doppelzimmer) double room

echt genuine
EDV-Literatur computer literature
Eier eggs
Einbahnstraße one-way street
Einfahrt freihalten keep entrance clear
Eingang entrance
Einheiten units
Einkaufszentrum/-passage shopping mall/arcade
Einkaufszone shopping area
einordnen get in lane
Einreisedatum date of arrival
Einrichtungen für Kinder facilities for children
Einrichtungshaus furniture warehouse
Einschiffung boarding point
einschließlich inclusive (room)
Einsteigebereit boarding now
Einsteigen nur mit gültigem Fahrausweis board only with a valid ticket
Einstieg (boarding) gate
Eintritt frei admission free
Eintrittskarten tickets
Eintrittspreise entry fees
Einwanderungsbehörde immigration control
Einzahlung deposits
Einzahlung und Auszahlung deposits and withdrawals
Einzelfahrschein/Einzelticket one way/single ticket
Einzelkabinen single berth cabins
Eis ice cream
Eislaufen ice skating
Elektrogeräte und -bedarf electrical appliances
Elektrogeschäft electrical store
Empfang reception
Ende der Umleitung end of diversion
Endstation terminus
Engagement gig
Entbindungsklinik maternity ward
Entfernung in Kilometer (km) distance in kilometers
entkorken uncork
entzündlich inflammable
Erdgeschoß first floor
Erfrischungsgetränke soft drinks
Erlebnispark amusement/theme park
erste Klasse/1. Klasse first class
erster Rang dress circle
erster Stock/Etage second floor

erster Weihnachtstag Christmas Day
Erwachsene: ... adults: ... *(dose)*
Erzbischof archbishop
Essen und Trinken food and drink
Essen verboten no food in the room
Etage floor/storey
EU-Staatsangehörige EU-Nationals
EuroCity (EC) intercity train
Explosionsgefahr explosive
EZ (Einzelzimmer) single room

F Fabrik factory
Fahrbahnschäden poor road
  surface
Fähre ferry
Fahrkarte entnehmen take ticket
Fahrkarten tickets
Fahrräder bicycles
Fahrradgeschäft bike shop
Fahrradhelm helmet *(bicycle)*
Fahrstuhl elevator
Fallschirmspringen parachuting
... fängt um ... an ... begins at ...
Farbfilm color film
(bitte) Fahrschein entwerten validate your
  ticket
Fasching carnival
Februar February
Federball badminton
Feinkost delicatessen
feinschmecker Art gourmet style
Feld field
Fensterplatz window seat
Feriendorf vacation village
Fernbahn long distance train
Fernsehraum television room
Fertiggerichte ready-to-serve meals
Fest festival
Festhalle concert hall
Festung fortress
fettarm low fat
feuerhemmende Tür fire door
Feuerlöscher fire extinguisher
Feuerwehr fire brigade
Feuerwehrwache fire station
Feuerwerk fireworks
Filmmusik movie soundtrack
Firn icy/old snow
Fisch fish
Fischen fishing
Fischen nicht erlaubt no fishing
Fischen nur mit Schein/Erlaubnis fishing
  by permit only
Fischhändler fish store
Fischspezialitäten fish

Fischstand fishstall
Fitnessstudio/-center
  fitness center/room
FKK-Strand nudist beach
Fleisch meat
Fluchtweg emergency exit
Flughafen airport
Flugnummer flight number
Flugplan flight schedule/timetables
Flugplatz airfield
Flugscheine tickets
Flugscheinkontrolle ticket control
Flugsteig gate
Flugzeit flight time
Flugzeug plane
Fluss river
Flussfahrt river trip
Folklore folk music
Fön hairdryer
Foto/Fotogeschäft camera shop
Fotoabteilung photography department
Fotografie photography
Fotografieren nicht erlaubt no
  photography
Frauen women *(restrooms)*
Frauenarzt gynecologist
Frauenparkplätze parking places
  reserved for women
frei for hire
Freibad outdoor pool
freier Verkauf unrestricted sale
freigegeben ab ... Jahren no children
  under ...; parental guidance *(film
  classification)*
Freigewicht luggage allowance
Freilandeier free range eggs
Freitag Friday
Freiwillig 30 speed limit - voluntarily 30
  km/h
Freizeitanlage country club
Freizeitkleidung informal wear
Fremdwährung foreign currency
Friedhof cemetery
frisch fresh
frisch gestrichen wet paint
frisches Obst fresh fruit
Frischwasser drinking water
Friseur hair dresser
Friseurgeschäft hairdresser's
Fruchtsäfte fruit juices
Frühling/Frühjahr spring
Frühstück/Frühstücksbüffet breakfast
Frühstückszimmer breakfast room
Führung guided tours

A-Z

A-Z

Fundbüro lost and found
für ... Tage for ... days
für Diabetiker for diabetics
für Familien mit Kindern family section
für fettendes Haar for oily hair
für Fortgeschrittene for intermediates *(piste)*
für normales Haar for normal hair
für trockenes Haar for dry hair
für unsere kleinen Gäste children's portion/selection
für zwei Personen for two
Fußball soccer/football
Fußgänger pedestrians
Fußgängerbereich traffic-free zone
Fußgängerüberweg pedestrian crossing
Fußgängerzone pedestrian zone
Fußpflegerin chiropodist
Fußweg footpath

G Gabel fork
Galerie gallery
Gänge gears
Gangplatz aisle seat
Gangschaltung gear shift
Garderobe coat check
Garten garden
Gartenbedarf und -geräte/Gartencenter garden center
Gasanschluss camping gas connection
Gasse alley
Gasthaus/-hof guest house (inn)
Gastspiel performance by visiting actors
Gebärdenspiel mime
Gebet prayers
Gebirge mountain range
Gebrauchsanweisung/-information instructions for use
Gebühren frei admission free
Gebührenpflichtige Straße toll road *(Switzerland)*
Geburtsdatum date of birth
Geburtshaus von ... birthplace of ....
Geburtsname maiden name
Geburtsort place of birth
Gedichte poems
Gefahr danger
gefährlich dangerous
gefährliche Abhang dangerous slope
Gefälle gradient
Geflügel poultry
gegen Schuppen dandruff shampoo

Gegenanzeigen contraindications
Gegenverkehr two-way traffic
Gehweg sidewalk
Gel ointment
gelandet arrived
Gelbe Seiten Yellow Pages
Geldüberweisung money transfer
Geldwechsel currency exchange
Geldwechselautomat change machine
Gemäldegalerie art gallery
Gemeinde parish
Gemüse fresh vegetables
Gemüse nach Wahl choice of vegetables
Gemüsekonserven canned vegetables
geöffnet von ... bis ... open from ... to ...
Gepäckannahme baggage acceptance
Gepäckaufbewahrung baggage checkroom/storage
Gepäckausgabe baggage claim
Gepäckträger carrier
Gepäckwagen luggage cart
Gericht(sgebäude) courthouse
Gesamtkilometer der Skiabfahrten length of ski runs
Geschenkartikel gifts
Geschenkladen souvenir shop
geschlossen closed
Gewerbegebiet industrial area
Gewürze spices
Gift poison
giftig poisonous, toxic
Gipfel peak
Glas glass
Glascontainer recycling container for glass
Glatteis(gefahr) icy road
Gleis platform, railway track
glutenfrei gluten-free
Gold- und Silberwaren jeweler
Gondel gondola *(ski-lift)*
Grab grave
Grabmal/Grabstätte tomb
Gram Fett fat content
Grenzübergang border crossing
Grillen verboten no barbecues
Grillplatz barbecue/grill pit
großer Saal large assembly room
Grundgebühr .... minimum ...
grüner Punkt green dot (recyclable material)
Grünglas green glass
Gruppen willkommen parties welcome
Gruppenführung group tours
gültig ab Kauf valid from time of purchase
gültig ab ... valid from ...
gültig bis ... expires ...
gültig für Zonen ... valid for zones ...

gut gekühlt servieren best served chilled

H

Hackfleisch hamburger meat
Hafen port, harbor, docks
Halbpension half board
Hallenbad indoor pool
Hält! bus stopping
Halten verboten no stopping
Handwäsche hand wash only
Hauptbahnhof main station
Hauptstraße main street
Haus house
Haus- u. Küchengeräte household appliances
Hausarzt family doctor
hausgebackenes Brot homemade bread
hausgemacht homemade
Haushaltswaren household goods, kitchen equipment
Haushaltswäsche household linen
Heiligabend Christmas Eve
heilige Messe Catholic mass
Helm crash helmet
Herrenbekleidung/-mode menswear
Herrenfriseur barber
Herren gentlemen *(restroom)*
herzlich willkommen welcome
heute today
heute abend this evening
hier abreißen tear here
hier abtrennen cut here
(bitte) hier anstellen please wait here
hier Erfrischungsgetränke refreshments available
hier öffnen open here
hier Parkschein lösen get your parking ticket here
hier Telefonkarten phone cards on sale here
(bitte) hier warten please wait here
hier wird Englisch gesprochen English spoken
(bitte) hier zahlen please pay here
hinten aussteigen exit by the rear door
historische Altstadt historical old town
historische Gebäude historical building
Hochspannung high voltage
höchst Geschwindigkeit maximum speed
höchstgelegene Bergstation highest mountain station
hochwertig excellent
Homöopathischer Arzt homeopath
Honig honey
Hörer abnehmen lift receiver

Hörsaal auditorium
Hotel garni bed & breakfast
Hotelverzeichnis list of available accommodation
Hubschrauber helicopter
Hügel hill
Hunde bitte an der Leine dogs must be kept on leash
Hunde erlaubt dogs allowed
Hunderennen greyhound racing

I

Ihr Standort you are here, your location
im Kühlschrank aufbewahren keep refrigerated
im Notfall benötigen Sie keine Münzen/Telefonkarte emergency calls are free
im Preis inbegriffen included in the price
in der Tiefkühltruhe aufbewahren keep frozen
Immobilien real estate
in Wasser auflösen dissolve in water
inbegriffen included *(bill)*
Industriegebiet industrial area
Information information desk/office
inklusive included
Inlandsflüge domestic flights
innerhalb von 3 Tagen verbrauchen use within three days
Intensivstation intensive care
InterCity (IC) intercity train
InterCityExpress (ICE) express train
internat. Verkehrsflughafen international airport
internationale Flüge international flights

J

Jacht yacht
Jachtbassin marina
Januar January
Jugendherberge youth hostel
Jugendhörspiel cassettes for children
Jugendliche ab 14 Jahre children 14 and over
Juli July
junge Erwachsene young adult *(books)*
Juni June
Juwelier jeweler

K

Kabarett cabaret
Kabinen cabins
Kaffee coffee

A-Z

kalorienarm low calorie
Kammermusik chamber music
Kanal canal
Kanu canoe
Kapelle chapel
Karte aufbewahren please retain your ticket
Karte einschieben insert card
Karten maps, tickets
Kartentelefon card phone
Käse cheese
Kasse checkout, toll booth, ticket office
Kassetten cassettes
Kathedrale cathedral
Kaufhaus department store
Kegeln bowling/ninepins
kein Ausgang no exit
kein Blitzlicht no flash photography
kein Durchgang no entry
kein offenes Feuer no fires
kein Zutritt no entry
(bitte) keine Abfälle zurücklassen no dumping
keine Anlegemöglichkeit no anchorage
keine Chemischreinigung möglich do not dry clean
keine Eurocheques no checks
keine Filmschwärzung film safe
keine Haftung at the owner's risk; the owners accept no responsibility for damage or theft
keine Kreditkarten no credit cards
keine Pause no interval
keine Rückgabe non-returnable
keine Rückgabe des Restgeldes exact change only, no change given
kein Rabatt no discounts
Kfz-Nummer car registration number
Kfz-Schein registration papers
Kieferorthopäde orthodontist
Kinderhörspiel cassettes for children
Kinder: ... children: ... *(dose)*
Kinderabteilung children's department, pediatric ward
Kinderarzt pediatrician
Kinderbekleidung children's wear
Kinderkino children's movie/cinema
Kindermesse children's mass
Kinderspielplatz playground
Kindertheater children's theater
Kino movie theater/cinema
Kinopolis multiplex cinema
Kiosk snack shop/newsstand
Kirche(nruine) church ruins
Kirchhof churchyard

kirchlicher Feiertag religious holiday
Klassik classical music
Klassiker classics
Klebeband sticky tape
Kleider- und Kostümverleih dress rental
kleine Mahlzeit for the small appetite
Klettern rock climbing
Klinik health clinic
Klippe cliff
Kloster monastery, abbey
Kochbücher cookery
Kochmöglichkeiten cooking facilities
Kofferkulis luggage carts
Köln Cologne
Komödie (stand-up) comedy
Konditorei cake store, confectioner's
Konferenzsaal/-raum conference room
Konfitüre preserves
Kongresshalle convention hall
Konserven canned goods
Konservierungsmittel preservatives
Konsulat consulate
Konzert für Klavier und Orchester piano and orchestra concert(o)
Konzertsaal concert hall
köstlich delicious
Krankenhaus hospital
Krankenkasse health insurance
Krankenpfleger male nurse
Krankenschwester nurse
Krankenwagen ambulance
Kreditinstitut savings bank
Kreditkartennummer credit card number
Kreuzfahrt (steam) cruise
Kreuzung crossing, intersection
Kritik review
Kuchen cakes
Kugelschreiber pen
kühl aufbewahren keep cool
Kundenberatung customer information
Kundendienst repairs, customer service
Kundenparkplatz customer car park
Kundentoilette customer toilet
Kunstbände coffee table art books
Kunstfaser manmade fiber
Kunstgalerie art gallery
Kunsthandlung art store/shop
Kurort spa
Kurzparkzone short-term parking
Küste coast
Kutsche horse-drawn coach

L

Lagerfeuer camp fire
Lagerverkauf factory shopping
Lammfleisch lamb

Landeplatz airfield
landschaftlich schöne Strecke scenic route
Landstraße road
Langlauf(ski) cross-country skiing
Langlaufloipen cross-country ski routes
bitte läuten please ring the bell
Lawinengefahr danger of avalanches
Lazarett sickbay
Lebensmittelgeschäft grocery store, supermarket
Leder leather
Leerung ... collection times
Leichtathletik athletics
Leinen linen
letzter Eingang/Einlass um .... latest entry at … p.m.
Leuchtturm lighthouse
Licht einschalten switch on headlights
Lieder songs
Liederabend ballad concert
Lieferverkehr frei deliveries only
Liegestuhl deck-chair
Lift elevator
Linienverkehr frei access for public transport vehicles only
Linksabbieger – Gegenverkehr beachten watch for oncoming traffic when turning left
(bitte) links halten keep to the left
Literatur literature
Live-Musik live music
LKW (Lastkraftwagen) truck
Loge box *(theater)*
Lotterie/Lotteriespiel lottery
Lotterielos lottery ticket
Lounge (für Passagiere) (passenger) lounge
Luft air
Luftkissenfahrzeug hovercraft
Luftpumpe pump
Lustspiel comedy

 Mädchenname maiden name
mager low fat
Mai May
Männer men *(restrooms)*
Mantel tire
Märchen fairy tales
Markt market
Markthalle covered market
Marktplatz market square
Marschgebiet marsh
März March
Maschinenwäsche machine washable
maßgeschneidert made to measure

Mauer wall
Maxi CD single
maximal 2 Stunden two hours only
Meer sea, ocean
Meeresbucht estuary
Menü set menu
Messe fair
Metall/Plastik cans and plastic bin
Metzgerei butcher's
mikrowellengeeignet microwaveable
Milch milk
mindestens haltbar bis Ende ... best before end of …
mit Schwimmbad with swimming pool
mittags geschlossen closed for lunch
Mittwoch Wednesday
Möbelabteilung furniture
Möbelgeschäft furniture warehouse
moderner Tanz modern dance
Molkerei(produkte) dairy (products)
Monatskarte monthly ticket
Mönchskloster monastery
Montag Monday
Moor bog
morgen tomorrow
Motor abschalten/ausschalten turn off your engine
Motor abstellen turn off motor
Mühle mill
München Munich
Mundwasser mouthwash
Münzen einwerfen, Parkschein entnehmen insert money and take ticket
Münztelefon coin operated phone
Museen museums
Musik music
Musikhaus music store
Musikinstrument und -zubehör musical instrument shop
MwSt. (Mehrwertsteuer) VAT/sales tax

 nachmittags p.m.
Nachmittagsvorstellung matinee
nächste Führung um ... next tour at …
nächste Leerung ... next collection at …
nächste Tankstelle ... km next gas station … km
Nachtbeleuchtung lit in the evenings
Nachtdienst night service
Nachtportier night porter
Nahverkehrszug local train
Name name
Name des Ehegatten name of spouse

A-Z

Nationalfeiertag national holiday
Nationalpark country/national park
natriumarm salt-free
Naturbücher nature books
Naturfaser natural fibers
Naturschutzgebiet nature reserve
Nebenwirkungen side effects
neu im Sortiment new product
Neujahrstag New Year's Day
nicht an die Tür lehnen do not lean against door
nicht aus dem Fenster lehnen do not lean out the window
nicht besetzt vacant
(bitte) nicht betreten please do not enter
nicht bügeln do not iron
nicht EU-Staatsangehörige non-EU citizens
nicht hinauslehnen don't lean out the window
nicht inbegriffen not included (bill)
nicht rennen no running
Nichtraucher(abteil) non-smoking (compartment)
nichts zu verzollen nothing to declare
Nichtschwimmerbecken non-swimmers
(bitte) nicht stehen no standing
(bitte) nicht stören do not disturb
(Nonnen-)Kloster convent
Normal verbleit regular leadedgas
Notarztwagen ambulance
Notausgang emergency/fire exit
Notbremse emergency brake
Notfall emergency
Notfallaufnahme accident and emergency
Notfallstation ambulance station
nur an Sonntagen und Feiertagen Sundays and holidays only
nur für Flughafenpersonal flight crew only
nur für Anwohner residents only
nur für Auslandsfluggäste international passengers only
nur für das Personal staff only
nur für Fluggäste passengers only
nur für Frauen women only
nur für Gäste mit Dauerkarten season ticket holders only
nur für Herren men only
nur für Radfahrer cyclists only
nur für Rasierapparate razors only
nur gültig mit Entwerteraufdruck only good when validated
nur Handgepäck hand luggage only
nur heute today only

nur im Besitz einer gültigen Fahrkarte enter only with a valid ticket
nur mit Erlaubnis with permission only
nur mit Schein permit-holders only
nur an Werktagen weekdays only
nur zur äußeren Anwendung for external use only
Nürnberg Nuremberg

O

Oberdeck upper deck
Obergeschoß second floor, upper floor
Observatorium observatory
Obst und Gemüse fruit and vegetables
Obst- und Gemüseladen vegtable store
Obstkonserven canned fruit
öffentliches Gebäude public building
Öffnungszeiten visiting/opening hours, hours of business
ohne Konservierungsstoffe without preservatives
ohne Umsteigen direct service (train/bus)
ohne Zucker sugar-free
Oktober October
Öl oil
Oper opera (house)
Operationssaal operating theater
Optiker optician's
Orchester orchestra
Orgel organ
Orgelkonzert organ music
Orthopäde orthopedic doctor
Ostermontag Easter Monday
Ostern Easter
Ostersonntag Easter Sunday
Ozean ocean

P

Paddelboot canoe, kayak
Paddeln canoeing
Pakete parcels
Palais/Palast palace
Pannenhilfe, Telefon ... in case of breakdown, phone/contact ...
Papier- und Schreibwaren stationer's
Papier/Zeitung paper/newspaper bin
Papierwaren stationery
Parkdeck car deck
Parken bis zu 2 Std. parking limited to 2 hours
Parken nur für Gäste customer parking only
Parken verboten unauthorized parking prohibited
Parkett stalls
Parkhaus/-platz parking lot/car park

Parkplatz mit WC rest area
Parkschein anfordern press button to get ticket
Parkschein hinter die Windschutzscheibe legen place ticket behind windscreen
Parkschein-Automat ticket machine
Parkverbot no parking
Pass pass
Passage arcade
Passbild passport photos
Passkontrolle passport control
Passnummer passport number
Pastor pastor
Pavillon pavilion
Pedal pedal
Personalausweis vorzeigen proof of identity required
Personenfähre passenger ferry
Personenwagen car
Pfad path
Pfand deposit *(on bottle)*
Pfandflaschen returnable bottles
Pfarrer father
Pferdeschlittenfahrt horse-drawn sleigh ride
pflanzlich suitable for vegetarians
pflegeleicht easy-care
Pflegemittel skincare
Picknikplatz picnic site
Piste geschlossen/gesperrt ski run closed
PKW (Personenkraftwagen) car
PKW-Stellplätze vorhanden with adequate parking
planmäßig on time
Plattfuß puncture
Platz square
Polizei police
Polizeiwache/-station police station
Polo(spiel) polo
Polyacryl acrylic
Pop International pop music
Popkonzert pop-concert
Porzellan china
Post/Postamt post office
Postanweisung postal/money orders
Preis/Liter price per liter
Preise prices, rates
Preise inkl. MwSt. room rate including VAT
private Krankenversicherung private health insurance
Privatgrundstück private
Programm program
Palmsonntag Palm Sunday
Psychiater psychiatrist
Putzmittel cleaning products

Q **Quelle** spring

R **Radarkontrolle** radar control area
Radfahren cycling
Radweg bicycle lane/path/ track
Rang balcony
Rasen bitte nicht betreten keep off the grass
Rastplatz lay-by, picnic area
Raststätte service area
Rathaus town hall
Rauchen verboten no smoking
Raucher(abteil) smoking compartment
Räumungsverkauf closing-down sale
(bitte) rechts halten keep to the right
reduziert reductions
Reflektor reflector
Reformhaus health food store
Regencape/-jacke waterproof jacket
Reifenpanne flat tire
Reihe row, tier
reine Baumwolle 100% cotton
reine Schurwolle pure new wool
Reinigung dry cleaner's
Reisebüro travel agent's
Reiseführer travel
Reisezentrum travel center
Reiseziel destination
Reisezug long distance trains
Reiten horse riding
reizend irritating to skin, charming
Rennbahn racetrack/course
Rente pension
Reparaturwerkstatt repairs
reserviert reserved
Reservierung reservations
Residenzschloss palace
Restmüll leftover garbage with no green dot
Rettungsboot lifeboat
Rettungsdienst ambulance station
Rettungsring lifebelt
Rettungswagen ambulance
Rettungsweg für die Feuerwehr freihalten keep clear: emergency road for fire service
Rezeption reception
Rindfleisch beef
Ringstraße ring-road
Rockkonzert rock concert
Rollstuhlgerechte Beherbergung accommodations suitable for wheel

A-Z

chair users
Rolltreppe escalator
Romane fiction
Röntgenabteilung X-ray
Rückerstattung refund
Rückfahrkarte return ticket
Rückgaberecht money-back guarantee
(bitte) Rückgeld sofort nachzählen please check your change
Rücklicht rear lamp
Ruderboot rowboat
Rudern/Rudersport rowing
Rugby rugby
Ruhetag day off
ruhige Lage in a quiet location
(bitte) ruhig verhalten please respect this place of worship
Ruine ruins
rund um die Uhr geöffnet 24-hour service
Rundblick panorama
Rundfahrt round-trip

S **Sackgasse** cul-de-sac
saisonbedingt in season
Salbe ointment
Salz salt
Samstag Saturday
Sandboden sand (camping site)
Sanitäranlage/-ausstattung washing facilities
Sattel seat
SB (Selbstbedienung) self-service
Schallplatten records
Schauspiel spectacle
Schiff ship
Schiffsverbindung ferry route
Schlachtfeld battle site
Schlafwagen sleeper, sleeping compartment
Schläger racket
schlechte Fahrbahn poor road surface
Schlepplift drag lift
Schleudergefahr danger for towed trailers
Schleuse lock
Schließfächer luggage lockers
Schlittschuhe ice skates
Schlittschuhlaufen ice-skating
Schloss lock; castle
Schlosshotel castle lodging
Schlucht canyon
Schmuck jewelry
Schneeketten sind vorgeschrieben use snow

chains
Schnellgerichte ready-to serve meals
Schnellimbiss take out
Schnellstraße main road/principal highway
Schokolade chocolate
schöner Ausblick/schöne Aussicht panoramic view
Schreibpapier stationery
Schuhabteilung shoes
Schuhmacher/-reparatur shoe repair
Schulbus school bus
Schule school
Schulweg caution, school ahead
Schweinefleisch pork
Schwimmbad swimming pool
Schwimmen swimming
Schwimmen nicht erlaubt no swimming/bathing
Schwimmreif rubber ring
Schwimmweste lifejacket
See lake
Seemündung estuary
Segelboot sailboat
Segelfliegen gliding
Segeln sailing
Seide silk
Seilbahn cable car
Seitenstreifen hard-shoulder
Sekt sparkling wine
selbst wählen pick and mix
Selbstbedienung self-service
selbstgemacht homemade
Selbsttanken self-service (gas)
Seniorenmenü senior citizens' meals
September September
Service 0130 toll-free number
Service Point service station
Serviervorschlag serving suggestion
Sessellift chair lift
Sicherheitskontrolle security check
Silber silver
Silvester New Year's Eve
Sitzplatz für Behinderte handicapped seating
Sitzplatz Nummer seat number
Skier skis
Skilaufen skiing
Skilehrer ski teacher
Skischule (mit Aufnahme von Kleinkindern) ski school (for children)
Skistiefel ski boots
Skistöcke ski poles
Skiverleih ski rental
Soldatenfriedhof cemetery for soldiers

Solist(in) soloist
Sommer summer
Sonderangebot bargain
Sonnabend Saturday
Sonnendeck sun deck
Sonnenmilch Schutzfaktor 8 factor 8 sun lotion
Sonnenschirm sunshade
Sonntag Sunday
sonstige Straße minor road
Souvenirladen gift shop
Speisekarte menu
Speisesaal dining room
Speisewagen dining car
Spezialität des Hauses specialty of the house
Spezialitäten der Region local specialties
Spielfilme videos/feature film
Spielkarten playing cards
Spielplatz playground
Spielwarengeschäft toy store
Spirituosen alcoholic beverages
Sportbekleidung sportswear
Sportgeschäft/-bedarf sports store
Sportplatz sports ground
Sportzentrum sports center
Sprechzimmer consulting room
Springbrunnen fountain
Sprungbecken diving pool
Sprungbrett diving board
Spur lane
Staatsangehörigkeit nationality
Staatstheater theater
Stadion/Stadium stadium/(grand)stand
Stadtfestung/-mauer city wall
Stadtmitte town/city center, downtown
Stahl steel
Standort you are here
Station ward *(hospital)*
Stau traffic jam
Staudamm dam
Stausee reservoir
Steigung gradient
Sternwarte observatory
Stock floor/storey
storniert cancelled
strahlensicher film safe
Strand beach
Straße (gesperrt) road/street (closed)
Straßenarbeiten road works
Straßenbahn streetcar
Straußwirtschaft winery's bar and restaurant
Strickwaren knitted garments
Strom river

Stromschnelle rapids
Stromzähler ablesen read the meter
Sturmwarnung storm warning
Sulzschnee slush
Sumpf swamp, bog
Super (Plus) bleifrei premium unleaded gas
Super verbleit premium leaded gas
Suppen soups
Surfbrett surfboard
Süßwaren candy/sweets; cookies
SW-Film (schwarzweiß Film) black and white film
Symphonieorchester symphony orchestra
synchronisiert dubbed

T **Tabak/Tabakwaren** tobacconist's
Tabletten pills, tablets
Tagesgedeck set menu
Tageskarte daily ticket
Tagesmenü dish/set menu of the day
Tagesticket daily ticket
täglich daily
Tal valley, canyon
Tankstelle filling station
Tanz dance
Tänzer(in) dancer
Tanzmusik dance music
Tarif rate
Taste-Nr. ... drücken push ... button number
Tauchausrüstung scuba diving equipment
Tauchen water diving
Taxistand taxi stand
Teich pond
Telebriefversand faxes sent
Telefax fax
Telefon telephone
Telefonbuch directory
Telefonkarten telephone cards
Telefonnummer telephone number
Telefonzelle public telephone
Telegramme telegrams
Tennis tennis court
Tennishalle indoor tennis
Tennisschläger tennis racket
Terminal terminal
Terrasse terrace
Textilien textile goods
Theater theater
Theaterstück play
Thermalbad mineral baths

A-Z

Tiefgarage underground parking/garage
tiefgefroren frozen
Tiefkühlprodukte frozen goods
Tiefschnee deep snow
Tierarzt veterinary
Tierbedarf pet store
Tiere cattle crossing
Tierhandlung pet shop
Tip serving suggestion
Tische in der 1. Etage seats upstairs
Tischtennis table tennis
Toiletten restrooms
Tor bitte geschlossen halten keep gate shut
Toto Lotto lottery
Touristenstraße scenic/tourist route
Tragflächenboot hydrofoil, hovercraft, jetfoil
Tragödie tragedy
Trambahn streetcar
Treffpunkt meeting point
Tretboot peddle boat
Tribüne viewing gallery
Triebsand quick sand
Trinkwasser drinking water
trocknergeeignet can be put in the clothes dryer
Tropfen drops
Trümmer ruins
Tunnel tunnel
(bitte) Tür schließen/zuziehen please close the door
Turm tower

U U-Bahn subway
Überführung walkway
Übergepäck excess luggage
Überholverbot no passing
Überweisungen drafts and transfers
Umgehungsstraße bypass
Umkleide changing rooms
Umkleidekabine changing cubicle
Umleitung detour
Umriß contour
umsteigen in ... change at ...
unbefestigte Straße unpaved road
Unfallstation casualty
Universität university
Unterdeck lower deck
Unterführung underground passage
Untergeschoss basement
Unterhaltungsmusik easy-listening
Unterhaltungsliteratur light fiction

Unterschrift signature
Untertitel subtitled
unzerkaut einnehmen swallow whole
Uraufführung premiere/first night

V Varietévorstellung variety show
vegetarisches Gericht suitable for vegetarians
Verbandskasten first-aid box
verbessert improved
verbleit leaded
Verbot für Fußgänger no thoroughfare for pedestrians
... verboten ... forbidden
verengte Fahrbahn narrow road
Vergiftung poison
Vergnügungspark amusement park
Vergrößerung enlargement service
Verkauf currency sold at
Verkehrskreis traffic circle
Verkehrspolizei traffic police
Versicherungsagentur insurance agent
Verspätung delayed
verwendbar bis: ... use by: ...
verzollen goods to declare
Videothek video rental
Viehtrieb cattle crossing
Villa stately home
Viskose rayon
Volksmusik folk music
Vollpension full board
von ... bis ... Uhr from ... to ...
vor Licht schützen keep out of light
Vorabendmesse evening mass
Vorderlicht headlight
Vorderrad front wheel
Vorfahrt achten yield/give way
vormittags a.m.
Vornamen given names
vorne einsteigen enter by the front door
Vorratspackung multipack
Vorsicht caution
Vorsicht! Stufen mind the step
Vorsicht! Taschendiebe beware of pickpockets
Vorspeisen appetizers
vorübergehend geschlossen temporarily closed
Vorverkauf advance sales/bookings
Vorwahl area code

W wählen Sie Ihre Fahrziele/Tarifgebiet/Fahrkarte
select destination/zone/ticket

wahlweise at your choice
Wahlwiederholung last number redial
Wald forest, wood
Wanderkarten hiking maps
Wanderweg nature trail
Warnung warning
Warteraum/-zimmer waiting room
Wartezeit: ca. .... Minuten waiting time: approx … mins.
Wäscherei launderette (not self-serve)
Wäscheservice laundry service
Waschmaschinen washing machines
Waschmittel laundry detergent
Waschsalon laundromat
Wasser water
wasserdicht waterproof
Wasserhahn water faucet
Wassermühle water mill
Wasserski/-schi waterskiing
Wasserturm water tower
WC restrooms
(bitte) Wechselgeld sofort nachzählen please check your change
Wechselkurs exchange rate
Wechselstube currency exchange office
wegen ... geschlossen bis ... closed until … due to …
Wegweiser store guide
Wegwerf(-flasche) disposable (bottle)
Weiher pond
Weihnachten Christmas
Wein wine
Weinberg vineyard
Weingut winery
Weinkelter winepress
Weinprobe wine tasting
Weißglas clear glass
weitere Vorstellungen other performances
Werk(sausfahrt) factory (exit)
Werkstatt repair shop, garage
werktags weekdays
Wettannahmen off-track betting
Wettkampf contest
wichtige Telefonnummern emergency services
Wiederaufnahme second half *(after interval)*
Wien Vienna
Wild venison and game
Willkommen welcome
Windmühle windmill
Winterschlussverkauf winter season sale
wir haben reduziert sale
wir zeigen jeden Diebstahl an shoplifting will be prosecuted

Wochenkarte weekly ticket
Wohnmobil/-wagen RV trailer
Wohnort home address
Wohnung zu vermieten apartment for rent
Wolle wool
Wurst(waren) cold meats/sausage

Z **Zahlmeister** purser
Zahlungsanweisung money order
Zahnarzt dentist
Zahnpaste toothpaste
Zahnseide dental floss
Zapfsäule gas pump
Zeitschriften magazines
Zeitungshändler/-kiosk newsagent's
Zelt tent
Zelten verboten no camping/tenting
Zeltplatz campsite/tenting grounds
Zentrum city center (downtown)
zerbrechlich – Glas fragile – glass
ziehen pull
Zimmer frei vacancies, rooms to let
Zimmerservice room service
Zimmer sind mit Dusche und WC ausgestattet rooms with en-suite bathroom
Zimmer sind mit Kabel-TV/Farbfernseher ausgestattet rooms with cable TV/ color TV
Zirkus circus
Zoll customs control
zollfreie Ware duty-free goods
Zone 30 speed limit 30 kilometers/hour
Zoo zoo
Zoohandlung pet shop
zu den Gleisen to the platforms
zu den Verkaufsräumen to the sales floors
zu Vermieten for rent
zum Halten, bitte drücken press button to request stop
zum Mitnehmen to take out/away
Zug des Nahverkehrs local train
Zuschauer spectators
Zuschlag supplement
Zutaten ingredients
Zweibett-Kabine two-berth cabin
zweite Klasse/2. Klasse second class
zweiter Rang upper circle

Reference

Numbers   GRAMMAR

When taking down tens and units, it is quicker to write the unit down as you hear it, then insert the ten before it.

siebenundachtzig (7 and 80 = 87)

zweihundertvierundfünfzug (200, 4 and 50 = 254)

On the telephone, **zwo** is often used for **zwei**, to avoid confusion with **drei**.

0	**null** *nul*		17	**siebzehn** *zeeptsayn*
1	**eins** *iens*		18	**achtzehn** *akhttsayn*
2	**zwei** *tsvie*		19	**neunzehn** *noyntsayn*
3	**drei** *drie*		20	**zwanzig** *tsvantsikh*
4	**vier** *feer*		21	**einundzwanzig** *iennunttsvantsikh*
5	**fünf** *fewnf*			
6	**sechs** *zeks*		22	**zweiundzwanzig** *tsvieunttsvantsikh*
7	**sieben** *zeebern*		23	**dreiundzwanzig** *drieunttsvantsikh*
8	**acht** *akht*			
9	**neun** *noyn*		24	**vierundzwanzig** *feerunttsvantsikh*
10	**zehn** *tsayn*		25	**fünfundzwanzig** *fewnfunttsvantsikh*
11	**elf** *elf*			
12	**zwölf** *tsvurlf*		26	**sechsundzwanzig** *zeksunttsvantsikh*
13	**dreizehn** *drietsayn*		27	**siebenundzwanzig** *zeebernunttsvantsikh*
14	**vierzehn** *feertsayn*			
15	**fünfzehn** *fewnftsayn*			
16	**sechzehn** *zekhtsayn*			

28	**achtundzwanzig** *akhtunttsvantsikh*	first	**erste** *ehrster*
29	**neunundzwanzig** *noynunttsvantsikh*	second	**zweite** *tsvieter*
30	**dreißig** *driessikh*	third	**dritte** *dritter*
31	**einunddreißig** *iennuntdriessikh*	fourth	**vierte** *feerter*
32	**zweiunddreißig** *tsvieuntdriessikh*	fifth	**fünfte** *fewnfter*
40	**vierzig** *feertsikh*	once	**einmal** *ienmaal*
50	**fünfzig** *fewnftsikh*	twice	**zweimal** *tsviemaal*
60	**sechzig** *zekhtsikh*	three times	**dreimal** *driemaal*
70	**siebzig** *zeebtsikh*	a half	**eine Hälfte** *iener hehlfter*
80	**achtzig** *akhtsikh*		
90	**neunzig** *noyntsikh*	half an hour	**eine halbe Stunde** *iener halber shtunder*
100	**(ein)hundert** *(ien)hundert*		
101	**hunderteins** *hundertiens*	half a tank	**ein halber Tank** *ien halber tank*
102	**hundertzwei** *hunderttsvie*	half eaten	**halb gegessen** *halp gegessern*
200	**zweihundert** *tsviehundert*	a quarter	**ein Viertel** *ien feerterl*
500	**fünfhundert** *fewnfhundert*	a third	**ein Drittel** *ien dritterl*
1,000	**(ein)tausend** *(ien)towzernt*	a pair of ...	**ein Paar ...** *ien paar*
10,000	**zehntausend** *tsayntowzernt*	a dozen ...	**ein Dutzend ...** *ien dutsernt*
35,750	**fünfunddreißig-tausendsieben-hundertfünfzig** *fewnfundrighssikh-towzerntzeebern-hundertfewnftsikh*	1997	**neunzehnhundert-siebenundneunzig** *noyntsaynhun-dertzeebernunt-noyntsikh*
		2001	**zweitausendeins** *tsvietowzerntiens*
1,000,000	**eine Million** *iener millioan*	the 1990s	**die neunziger Jahre** *dee noyntsiger yaarer*

217

Days Tage

Monday	**Montag** *moantaag*
Tuesday	**Dienstag** *deenstaag*
Wednesday	**Mittwoch** *mitvokh*
Thursday	**Donnerstag** *donnerstaag*
Friday	**Freitag** *frightaag*
Saturday	**Samstag/Sonnabend** *zamstaag/zonnaaberni*
Sunday	**Sonntag** *zontaag*

Months Monate

January	**Januar** *yanuaar*
February	**Februar** *faybruaar*
March	**März** *mehrts*
April	**April** *april*
May	**Mai** *mie*
June	**Juni** *yooni*
July	**Juli** *yooli*
August	**August** *owgust*
September	**September** *zeptember*
October	**Oktober** *oktoaber*
November	**November** *novvember*
December	**Dezember** *daytsember*

Dates Daten

It's …	**Es ist …** *ess ist*
July 10	**der zehnte Juli** *dehr tsaynter yooli*
Tuesday, March 1	**Dienstag, der erste März** *deenstaag dehr ehrster mehrts*
yesterday/today/tomorrow	**gestern/heute/morgen** *gestern/hoyter/morgern*
this week/month/year	**diese Woche/diesen Monat/dieses Jahr** *deezer vokher/deezern moanat/deezerss yaar*
last week/month/year	**letzte Woche/letzten Monat/letztes Jahr** *letster vokher/letstern moanat/letsterss yaar*
next week/month/year	**nächste Woche/nächsten Monat/nächstes Jahr** *naikhster vokher/naikhstern moanat/naikhsterss yaar*
every week/month/year	**jede Woche/jeden Monat/jedes Jahr** *yayder vokher/yaydern moanat/yayderss yac*
at the weekend	**am Wochenende** *am vokhernender*

Seasons Jahreszeiten

spring/summer	**der Frühling/der Sommer**	
	dehr frewling/dehr zommer	
fall/winter	**der Herbst/der Winter**	
	dehr hehrpst/dehr vinter	
in spring	**im Frühling** *im frewling*	
during the summer	**während des Sommers**	
	vairernt dess zommerss	

Greetings Grüße und Wünsche

Happy birthday! **Herzlichen Glückwunsch zum Geburtstag!**
hehrtslikhern glewkvunsh tsum gerboortstaag!

Merry Christmas! **Fröhliche Weihnachten!**
frurlikher vienakhtern

Happy New Year! **Ein Glückliches Neues Jahr!**
ien glewklikherss noyerss yaar

Happy Easter! **Frohe Ostern!** *froaer oastern*
Best wishes! **Alles Gute!** *allerss gooter*
Congratulations! **Herzlichen Glückwunsch!**
hehrtslikhern glewkvunsh

Good luck!/All the best! **Viel Glück!/Alles Gute!**
feel glewk/allerss gooter

Have a good trip! **Gute Reise!** *gooter riezer*
Give my regards to … **Grüßen Sie … von mir.**
grewssern zee … fon meer

Public holidays Feiertage

National holidays in Germany (D), Austria (A) and Switzerland (CH):

January 1	Neujahr	New Year's Day	D	A	CH
January 2					CH*
January 6	Dreikönigstag	Epiphany		A	
May 1	Tag der Arbeit	Labor Day	D	A	
August 1	Nationalfeiertag	National Holiday			CH*
August 15	Maria Himmelfahrt	Assumption Day		A	
October 3	Tag der Deutschen Einheit	National Unity Day	D		
November 1	Allerheiligen	All Saints Day		A	
December 8	Maria Empfängnis	Immaculate Conception		A	
December 25	1.Weihnachtstag	Christmas	D	A	CH
December 26	2. Weihnachtstag	St Stephen's Day	D	A	CH
Movable dates:					
	Karfreitag	Good Friday	D		CH*
	Ostermontag	Easter Monday	D	A	CH*
	Christi Himmelfahrt	Ascension	D	A	CH
	Pfingstmontag	Whit Monday	D	A	CH*
	Fronleichnam	Corpus Christi		A	

*most cantons

Time Uhrzeit

The official time system uses the 24-hour clock. However, in ordinary conversation, time is generally expressed as shown below, often with the addition of **morgens** (morning), **nachmittags** (afternoon) or **abends** (evening).

Excuse me. Can you   **Entschuldigen Sie. Können Sie mir sagen,**

tell me the time?	**wie spät es ist?** *entshuldigern zee.*
	kurnern zee meer zaagern vee shpait ess ist
It's …	**Es ist …** *ess ist*
five past one	**fünf nach eins** *fewnf naakh ienss*
ten past two	**zehn nach zwei** *tsayn naakh tsvie*
a quarter past three	**Viertel nach drei** *feerterl naakh drie*
twenty past four	**zwanzig nach vier** *tsvantsikh naakh feer*
twenty-five past five	**fünf vor halb sechs** *fewnf foar halp zeks*
half past six	**halb sieben** *halp zeebern*
twenty-five to seven	**fünf nach halb sieben**
	fewnf naakh halp zeebern
twenty to eight	**zwanzig vor acht** *tsvantsikh foar akht*
a quarter to nine	**Viertel vor neun** *feerterl foar noyn*
ten to ten	**zehn vor zehn** *tsayn foar tsayn*
five to eleven	**fünf vor elf** *fewnf foar elf*
twelve o'clock	**zwölf Uhr** *tsvurlf oor*
noon/midnight	**Mittag/Mitternacht** *mittaag/mitternakht*

at dawn	**bei Tagesanbruch**
	bigh taagersanbrukh
in the morning	**morgens** *morgerns*
during the day	**tagsüber** *taagsewber*
before lunch	**vor dem Mittagessen**
	foar daym mittaagessern
after lunch	**nach dem Mittagessen**
	naakh daym mittaagessern
in the afternoon	**nachmittags** *naakhmittaags*
in the evening	**abends** *aabernts*
at night	**nachts** *nakhts*

I'll be ready in five minutes.
Ich bin in fünf Minuten fertig.
ikh bin in fewnf minootern fehrtik

He'll be back in a
quarter of an hour.
Er ist in einer Viertelstunde wieder da.
ehr ist in iener feerterlshtunder veeder daa

She arrived half an hour ago.
**Sie ist vor einer halben Stunde
angekommen.** *zee ist foar iener halbern
shtunder angerkommern*

The train leaves at …
Der Zug fährt um … *dehr tsoog fairt um*

13:04
dreizehn Uhr vier *drietsayn oor feer*

0:40
null Uhr vierzig *nul oor feertsikh*

He came 10 minutes early/late.
Er kam zehn Minuten zu früh/zu spät.
*ehr kaam tsayn minootern tsoo
frew/tsoo shpait*

The clock is 5 seconds fast/slow.
Die Uhr geht fünf Sekunden vor/nach.
dee oor gayt fewnf zekundern foar/naakh

from 9:00 to 5:00
von neun bis siebzehn Uhr
fon noyn biss zeeptsayn oor

between 8:00 and 2:00
zwischen acht und vierzehn Uhr
tsvishern akht unt feertsayn oor

I'll be leaving by 11 o'clock.
Ich reise vor elf Uhr ab.
ikh riezer foar elf oor ap

Will you be back before 8 p.m.?
Kommen Sie vor zwanzig Uhr wieder?
kommern zee foar tsvantsikh oor veeder

We'll be here until Friday.
Wir sind bis Freitag hier.
veer zint biss frietaag heer

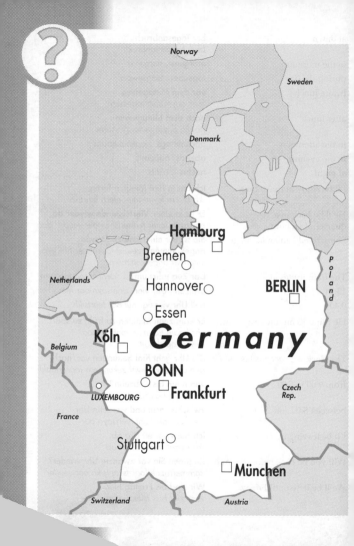

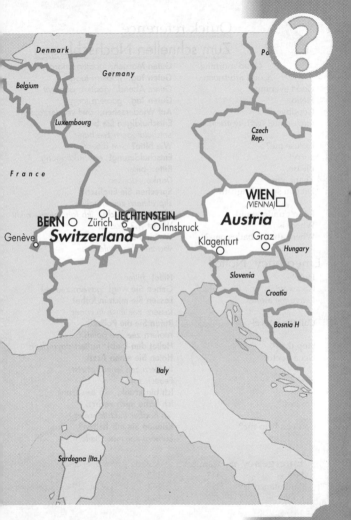

Quick reference
Zum schnellen Nachschlagen

Good morning.	**Guten Morgen.** *gootern morgern*
Good afternoon.	**Guten Tag.** *gootern taag*
Good evening.	**Guten Abend.** *gootern aabernt*
Hello.	**Guten Tag.** *gootern taag*
Goodbye.	**Auf Wiedersehen.** *owf veederzayern*
Excuse me! *(getting attention)*	**Entschuldigen Sie bitte!** *entshuldiggern zee bitter*
Excuse me?	**Wie bitte?** *vee bitter*
Sorry!	**Entschuldigung!** *entshuldiggung*
Please.	**Bitte.** *bitter*
Thank you.	**Danke.** *danker*
Do you speak English?	**Sprechen Sie Englisch?** *shprekhern zee ennglish*
I don't understand.	**Ich verstehe nicht.** *ikh fehrshtayer nikht*
Where is …?	**Wo ist …?** *voa ist*
Where are the bathrooms?	**Wo sind die Toiletten?** *voa zint dee twalettern*

Emergency Notfall

Help!	**Hilfe!** *hilfer*
Go away!	**Gehen Sie weg!** *gayern zee vek*
Leave me alone!	**Lassen Sie mich in Ruhe!** *lassern zee mikh in rooer*
Call the police!	**Rufen Sie die Polizei!** *roofern zee dee pollitsie*
Stop thief!	**Haltet den Dieb!** *haltert dayn deep*
Get a doctor!	**Holen Sie einen Arzt!** *hoalern zee ienern aartst*
Fire!	**Feuer!** *foyer*
I'm ill.	**Ich bin krank.** *ikh bin krank*
I'm lost.	**Ich habe mich verirrt.** *ikh haaber mikh fehreert*
Can you help me?	**Können Sie mir helfen?** *kurnern zee meer helfern*

Emergency ☎	Germany	Austria	Switzerland
Fire	112	122	118
Ambulance	112	144	114 or 117 in major towns
Police	110	133	117

ABOUT BERLITZ

In 1878 Professor Maximilian Berlitz had a revolutionary idea about making language learning accessible and enjoyable. One hundred and twenty years later these same principles are still successfully at work.

For language instruction, translation and interpretation services, cross-cultural training, study abroad programs, and an array of publishing products and additional services, visit any one of our more than 350 Berlitz Centers in over 40 countries.

Please consult your local telephone directory for the Berlitz Center nearest you or visit our web site at http://www.berlitz.com.

Helping the World Communicate

Also from Berlitz

German
phrase book & dictiona.

- World's bestselling phrase boo
  series
- Practical, up-to-date words an
  phrases
- Color-coding makes words and
  phrases easy to find

<table>
<tr><td>▭</td><td>Basic Expressions/
Accommodations</td></tr>
<tr><td>▭</td><td>Eating Out</td></tr>
<tr><td>▭</td><td>Travel</td></tr>
<tr><td>▭</td><td>Sightseeing</td></tr>
<tr><td>▭</td><td>Stores & Services</td></tr>
<tr><td>▭</td><td>Health</td></tr>
<tr><td>▭</td><td>Bilingual Dictionary</td></tr>
<tr><td>▭</td><td>Reference</td></tr>
</table>

ISBN 2-8315-6240-6

9 782831 562407

90000

US $ 7.95 UK £ 3.95

0 52106 06240 6